The Ethics of Superintelligent Design

The Ethics of Superintelligent Design

A Christian View of the Theological and Moral
Implications of Artificial Superintelligence

PAUL GOLATA

WIPF & STOCK · Eugene, Oregon

THE ETHICS OF SUPERINTELLIGENT DESIGN
A Christian View of the Theological and Moral Implications of Artificial Superintelligence

Copyright © 2018 Paul Golata. All rights reserved. Except for brief quotations in critical publications or reviews, no part of this book may be reproduced in any manner without prior written permission from the publisher. Write: Permissions, Wipf and Stock Publishers, 199 W. 8th Ave., Suite 3, Eugene, OR 97401.

Wipf & Stock
An Imprint of Wipf and Stock Publishers
199 W. 8th Ave., Suite 3
Eugene, OR 97401

www.wipfandstock.com

PAPERBACK ISBN: 978-1-5326-3223-5
HARDCOVER ISBN: 978-1-5326-3225-9
EBOOK ISBN: 978-1-5326-3224-2

Manufactured in the U.S.A.   MARCH 6, 2018

Dedicated to my wife, Dianna Golata

Contents

Preface | xi
Summary | xiii

Chapter 1 Introduction | 1
    Artificial Intelligence
    Questions to Be Answered
    Thesis
    Points to Demonstrate
    Literature
    Methodology

Chapter 2 The Creature—Man | 13
    Creature
        Order and Chaos
        Homo Faber
            Technology
            Imago Hominis
        Ethics
    Man
        Human Exceptionalism
        Biological Machine vis-à-vis *Imago Dei*

CONTENTS

    Humans as Machines Only
    Humans as Image-Bearers
    Monism (Body Only) vis-à-vis Holistic Dualism (Body and Soul)
    Mind and Intelligence: The Impact of Sin
Summary

Chapter 3   Intelligence | 42

What Is Intelligence?
Natural Intelligence
    Increasing Natural Intelligence
    The Bible on Intelligence
Artificial Intelligence
    The Pursuit of Artificial Intelligence
    The Possibility of Artificial Superintelligence
    Weak and Strong
Epistemology
Cognition
Language
Identity
Agency
Imaging
Summary

Chapter 4   Singularity | 73

The Potential of Artificial Superintelligence
    Technological Advancement
    Pursuit of Perfection
    Decision-Making
    Safety, Defense, and Crime
    Medicine
    Biological Enhancement
    Stewardship

Achieving Artificial Superintelligence via External and Internal Transformation
    Artificial Intelligence
    Whole Brain Emulation
    Biological Cognition
    Brain and Computer Interface and Implants
    Networks
Forms of Artificial Superintelligence
    Speed
    Collective
    Quality
Separation of Biology from Purpose
Human Existential Risks
    Orthogonal Goals
    Instrumental Goals
    Decisive Strategic Advantage
    Pandora's Box
        Perverse Instantiation
        Infrastructure Profusion
        Mind Crime
Moral Enhancement
Transhumanism
Life Extension and Immortality
    Singularity Advocates
A Biblical Perspective
Summary

Chapter 5   Artificial Superintelligence Ethics | 120

    Anthropomorphizing Artificial Superintelligence
    Artificial Superintelligence Motivations
        Rationality
        Ordered Efficiency
        Ends
        Survival

CONTENTS

    What Is the Good?
        Beyond Good and Evil
    Artificial Superintelligence and Functional Autonomy
        A Closer Look at Functional Autonomy
        Where There Is a Will There Is a Way
    Summary

Chapter 6   Conclusion | 162

    Artificial Superintelligence vis-à-vis Imago Hominis
    Artificial Superintelligence vis-à-vis Imago Dei
    Moving Forward

Bibliography | 169
Subject Index | 189
Scripture Index | 217

Preface

Intelligence is a complex topic. The idea that man is about to increase his level of intelligence exponentially over the coming generations is based upon a technological revolution and the potential for superintelligence. Its potential impact is so enormous that no one has yet grasped the magnitude of its impeding arrival. As a global phenomenon, it is anticipated that this will impact every society and person on the planet. This technological revolution has been called the next industrial revolution, and is characterized by the intersection of the realms of digital electronics, biology, and the relationship interface between man and machine. Its arrival is appearing with exceptional haste and will disrupt historical and current understandings of mankind.

It is within this context that there is a prevailing need for a discussion of its ethical implications. As a Christian ethicist, the need for this conversation to be informed by Christian principles is imperative. While proponents of ASI largely look to science and empirical methods for their authority, Christian orthodoxy looks to general revelation, as revealed in nature, but more importantly relies on special revelation as related to the Holy Bible as the inspired word of God. People who claim to be Christians have compromised their position regarding the authority of the Bible as special revelation relative to that which seems to be revealed through a study of the natural sciences.

Superintelligence, in one manner, is a move toward the proper handling of information. However, how a society interprets and applies this information is actually more pertinent than the raw amount of information

Preface

it possesses. To date, there are limited and deficient articulations as to how those affirming a biblical worldview should proceed.

This work endeavors to take one step forward in taking seriously the potential future reality of advanced intelligence in many forms while maintaining an affirmation of (a) biblical authority, (b) biblical inerrancy, and (c) creation originating from God's supernatural creative action. These specific positions have more than twenty centuries of theological and philosophical support, but have now often fallen into disrespect in many domains, even among orthodox Christians, and particularly have little, if any, support from people within the AI community. This study seeks to make a unique contribution to establish a baseline from which those who acknowledge and maintain a belief in the sovereignty of God, the lordship of Jesus Christ, and the authority of Scripture may perform further research.

This work was inspired by my own working in the field of technology over the past thirty-plus years coupled with my present theological and pastoral work. This exciting and expanding field presented itself in need of Christian support and articulation. It is desired that the necessary discussions regarding the ethical implications take place, but are done in a manner that does not dismiss the Christian and biblical understanding from the outset. To date, evolutionary naturalistic thinking has largely precluded bringing Christian understanding into the discussion. If evolutionary naturalism is incorrect, as is contended, then the elimination of Christian principles in the discussion means that the derived ethical conclusions will also be incorrect. Evolutionary naturalism fails to understand mankind as made in the *imago Dei*, as existing in a state of sin, and in need of redemption. Lacking the proper biblical understanding of the state of man, every decision of any ASI not employing Christian ethics is deficient in its ability to come properly to the correct ethical conclusions and actions. For Christians, there is a need to speak boldly and with conviction for the incorporation of biblical ethics into the conversation, lest the future be void of Christian ethical understandings and be reframed entirely along materialistic grounds.

Paul Golata
Frisco, Texas
August 2017

Summary

This work argues that any technological enhancements to humankind's cognitive intelligence, whether achieved through biological or artificial manipulations of human nature or resulting from human creation, are subject to the commands, prescriptions, and principles revealed through God's unified revelation, taking into account that man is created as his image-bearer.

Chapter 1 introduces the statement of the problem and discusses the necessity of properly understanding man and intelligence, and provides definitions and research methodology.

Chapter 2 discusses human anthropology and discusses man's relationship to the cosmos in the context of him making technology for his use. It investigates the need for proper theological understandings in order to understand the ethics of his creation of ASI.

Chapter 3 investigates the understanding of intelligence and provides insight to how it is viewed from the context of natural and artificial understandings.

Chapter 4 looks at the technological singularity and its implications, including extending human lifetimes. It acknowledges the power of potential of ASI while discussing its separation of purpose from biology and its existential risks to humanity.

Chapter 5 tackles the issue of ASI ethics. It looks at ASI's ethical relationship to mankind as a human invention and examines from whence its motivations and values stem. The issue of functional autonomy is examined and deemed ethically unsatisfactory.

Chapter 6 concludes by suggesting that all developments in AI/ASI be employed within a Christian ethical framework.

Chapter 1

Introduction

Man is a rational animal and he is also a creator. He creates, fabricates, and utilizes tools to help increase his efficiency and effectiveness. The applications and uses of these tools, many of them just coming into being, constitute technology, which continues to advance as mankind is discovering new ways to collect and disseminate information. Mankind advances in technology because he is able to use his rational faculties by application of his native intelligence to create possibilities that enable him to help meet his needs and desires. Technology is one component of culture and assists in the development of our conceptual framework from which we define meaning in life.

Man is also a finite creature. Man's capacity to create is neither infinite nor unbounded. Christianity, like science, affirms that the world had a beginning in time (Gen 1:1; Heb 11:3). Christianity maintains that no finite creatures could (a) conceivably make themselves, nor (b) could they create the world or other creatures. Christianity claims that creation comes from an infinite, eternal, independent being who is the first cause of everything and is known as God (Exod 3:13–15; Ps 41:13; 90:2; 100:3; 102:27; Rom 11:33). If, as Christianity claims, creation is the result of God, then mankind is morally bound to obey the will of the sovereign God as it has been revealed in nature, history, the Scriptures, and Jesus Christ (Gen 1–3). If God is not the creator of both the universe and mankind, then mankind is not under any ethical obligation to God; hence, man himself becomes the measure of all things, including morality.[1]

---

1. The first mention of this philosophy is attributed to pre-Socratic Sophist

The Ethics of Superintelligent Design

After World War II, advances in technology have led to what is now known as artificial intelligence (AI), which involves the processing performance and capabilities of computers, robots, machines, and software. According to technologists and futurists, the advent of artificial superintelligence (ASI) is on the horizon. ASI is defined as an artificial "intellect that is much smarter than the best human brains in practically every field, including scientific creativity, general wisdom and social skills."[2] Mankind would be wise to understand the theological and ethical implications prior to its arrival. This work will undertake an examination and evaluation of ASI and its implications as it relates to orthodox historical Christianity as revealed in the sixty-six canonical books of the Old and New Testament, which are under the authority of *sola scriptura*.[3]

Man lives and understands himself in the context of his surroundings and all other forms of animal life, which, on a first order, encompasses his natural surroundings available to his immediate senses on the Earth and, by extension, to nature that is assessable for investigation beyond his immediate senses through the aids of technology, reason, and deduction. Man utilizes his mind through the employment of his intellectual capacities to understand the cosmos that surrounds him. Man's high level of intelligence, relative to his natural surroundings, makes intelligence one of the distinguishing characteristics of mankind. Mankind is able to supplement his intelligence by creating tools that help him increase his knowledge. ASI is a tool that mankind is presently working towards in order to provide him with greater knowledge of his surroundings. Mankind has not yet taken proper pause to reflect on the theological and ethical implications ASI presents upon its arrival.

What ethical perspective will ASI assume? The present trajectory is that its ethics will largely be reflective of the ethical characteristics of mankind. If, as the Christian claims, mankind apart from a relationship with

---

philosopher Protagoras (c. 490–c. 420 B.C.). "... only Protagoras puts it rather a different way. For he says, you know, that 'Man is the measure of all things: of the things which are, that they are, and of the things which are not, that they are not.'" Protagoras is claiming that truth is subjective and not beholden to an external objective reality. Plato, *Theaetetus*, 152a, 69.

2. Bostrom, "How Long before Superintelligence?" For an early, if not the first, mention of this idea refer to Good, "Speculations Concerning the First Ultraintelligent Machine."

3. When properly understood, this means that Scripture is not the only authority, just the final authority. "For evangelical theology Scripture remains the final authority to which one can appeal." Lane, "Sola Scriptura?," 327.

God is depraved, then what are the theological implications in bringing ASI to reality? The thesis of this work is that ASI falls under the lordship and authority of Jesus Christ and, as such, the creation, fall, and redemption aspects of the gospel metanarrative should be considered in order to formulate and address appropriate and proper ethical understandings of how to deal with the existence of ASI.

ARTIFICIAL INTELLIGENCE

Artificial intelligence (AI) is a derived intelligence that comes from man's development and employment of technology.[4] AI can be classified into three macro-categories based upon their relationship to mankind's general innate intelligence level. Advances in technology have, to date, led to the first level, what is now known as artificial narrow intelligence (ANI). ANI is machine intelligence that equals or exceeds human intelligence or efficiency at a *specific* function. The next category level is artificial general intelligence (AGI). This level of intelligence is where the machine intelligence is equal to or exceeds average human intelligence in all aspects. The final frontier is called artificial superintelligence (ASI). ASI is characterized as being anywhere from one (1) to one trillion (1,000,000,000,000) times higher in intelligence than average human intelligence in every aspect.[5]

AI has come into its own since the end of World War II and is thus of relatively recent origin. It has matured in a philosophical and theological context that has been shaped by evolutionary naturalism, which believes that physical determinism allows for biological properties such as intelligence to develop emergently. Evolutionary naturalism's counterpart, philosophical naturalism, posits that no supernatural or transcendent beings or processes operate inside the cosmos.[6] They see the cosmic system as closed.

---

4. Critic and educator Neil Postman (1931–2003) asserts that technology is part of what is physical and that it can be compared to a machine. In distinction from technology is the medium that, to Postman, conjures conceptions of use and utility that arise from creation in a social context. Postman interestingly analogizes technology to the brain, holding that the brain is the physical machine part of the body that performs intellectual operations but it is the mind that is the medium that determines how this intelligence is used and applied. Postman, *Technopoly*.

5. Bostrom, *Superintelligence*, 18, 22. Goertzel and Pennachin, *Artificial General Intelligence*; Kurzweil, *Singularity Is Near*; Wang and Goertzel, eds., *Theoretical Foundations of Artificial General Intelligence*.

6. Plantinga, *Warrant and Proper Function*, 216–37. See also Beilby, *Naturalism*

This understanding of a closed cosmic system is based upon empirical inductive study of the cosmos in various domains of investigation that operates under the classification of science.

In contrast to a closed cosmos, Christians understand that God exists outside of and prior to the cosmos. The Christian understands God as an eternally existing, transcendent personal being with perfect attributes. This understanding is not informed solely by empirical inductive studies but comes uniquely through special divine revelation, whereby God has chosen both to speak through divine communication to man through thoughts and words given through divine inspiration to prophets to record as Scripture and to reveal himself by becoming incarnated, living as a human, and dying as a sacrificial atonement to reconcile creation to himself (Phil 2:5–11; Col 1:15–20).

Relationships give rise to the discussion of morality. Atheist social critic, philosopher, and public intellectual Paul Goodman (1911–1972) realized that, "Whether or not it draws on new scientific research, technology is a branch of moral philosophy, not science."[7] Ethics (moral philosophy) is the study of what is good and right. Ethics may be defined as the subject matter of the proper ordering of an agent's external deontological actions and behaviors practiced through social conduct in combination with its internal ontological motivations and volitional character coupled with its teleological purposes.[8]

As a creature capable of building systems incorporating AI, any discussion related to its associated ethical standards requires a discussion of metaethics. Metaethics is the study of the foundational concepts regarding the nature of morality (metaphysics of morals), how one knows what is good, true, and beautiful (moral epistemology), and how one subjectively understands what is good, true, and beautiful (moral psychology). A primary concern of this work is to show that the ethical foundations and concepts of ASI are deficient because, relative to Christian ethics, it (1) possesses an incorrect metaethical foundation, (2) is presently operating under an ungrounded metaethic, and (3) employs an insufficiently robust and comprehensive metaethic. On the positive side, it will be articulated that God's

---

Defeated?.

7. Goodman, *New Reformation*, 40.

8. Agent's external deontological actions mean actions taking towards others based upon realized duties and responsibilities. Internal ontological motivations mean subjectively perceived driving forces happening in time and space initiated by a cause.

establishment of a moral law and a natural order provide warrant for consideration of Christian ethics to be utilized within any AI/ASI frameworks.

The question then arises how the ethics of ASI will be implemented. Will it be subject only to the rules found from within science or will it be open to the full study of moral philosophy?[9] Will it align with the understanding arising from a philosophical understanding of a closed cosmos that lacks any ethical obligations that derives from an object outside of mankind—a man-centric (anthropocentric) ethic? Conversely, should it consider incorporating the possibility, or the reality, of a transcendent ethic such as what Christians lay claim to based upon the authority of the biblical scriptures?

In taking both sides into account it will be proper to consider their respective views pertaining to creation, explaining how things came into being. Significant differences are to be observed at the outset. Christians account for rationality and intelligence as part of being made in the image of God (*imago Dei*). In contrast, thinkers associated with ASI reject this as a myth and hold to evolutionary naturalism. Evolutionary naturalists maintain that intelligence emerged over time through determined and random processes until such time as mankind was thought to be the most intelligent animal on the planet. Evolutionary naturalists believe that it is through man's intelligence that he has been successful in obtaining dominion over much of the planet. In fact, many proponents of ASI strongly oppose anthropocentric claims of dominion over creation. They argue rather that mankind's intelligence is responsible for "anthropogenic climate and environmental changes" that are harmful.[10]

Similarly, both sides have different understandings of man and his anthropology. ASI proponents believe that intelligence is one particular attribute of man that has enabled him to employ technology, but otherwise man is of no inherently greater value than other biological life forms. Biblical Christianity understands intelligence as a connection point to the Creator and so sees that mankind is exceptional from other life forms because mankind is spiritual in nature; that is, he can relate to God.

The nature of intelligence itself is an important issue. How is one to understand the issue of intelligence relative to the ideas of a brain, a mind,

---

9. Prominent social critic and atheist Paul Goodman maintained the position that "whether or not it draws on new scientific research, technology is a branch of moral philosophy, not science." Goodman, *New Reformation*, 208.

10. Persson and Savulescu, *Unfit for the Future*, 73.

and a machine? If intelligence is an emergent biological property, what is it grounded on so that it can be considered to be epistemically reliable?

Exponential growth in technologies provides a potential future forecast where machines or enhanced humans can outperform all intelligent systems that are presently viable. Such an explosion in intelligence may create a situation where the current rules no longer apply. These events, known as a "technological singularity," seek answers to whether a created intelligence could, in effect, take over running the cosmos for humans.[11] If so, what are the implications? Christians would recognize such a technological singularity as a manufactured god. What are the implications if this creation becomes a reality?[12]

There is a future era when, besides doing plastic surgery on their bodies, people may elect to perform an implant surgery, take medications, or upload and download their minds into machines in order to have functionally more intelligence at their disposal in a manner similar to what computers and portable devices have done extra-bodily over the past generation. This enhancement of intelligence, both in the natural and artificial domain, warrants an ethical discussion.

With the coming of intelligence enhancement and ASI, it may someday be possible to take information stored in the brain and map it digitally into computers. Is this a way for humans to cheat and escape death by keeping the information on ASI? This leads to pertinent questions regarding the understanding of intelligence and whether intelligence is lost at natural death when the brain ceases to function. Is intelligence something that can be captured and contained, or is it so abstract that containing it leads to some type of reductionism?

ASI ethics currently are largely based upon functional and utilitarian considerations, and with the advent of ASI there is a large emphasis on functional autonomy for machines, computers, and enhanced humans that may be performing AI. Functional autonomy largely places ethics under

---

11. For further reading on the topic of technological singularity, look at Barrat, *Our Final Invention*; Chalmers, "Singularity"; Del Monte, *Artificial Intelligence Revolution*; Eden et al., *Singularity Hypotheses*; Kurzweil, *Singularity Is Near*; Sandler, *Ethics and Emerging Technologies*; Sirius and Cornell, *Transcendence*; Tipler, *Physics of Christianity*; Vinge, "Coming Technological Singularity"; Yampolskiy, "What to Do with the Singularity Paradox?"

12. *Limitless* is an American drama television series based on the novel *The Dark Fields*. The premise is that a drug named NZT-48 increases the character's IQ by an order of magnitude, giving him amazing powers of intelligence. It debuted on television on September 22, 2015. Glynn, *Dark Fields*; Glynn, *Limitless*.

INTRODUCTION

the subjective control of the operating agent. Is such an ethic properly warranted and useful to navigate through an ethical dilemma in view of either external objective considerations and/or society relationships?

QUESTIONS TO BE ANSWERED

Given that ASI, as presently formulated and conceived, is entirely naturalistic in its philosophical understanding, what do present articulations of possible and actual ASI ethics look like in comparison to Christian ethics? Is ASI some utopian dream or perhaps a modern tower of Babel that God would not allow (Gen 11:1–9)? What is the role and responsibility of the people of God in shaping AI, ASI, and transhumanism (H+)?[13] What are the ethical implications of a predominately transhumanistic culture? Is the next evolution of our postmodern culture a move to becoming transhumanistic, and what would that mean morally and politically? Could ASI be the tipping point? If ASI is realized and becomes part of the human condition, how does the potential for life extension of one's own intelligence relate to Christian understandings of anthropology, sin, and redemption? What challenges do ASI ethics encounter relative to Christian ethical approaches?

THESIS

The thesis of this work is that any technological enhancements to humankind's cognitive intelligence, whether achieved through biological or artificial manipulations of human nature or resulting from human creation, are subject to the commands, prescriptions, and principles revealed through God's unified revelation—taking into account that man is created as an image-bearer of God.[14] It will be asserted that Christians should articulate

---

13. Advances in AI, in all its forms, will be congruent with a rise in transhumanism (H+), which "is an international cultural and intellectual movement with an eventual goal of fundamentally transforming the human condition by developing and making widely available technologies to greatly enhance human intellectual, physical, and psychological capacities." "What Is Transhumanism?—the 3 Supers," http://ieet.org/index.php/IEET/more/pearce20140916. Such a philosophical system and this particular worship of what man has created have far-reaching effects into the ethics of society and culture.

14. As image-bearers, human beings are theologically and morally responsible and accountable to their Creator, the triune God of the Bible, as the norm for being and doing; as such, they are called to love God to the utmost with all their "heart," or their entire

an ethic for ASI that is biblical in its worldview perspective rather than naturalistic, because ASI, regardless of its extraordinarily high intelligence level, is still a finite creation that is encompassed within God's created realm. Specifically, it will be argued that human beings are morally accountable to the triune God and biblical teachings and that Christian ethics would be a superior conceptual ethical framework to employ with ASI.

POINTS TO DEMONSTRATE

The first point to demonstrate is that intelligence should properly involve discussions of God, even if it is just the possibility of the existence of God, as God provides the best framework from which to understand intelligence. Atheistic understandings of intelligence are lacking in unity and cohesion largely due to the issue of evolutionary argument against naturalism.[15]

The second point to demonstrate is a proper understanding of man. Because this work looks at the ethical implications as it pertains to ASI, it is necessary to understand correctly man (*homo*) before considering any relationships to what he creates. From this, it will need to be understood that if man creates out of finite substances, there are limits regarding the ideal final results of what he can create.

The third point to demonstrate is that even if one does not accept Christianity, Christian ethics can properly account for and handle significant and relevant ethical issues that are presented. Christianity articulates itself as a system of truth with God at its nexus. If all truth is God's truth, then Christianity can be expected to handle ethical issues in a manner that is superior to other ethical systems. It will be demonstrated that a Christian ethic can be applied in all cases of ASI and deliver virtuous results.

---

being; thus, any technological enhancements to humankind's cognitive intelligence as conceived and envisioned within H+, whether achieved through biological or artificial manipulations of human nature or through intelligence emanating as a result of human creation and innovation, are fundamentally and completely subject to the Creator's commands, prescriptions, and principles as revealed in his unified revelation and must properly take into account the implications of being such an image-bearer.

15. "Evolutionary argument against naturalism" (EAAN) is a phrase first formerly introduced by Christian philosopher Alvin Plantinga. For a further look into EAAN consider Lewis, *Miracles*; Plantinga, *Warranted Christian Belief*, 194–237; Reppert, *C. S. Lewis's Dangerous Idea*.

INTRODUCTION

LITERATURE

At its philosophical inception, ASI was largely in the purview of science fiction writers. However, ASI has garnered specific and identifiable key personnel that are leading representatives that speak out on its thought and possible implications. Some of the most notable names discussing ASI include Zoltan Istvan, a writer and futurist; philosopher Nick Bostrom; author, inventor, and futurist Ray Kurzweil; and Stephen Hawking, physicist and cosmologist. This work will focus on published works of Kurzweil and Bostrom, two of the most successful writers on the topic of ASI over the past twenty years.

In 1999 Kurzweil, a top-selling author, published *The Age of Spiritual Machines: When Computers Exceed Human Intelligence*, which became a number one seller on Amazon in the category of science.[16] In this work, Kurzweil forecasts a day when ASI will exceed normal human intelligence in every category and in every way. He would go on to write *The Singularity Is Near: When Humans Transcend Biology*, released in 2005. It outlined his thesis that ASI will shortly be embedded into human bodies and brains. This work became a *New York Times* bestseller and additionally became a number one seller on Amazon in the areas of both science and philosophy. His latest 2012 release, *How to Create a Mind: The Secret of Human Thought Revealed*, has also become a *New York Times* bestseller. In this work, Kurzweil articulates how the brain is successful at performing as a self-organizing hierarchical system of pattern recognizers. He argues that the brain's ability to recognize patterns forms the basis for intelligence. By taking what

---

16. Kurzweil, *Age of Spiritual Machines*. "Ray Kurzweil first achieved notice as an inventor. He is credited with creating the charge-coupled device (CCD), the first CCD flatbed scanner, the first omni-font optical character recognition (OCR), the first print-to-speech reading machine for the blind, the first text-to-speech synthesizer, the first music synthesizer capable of recreating the grand piano and other orchestral instruments, and the first commercially marketed large-vocabulary speech recognition. Kurzweil is the recipient of the $500,000 MIT-Lemelson Prize; the world's largest for innovation. In 1999, he received the National Medal of Technology, the nation's highest honor in technology, from President Clinton in a White House ceremony. In 2002, he was inducted into the National Inventors Hall of Fame, established by the US Patent Office. He has received twenty honorary doctorates, and honors from three US presidents. His website, KurzweilAI.net, tracks daily breakthroughs in science and technology and has over three million new readers annually. In 2012, Ray Kurzweil was appointed a Director of Engineering at Google, heading up a team developing machine intelligence and natural language understanding." KurzweilAINetwork, "Ray Kurzweil Biography."

is understood of the human brain, Kurzweil desires to articulate how these ideas and concepts can be used to develop ASI.

Nick Bostrom is a professor of philosophy at the Oxford Martin School, director of the Future of Humanity Institute, and a founding director at the Oxford Martin Programme on the Impacts of Future Technology at the University of Oxford. Bostrom has a background in physics (astrophysics and general relativity) and computational neuroscience (MSc, King's College, University of London), mathematical logic (BA in philosophy, mathematics, mathematical logic, and artificial intelligence, University of Goteborg) and philosophy (PhD, London School of Economics). To date, he has published four books, two of which are specifically applicable to the subject of this work.

In 2009, Bostrom published *Human Enhancement* with Julian Savulescu. It a collection of essays from philosophers and thinkers on what the future may hold related to humanity incorporating technological enhancements in order to make their human biology perform better and/or longer. In 2014, Bostrom released the most thorough discussion on the topic of ASI to date in *Superintelligence*. Recognizing the impact of realized ASI, Bostrom looks at what might happen if such powerful machine intelligence came into existence. Bostrom identifies what may be the existential risks for humanity and looks into how humanity gets to make the first move by contemplating how it will design and make the best of a potentially soon-to-be reality. In addition to his books, he has written extensively in journal articles and other publications. Some of the relevant works he has written on the subject at hand include "A History of Transhumanist Thought" (2005), "In Defense of Posthuman Dignity" (2005), "How Long Before Superintelligence" (2006), "The Future of Humanity" (2009), "Dignity and Enhancement" (2009), "The Superintelligent Will: Motivation and Instrumental Rationality in Advanced Artificial Agents" (2012), and "Why We Need Friendly AI" (2014). Bostrom recognizes that the challenge is to program any superintelligence with alogrithms that are necessarily more ethical than humans yet is not able to articulate how this will be accomplished.

Along with these personnel there are several organizations that discuss and promote these ideas, including Humanity+ (H+), Institute for Ethics and Emerging Technologies (IEET), and Machine Intelligence Research Institute (MIRI).[17] Interaction with primary sources will largely come from

---

17. "Humanity+ (H+) is an international nonprofit membership organization that

INTRODUCTION

people associated directly or with strong affinities, respect, and sympathies towards these philosophical ideas.

From the Christian perspective, no single work or author stands out as primary resources for argumentation in this endeavor. Christian theological sources that hold to a strong sense of the authority of the Bible and Christian orthodoxy articulated at the inception of the church as demonstrated in such manifestations as the Nicene Creed will be employed to argue the Christian position.

METHODOLOGY

ASI is a dynamic and fast-moving field that is rapidly increasing in its scope and capabilities such that what is cutting edge today is replaced and obsolete within a matter of a few seasons or even months. This rapidity of change requires that any and all research be both current and forward-looking so as to capture the latest trends and trajectories. The quantity of people involved in written and presentation communication on the topic of ASI is relatively small due to its highly technical nature and relatively recent origins. Because of the technology and the global nature of this endeavor, much of what is written and/or presented is available in some form or another digitally through the Internet.

The primary focus will be on assessing information presented by recognized and acknowledged leaders in this field. This information will consist of primary sources through published books by individual authors, edited books, which are often collections of many people outside

---

advocates the ethical use of technology to expand human capacities. In other words, we want people to be better than well." Humanity+ adopted the Transhumanist Declaration; see http://humanityplus.org. "The Institute for Ethics and Emerging Technologies is a nonprofit think tank which promotes ideas about how technological progress can increase freedom, happiness, and human flourishing in democratic societies. We believe that technological progress can be a catalyst for positive human development so long as we ensure that technologies are safe and equitably distributed. We call this a 'techno-progressive' orientation. Focusing on emerging technologies that have the potential to positively transform social conditions and the quality of human lives—especially 'human enhancement technologies'—the IEET seeks to cultivate academic, professional, and popular understanding of their implications, both positive and negative, and to encourage responsible public policies for their safe and equitable use." Institute for Ethics and Emerging Technologies, http://ieet.org. "We do foundational mathematical research to ensure smarter-than-human artificial intelligence has a positive impact." Machine Intelligence Research Institute, https://intelligence.org.

the editors, and journal articles. As this primary information is generated after 1945, it is largely available in English and thus there is no anticipated need for having to interact with any other languages on the topic of ASI. In contrast, biblical, theological, and philosophical primary sources have a long history and may include research into primary sources with languages including Hebrew, Greek, and Latin.

There is no key Christian ethical primary source on the subject of ASI. As such, ethical, biblical, theological, and philosophical issues were researched utilizing primary sources from across the broad spectrum of Christian orthodoxy. The research did not incorporate any firsthand contact with any sources, whether through personal interviews, through meeting or hearing at conventions, conferences, or trade shows, or through other one-on-one methods such as telephone, email, or similar communication methods.

The Word of God is constant and unchanging. Source materials utilized to discuss theological and ethical issues may thus range across historical eras. A heavy reliance will be placed upon what the Bible has stated on the topic, as it is considered for the purposes of this work to be the source of revealed authority of God.

Chapter 2

The Creature—Man

CREATURE

Man is a creature with an intelligent mind.[1] How did man come to have his mind and his intelligence? One's understanding of the mind's origins will impact one's perspective regarding ASI ethics. The first part of the thesis to be proved is that human beings are morally accountable to the triune God and biblical teachings.

Ethics is the study of how one applies good and right actions in relationship to oneself and other persons within complicated and ongoing situational contexts.[2] If a rational agent attempts to employ the most efficient

---

1. Satisfactorily defining intelligence is no easy task. Simplistically, it may be considered to be the ability to reason in order to accomplish goals in various environments. Hutter proposes a formal definition for intelligence in AI, called AIXI. It attempts to unify aspects of universal induction, probabilistic planning, and reinforcement learning. The goal is the highest reward calculated based on sequential decision theory and algorithmic information theory. Armstrong, *Smarter Than Us*, 8–9; Hutter, *Universal Artificial Intelligence*, 3.

2. For the purposes of this work, ethics is defined as the subject matter of an agent's external deontological actions and behaviors practiced through social conduct in combination with its internal ontological motivations and volitional character coupled with its teleological purposes. Christian ethics is defined as the wisdom of an agent's external deontological actions and behaviors practiced through social conduct in combination with its internal ontological motivations and volitional character coupled with its transcendent teleological purposes with the requirement that everything give proper respect, attention, and application to the commands, principals, and prescriptions of the triune God revealed through his unified revelation, which culminated in the gospel of Jesus Christ, the wisdom of God—given the objective reality that all human agents are created in the *imago Dei*.

means to achieve its objectives, how are various situational aspects to be resolved? A reliance on the most favorable expected outcome prompts the question of who and how these expected outcomes are to be calculated and programmed, since they may fail to take into account all the factors and weigh them properly because, by definition, the machine is only finite and thus not capable of an infinite and thus perfect perspective. How are these challenges to be faced? It will be subsequently argued that biblical ethics provides the best ethical framework for ASI.

This chapter will discuss the theological and philosophical implications of position that assumes *a priori* that Scripture is God's divine revelation to mankind providing him with both the necessary and sufficient knowledge of him as the Creator of mankind, to whom mankind is held responsible and accountable to obey, in contrast to the evolutionary naturalistic worldview that believes that man is not morally accountable to any supernatural being and is able to operate in the domain of ethics as he ascertains is best for his survival, reproduction, and personal subjective pleasure.

Different worldviews are the starting and constant source of conflict in discussions related to ASI. Naturalistic worldview perspectives that support evolution dominate ASI worldviews. This chapter will articulate a biblical worldview of man that derives from the special revelation of God as articulated in the book of Genesis. It will maintain that the cosmos was created as a special act of the triune God of the Bible at a distinct point in time in the relatively recent past, when compared to the billions of years generally claimed by evolutionary naturalists. This work will not attempt to resolve this issue but allow this tension to distinguish two diametrically opposed theological starting points.

Evolutionary naturalism articulates the starting point of time, space, and matter as the Big Bang, happening an estimated fourteen billion years ago.[3] Cosmologically, the universe had a beginning in time. For the evolutionary naturalist it is not clear how this cosmological beginning was initiated or why it gives the appearance that it so finely tuned to support human life. To date, they have offered no explanatory principle behind what

---

3. Ade et al., "Planck 2013 Results," 55–57. Evolutionary naturalism subscribes to scientism, a worldview perspective that believes that empiricism and the scientific method are the ultimate source of knowledge and authority. Scientism fails because (1) it cannot explain abstract (nonempirical) concepts such as color, time, space, the self, mathematics and (2) cannot provide philosophical grounding for necessary and universal judgments.

initiated this sequence, meaning there is no ability to identify a first cause.[4] Besides not being able to ascertain what initiated the supposed Big Bang, evolutionary naturalism has not been able to give any justifiable answers for how life spontaneously arose since it has never been observed that nature is able to generate life out of non-life. Evolutionary naturalism theorizes that mental processes are nothing more than the result of material properties acting within the brain and are not the result of self-determining agents that have the ability to make uncoerced choices of their own. Evolutionary naturalists limit themselves to only looking for possible explanatory causes from within the material cosmos.[5]

A proper understanding of God's divine revelation as an external and necessary communication by God as an agent outside the cosmos (transcendent) allows Christians to have additional insight into metaphysical realities. Biblical creationism, as articulated in Genesis 1, occurred over a period of six days, with the seventh day intended to model a day of rest.[6]

---

4. This is sometimes referred to as the cosmological argument. For classical articulations on this argument start with Aristotle, *Metaphysics*, bk. Λ (12). Also see Aquinas, *Summa Theologica*, I.2.3. For discussion on the cosmological fine-tuning look at Craig, "Teleological Argument and the Anthropic Principle"; McGrath, *Fine-Tuned Universe*.

5. Wallace, *God's Crime Scene:*, 19–46.

6. Not all Christians hold to an interpretation of creation in a literal six twenty-four-hour days. However, a debate in that topic is beyond the scope of this work. Throughout this work the following principles of biblical interpretation will be employed: (1) Scripture is read from the perspective of it as God speaking and communicating to mankind; (2) accepting the primacy of the biblical languages; (3) understanding the importance of context/background; (4) Scripture interprets Scripture (*Scriptura Scripturae interpres*), meaning interpret Scripture by other Scripture; (5) affirmation and presupposition of the theological unity of Scripture; and (6) Scripture is approached with an attitude of faith seeking understanding: (a) believe that you may understand (*crede ut intelligas*) (Augustine, *Tractate* 29.6 [John 7:14–18]); (b) faith seeking understanding (*fides quarens intellectum*) (Anselm of Canterbury, preface of *Proslogium*); (c) I believe in order to understand (*credo ut intelligam*) (Anselm of Canterbury, *Proslogium*, ch. 1). This work is written from the perspective of affirming "The Chicago Statement on Biblical Inerrancy" (1978). International Council on Biblical Inerrancy, http://library.dts.edu/Pages/TL/Special/ICBI_1.pdf. There are some Christians who reject a six-day creation and believe that it is possible for the cosmos to have been in existence for possibly millions to billions of years. This position believes that Scripture does not indicate how creation happened but only that it was the result of God. It rejects the idea that Genesis 1–11 is descriptive historical narrative and claims that God is not limited and is open to work through processes and time. Such speculations are largely built upon scientific and literary claims rather than the scriptural texts. Reasons for rejecting such claims include but are not limited to: (1) the determining texts in Genesis 1–11 are written in historical narrative form; (2) God cannot lie and so any revelations he has provided must be truthful; (3) Adam

The Bible provides an explanation as to the first cause of all creation and identifies it as God (*elohim*), a personal, transcendent, and infinite being (Gen 1:1—2:3).[7]

This leads to some provocative questions. From where comes order such as is evident in what mankind observes as scientific laws and principles? What holds things in place and causes them to be preserved? What place does intelligence have in this concept? How is chaos held in check so that it does not overtake that which is ordered? The evolutionary naturalist and the biblical creationist will answer these questions differently. Since evolutionary naturalists state that empirical evidence is primary, they must answer these questions using their own requirements.

Order and Chaos

Modern scientific understanding believes that physical laws are able to characterize and describe reality accurately. The belief is that nature reflects an ordered structure that science and technology can rely upon in order to enable pragmatic human results. A key question that arises from this understanding is upon what foundation this created order operates.

By way of comparison, modern scientific thinking largely takes for granted that social laws are culturally determined and defined and not inherently connected to physical realities. In short, David Hume's (1711–1776) fact/value dichotomy is accepted as correct.[8] Moral facts are rejected and moral realism is dismissed as invalid.

Not by empirical methods, but rather by divine revelation, the Christian understands that the created order is a result of a Creator God (*elohim*) (Gen 1:1—2:3).[9] The creation is a reflection of his will, his power, and his

---

was created in the *imago Dei*; (4) the biblical genealogies; (5) the testimony to the reality of Adam in both the Old and New Testaments; (6) Jesus Christ pointing to the creation narrative as historical reality; (7) the biblical claim of common descent from one man; (8) the impact of sin on the created world; and (9) the reality of death through Adam and the hope of life through Jesus Christ.

7. According to time lines recorded in Scripture, the biblical creation of mankind is much more recent than the theory of evolution proposes, by up to perhaps six orders of magnitude: thousands (10^3) as opposed to billions (10^9) of years.

8. Hume, *Treatise of Human Nature*.

9. Augustine (354–430) understood that there were only two ways to arrive at a first principle. The first is through reason and the second through authority. Augustine contended that philosophy can only teach a first principle of all things, without itself

purpose. Everything that God created was deemed to be good (*tob*) and appropriate to its purpose and function (Gen 1:4, 10, 12, 18, 21, 25, 31). The creation is a reflection of God's nature and glory (Ps 19; 57:5, 11; 108:5; 113:4).[10] One aspect of the created order is the natural order, which consists of every physical aspect of reality, including the laws of physics (fundamental principles and forces of physical phenomena), chemistry (physical interaction and change of matter), and biology (life). As Creator, all these physical aspects of reality are subject to his sovereign control; meaning that at any time God as Creator can intervene in the physical aspects of reality. By definition, such interventions may be characterized as miracles. The incarnation, life, death, and resurrection of Jesus Christ should be understood as being the most significant historical example of this case.[11]

Christians believe that God's created order extends into the social order. It will be shown that besides not believing that God established the created physical order, evolutionary naturalists reject that God created social order. This denial ultimately has ethical and moral implications because it rejects the connection between fact and value. Christians understand that God ordained social institutions, including the family, the state, and the

---

having a foundational principle. In contrast to philosophy, Augustine believed that all authority comes from God (Rom 13:1). Augustine viewed Scripture as revelation from God almighty, triune (three persons) in nature. Scripture is provided to reveal mysteries to liberate people and nations. The incarnation of Christ, whereby for mankind's sake God assumed a human body, was done for our sakes and is beyond the grasp of the proud minds of men. Augustine, *On Order (De Ordine)*, bk. 2, debate 1, sec. 5, pp. 67–71.

10. The Scriptures provide meaning and insight to the created order through indicating God's purposes and his character as well as his actions through his design (providence). There are two complimentary elements identified in Psalm 19. Psalm 19:1–6 points to general revelation/natural theology, whereas Psalm 19:7–14 alludes to specific revelation. Psalm 19:1–6 makes an appeal to the heavens, explaining that its desirability is more than gold. The functionality of this section warns people and leads them toward a reward through the knowledge of our own faults and the overcoming of sin. It calls us to the need for forgiveness of sins. Secondly, the name of God is different in these two sections. In v. 1 his name is *El*, meaning God, and in vv. 7–9 his name is *Yahweh*, meaning LORD. The claim it makes about general revelation is that God speech is a restrained way of him revealing his first-hand knowledge to mankind. General revelation is a clearing of the throat by God in order to get the attention of mankind.

11. For a discussion of the relevance and importance of God coming in the flesh and raising himself back to life in a bodily human resurrection, see Clark, "Bodily Resurrection Scientifically Sound."

church.¹² Morality should be properly understood to be one's actions operating in accordance with God's ordained order.¹³

Philosopher and intellectual historian Arthur Lovejoy (1873–1962) called the Christian conception of order the "Great Chain of Being."¹⁴ In this pre-Darwinian worldview conception, order and chaos are seen as part of a hierarchy that stops at the top with God and proceeds downward in graduations: God → Mind → Design → Order → Chaos → Nothing.¹⁵ This conception places mankind as part of the created order. Man's intelligence derives from a design that God originated in his mind.¹⁶ The takeaway from this is that God's mind is first and prior to design and order.¹⁷

Darwinian evolutionary understanding sees this process in reverse. In the outlook of philosopher, writer, and cognitive scientist Daniel Dennett (1942–), design is nothing more than "a living thing or a part of a living thing or the artifact of a living thing organized in any case in aid of the battle against disorder," while in the view of Kurzweil such biological processes do not emanate from the mind of God, "but rather are a result of a godless natural selection."¹⁸ Inherent in both men's thinking is the belief that from

---

12. (1) family: Gen 1:28; 2:18–24; Ps 127:3–5; Matt 19:4–6; 1 Tim 5:8; (2) state: Rom 13:1–7); (3) church: Isa 2:2–3; Dan 2:44; Matt 16:18–19; Luke 24:49; John 16:13; Acts 1:5, 8; 2:1–4, 37–39, 41–43, 47.

13. It is recognized that morality warrants a much larger discussion. The issue of morality and ethics will be discussed in an ongoing manner throughout.

14. Lovejoy, *Great Chain of Being*.

15. Design in this chart is conceived of in a manner similar to that articulated by Aristotle's *telos* meaning: end, goal, or purpose. Aristotle, *Nicomachean Ethics*.

16. This idea will be examined more closely when the discussion centers on man created in the *imago Dei* (image of God).

17. Such a conception means that the mind of God and his design plans are eternal (Exod 3:14; Num 23:19; Ps 90:2; 102:25–27; Isa 40:8, 28; Mal 3:6; Heb 6:17–18; 7:24; 13:8; Jas 1:17). This matter of the eternal status of the conscious minds of mankind as well as the status of artificial intelligence are further addressed under the subject of ethics.

18. Dennett, *Darwin's Dangerous Idea*, 69. Kurzweil proposes the Law of Time and Chaos: In a process, the time interval between salient events (that is, events that change the nature of the process, or significantly affect the future of the process) expands or contracts with the amount of chaos. From this Kurzweil generates the following two laws. (1) The Law of Increasing Chaos: As chaos exponentially increases, time exponentially slows down (that is, the time interval between salient events grows longer as time passes). Kurzweil holds that the Law of Increasing Chaos applies to the universe and life of an organism. (2) The Law of Accelerating Returns: where evolution draws upon chaos and order, then increases exponentially, making time speed up and the returns accelerate. This law is applied to the evolution of life forms. These life forms lead to the evolution of technology leading onwards to computation. Kurzweil views computation as the essence

order and extended time all of life (biology) was able to arise.[19] In this view, it is not the mind of God that creates everything, but rather an emergent order. The Genesis account is rejected in favor of abiogenesis (life arising from non-life). One may question how Darwinian evolutionists can ensure that order exists, since it would be conceivable that, rather than order, all might be either (1) existing as complete and total chaos or (2) nothing (*nil*). Abiogenesis and Darwinian evolutionary accounts of man's origin are unsatisfactory based upon probability theory. Origins beg an explanation and a more satisfying probability is found in a first cause, a Creator. The biblical worldview identifies the first cause as the Creator God (*elohim*) (Gen 1:1).

Both sides have chosen different starting points, and two different first principles. Evolutionary naturalism chooses as its first principle the reason of man. This is employing reason simply as an artifact, devoid of any special creation through the process of a great and powerful mind. Against this theory of evolutionary naturalism, Christians choose as their starting point the revelation of God's mind through the Scriptures, understanding that he has created mankind's mind and intelligence to exist in his created realm. James Sire, Christian author, speaker, and editor, cautions against the autonomy of human reason, stating that worldviews constructed in such a manner are subject to the dangers inherent in each person's human ego and the community's sense of reason. Sire stresses that ontology (being) precedes epistemology (knowing) in worldview formation. Sire must be taken seriously in this matter because, as has been shown, both sides of this issue recognize and understand ontology as preceding epistemology and hermeneutics (interpretation).[20] Evolutionary naturalists appear to undercut their argument for autonomous reason by claiming their being is a result of nonintelligent natural selection that provides no account for where intelligence ultimately originates.

Creation by God and natural selection are thus at opposite ends of the spectrum and cannot be reconciled because one affirms God and the other rejects God. By way of the law of noncontradiction, only one may be

---

of order in technology. Kurzweil, *Age of Spiritual Machines*, 25–35.

19. Proponents of the Intelligent Design (ID) movement argue that, contrary to Darwinian claims, biology in fact shows evidence of intelligent design. Dembski, *No Free Lunch*; Dembski and McDowell, *Understanding Intelligent Design*.

20. Lyotard, *Postmodern Condition*. Lyotard (1924–1998) argues that no grand narrative, such as the Bible, will contain the ultimate answers. He contends that little narratives will do the work of accounting for the differences and that one day all knowledge will need to be on computers. Sire, *Naming the Elephant*, 72–73.

considered true.[21] The idea of natural selection as a mindless process has assumed validity in modern science and philosophy. The resultant implications as they pertain to ethics will be seen.[22]

Homo Faber

Both of these worldviews maintain that man is a creator and maker of things that are useful for his own purposes, the so-called *Homo faber* (man as maker), with the capability to plan with greater intentionality than other species.[23] Evolutionary naturalists see technology as a development of mankind that has progressed, in their view, since man's advent. As a result of a long period of time of evolutionary change, humans are thought now to be the most intelligent creatures on Earth. It is the human mind, not the human biological body, that is understood to produce the capability to survive and thrive relative to other species.

Technology

Technology is the collection of tools, including machinery, modifications, arrangements and procedures, used by humans to reach desired ends.[24] Kurzweil adds to this general definition, stating that as it is generally understood it is "not entirely sufficient."[25] He maintains that such a definition fails to distinguish how human technology is different from technology employed by other primates and the like. Kurzweil suggests that a unique feature of human technology is "application of knowledge—recorded

---

21. Aristotle, *Metaphysics*, bk. Γ (4), 3–6, e.

22. Nagel, *Mind and Cosmos*.

23. Foerst claims to be a Christian and maintains that evolution and biblical creation are in conflict. She characterizes those that believe in biblical creationism being a literal-historical reality as outlined by a historical-grammatical approach to Genesis as extremists and fundamentalists. Thus, she dismisses them out of hand, thereby prioritizing human inductive reasoning over and above divine revelation. Her mistake is to believe that mankind necessarily has it right in explaining God to mankind, rather than that God has it right in explaining himself to mankind. Foerst, *God in the Machine*, 43–4, 93.

24. Technology comes from two Greek roots: (1) *techne*, meaning "art, skill, craft, manner, way, or the means"; and (2) *logos*, meaning "the word." An important theological point is that technology is teleological in nature, meaning that it is focused on rational ordering that moves in the direction of a particular end.

25. Kurzweil, *Age of Spiritual Machines*, 14–17.

knowledge—to the fashioning of tools" and that technology can "transcend the materials that it is composed of."[26] Kurzweil, in contrast to the biblical account, suggests that language is a human-created technology (Gen 2:19–20, 23). Kurzweil believes that "all forms of technology including art, language, and machines represent evolution by other means."[27]

Evolutionary naturalists claim that technology has increased relatively linearly over the time frame that mankind reportedly has been in existence. However, they claim that over the past few centuries technology has grown exponentially and shows little, if any, signs of slowing. Evolutionary naturalists believe that with the advent of the industrial revolution and new methods of transportation, communication, and manufacturing the recent past has seen exponential growth that will lead to an explosive increase in the amount of technology employed. This technology will find itself advancing first with AI in general and subsequently ASI. AI and ASI are derived intelligence, meaning they come from the programming, motivations, and ends that mankind has initially inserted into their functional capabilities. AI and ASI thus may be considered at this juncture a sort of creation that is made in the *imago Hominis* (image of man or alternatively image of the human). Julian Huxley (1887–1975), evolutionary biologist, eugenicist, and humanist, proposed that the increase in technology will lead to a new understanding of mankind, a concept he called transhumanism.[28]

---

26. Ibid.

27. By other means, Kurzweil is articulating that the seven-step life cycle of technology, consisting of (1) precursor, (2) invention, (3) development, (4) maturity, (5) pretenders, (6) obsolescence, and (7) antiquity, is not based on the chemical genetic code of biological life forms but rather is based upon the tools themselves, the written record and communication of them in writing, and finally from the technology itself. Ibid.

28. "The human species can, if it wishes, transcend itself—not just sporadically, an individual here in one way, an individual there in another way, but in its entirety, as humanity. We need a name for this new belief. Perhaps transhumanism will serve: man remaining man, but transcending himself, by realizing new possibilities of and for his human nature. 'I believe in transhumanism': once there are enough people who can truly say that, the human species will be on the threshold of a new kind of existence, as different from ours as ours is from that of Peking man. It will at last be consciously fulfilling its real destiny." Huxley, *New Bottles for New Wine*. Refer to Luke 5:33–39 for the biblical story to which this title has reference. Transgender lawyer, author, and entrepreneur Martine Rothblatt holds that technology has demolished the natural division of labor. This means that technology has made us transhuman and allows for the future of humanity to be (1) transbiologically receptive, (2) adaptational, and (3) noetically synthetic. Rothblatt, *From Transgender to Transhuman*, 104–9.

Those affirming the biblical creation account would consider technology to be a development of mankind whereby man goes about being a culture maker within the creation God has made.[29] Christians hold that mankind expresses the *imago Dei* (image of God) as technology is developed because it is a creative act that exhibits the various facets that are subsumed within the concept of the *imago Dei*.[30]

Imago Hominis

Christian understanding includes the notion that mankind is made in the *imago Dei*, but the evolutionary naturalists reject this view because they reject God as Creator. Putting aside for the moment the meaning of made in the *imago Dei*, the project will take a closer examination of what it means for *Homo faber* (man as maker) to use technology to create and fashion items that in some manner are built in the *imago Hominis*.[31] Two examples that come to mind are computers—which image man in calculating (primarily arithmetic and logic)—and robots—which image man in acting and performing tasks.

Noreen Herzfeld has done work as it pertains to the intersection of AI and theology. Herzfeld looks at the spiritual implications of AI by examining the *imago Dei* through three distinct perspectives and applying them to the idea of *imago Hominis*. The three perspectives she offers are: (1) Reinhold Niebuhr's (1892–1971) substantive (reason) approach leading to cybernetic immortality; (2) Gerhard von Rad's (1901–1971) functional (regency) view leading to expanded dominion; and (3) Karl Barth's (1886–1968) relational interpretation leading to human-machine relationships.

---

29. Technology, in this regard, may be considered as "the use of brain power to discover new products and less costly methods of production." Gwartney et al., *Common Sense Economics*, 30–31.

30. The concept of the image of God is divinely revealed throughout the Bible (Gen 1:26–27; 5:1–3; 9:6; Refer also to Rom 8:29; 1 Cor 11:7; 2 Cor 3:18; 4:4–7; Col 1:13–15; Heb 1:3; Jas 3:9). Note in Gen 5:3 the Hebrew distinguishes that Seth, Adam's son, is born in the image of Adam. Image of God: Hebrew transliteration, *tzelem elohim*; Latin, *imago Dei*. Tzelem is an image representation that is both concrete and abstract. Freedman, *Anchor Bible Dictionar*, 3:390. The image of God may include concepts containing aspects such as (1) intelligence, (2) rationality, (3) spirituality, (4) personality, (5) morality, (6) authority, (7) self-transcendence, and (8) creativity, but "which are expressions within a unified image." Clark, "Image of God."

31. *Imago Hominis*: "image of man" or alternatively "image of the human."

Herzold's conclusion is that there is much for us to learn from Barth's relational approach that can be applied to future human-AI convergences.[32]

While Herzfeld's three-perspective approach is enlightening on different aspects of the issue, it is open to critique. Herzfeld accepts evolution as scientific fact, giving priority to empiricism over the authority of Scripture through the lens of historical-grammatical methods of hermeneutics. Her selection and affinity for this viewpoint is sustained by the selection of three Neo-orthodox theologians as the basis for her evaluations. An object of this work will be to provide some additional insights into *imago Hominis* based upon insights obtained from the presuppositions assumed throughout this effort.

Evolutionary naturalism views the human as only a biological being, not as a spiritual being. Any *imago Hominis* found in AI and/or ASI would thus be anticipated to pertain to only the biological characteristics and capabilities found in humans. A primary focus for ASI is to produce intelligence that far exceeds the human limits possible through traditional biological means of birth, growth and development in youth, and finally reaching intellectual maturity in adulthood. Kurzweil's law of accelerating returns and Moore's law give reason to speculate that exponential growth in intelligence is possible.[33] As cognitive science learns more about the human brain, it is believed that machines and AI appear more closely to resemble human intelligence. Whether the various human intelligence nuances, besides simply raw computational power, can be captured within the AI's intelligence is a challenge that is still unfolding. Evolutionary naturalists believe that with increased science and technology it is simply just a matter of time, because if the brain is nothing it just "happens to be a meat machine."[34]

---

32. Herzfeld, *In Our Image*.

33. Moore's law observes that the transistor count doubles every two years on an integrated circuit chip (IC) while performance increases by a factor of two every eighteen months. Moore, "Cramming More Components onto Integrated Circuits."

34. This quote is attributed to cognitive scientist Marvin Minsky (1927–2016). Minsky is acknowledged, along with John McCarthy (1927–2011), as establishing the basic concepts of artificial intelligence and founding the MIT Computer Science and Artificial Intelligence Laboratory (CSAIL).

Ethics

It is taken for granted within the AI community that biblical creation is not scientifically and historically the best explanation for the creature man and, by implication, the origins of the cosmos. Evolutionary naturalism is looked to as the process by which mankind came into being. Such a perspective dismisses the possibility of the influence of metaphysical realities outside the empirically observable time-space-matter realm, hence only physical in nature. Does such an account provide a sufficient claim to a satisfactory explanation for ethics as it pertains to mankind and by extension to his technological creation of AI?

AI, technology, and science are valued in society based upon the practical results that they produce for humans. Science is deemed by society to be the best way to arrive at the truth. The current scientific paradigm in AI requires a mechanical metaphysic; it allows no room for transcendent aspects because it believes that everything in the cosmos is physical. Given the necessity of understanding the metaethical foundations for evolutionary naturalism based upon the claims of science, a look at how science claims to obtain knowledge and what the science actually tells mankind is warranted. From there the issue of a metaethic of ASI based upon science will be examined.

Epistemological knowledge by man's efforts is obtained by way of two broad categories: inductive logical reasoning (rationalism) and sensory observational experience (empiricism). It will be argued that both of these methods, whether standing alone or operating in concert, are insufficient. Take first the case of rationalism. Rationalism fails because it has to posit that there are universal ideas that can be understood consistently among mankind regardless of the varying sensory observations of different people. This is observably not the case. Different people, through their reasoning processes, come to different conclusions regarding the concept of a universal idea. Similarly, empiricism, starting with a blank mind that does not possess universal innate ideas is unable to explain how sensations are turned into concepts which are then categorized. In simplistic terms, rationalism as a philosophical system is insufficient to connect properly universal concepts to particular things and empiricism as a philosophical system is unable to bridge from particular things to universal concepts. Kant (1724–1804), realizing these issues, looks inward at man claiming that the mind of man (human intellect) contains the universal forms *a priori* and the mind assembles the particular sensory inputs into the correct categories.[35] How is this possible given that the mind prior to the experience had no understanding of what was to be received? Kant proposes a solution to this problem by articulating a transcendental schema, making appeal to something both nonempirical and nonrational.[36] Evolutionary naturalism is unable to account for Kantian conjectures because a transcendental schema is by definition unknowable. Nietzsche (1844–1900), under the influence of evolutionary naturalism, would go on to respond that "morality grows out of triumphant self-affirmation"—the will to power.[37] Nietzsche's philosophy gives rise to postmodern philosophical conceptions that give primacy to power and the human will over and above a transcendent order, logic, and rationality.

The scientific endeavor requires the laws of nature to be uniform; if they are not, then no statement of science would be seen as having a basis for confidence. While science desires to deal only with empirical methods, its foundational assumption of assuming the uniformity of nature cannot be established through observation. There must be something that ensures the required uniformity of nature. Kantian categories do not provide this because they are not able to define and bound the comprehensive aspects of the relationship between existing conditions. In actuality, science is a mere description of a set of empirical observations, but it is not capable of articulating the underlying workings of nature. It cannot justify its own mechanical metaphysic and thus cannot lay claim to even a mechanically derived metaethic.

Kant argues that the "morality of an act is not derived from its intentional end but is a result of one's motivation and is based upon duty."[38] Kant's failure to develop a suitable ethic uniting rationalism and empiricism epistemology is evident by his theory's failure to acknowledge the anticipated outcome (teleological good) to come from an action as well as its inability to articulate an explanation for the mechanistic nature of the phenomenal world contrasted with the agency of the mind in the noumenal world.[39] Post-Kantian conceptions on morality came first from the pen of Jeremy Bentham (1748–1832), who articulated morality as deontological (rules based) with its primary principle being that of utility, the greatest

35. Kant, *Groundwork of the Metaphysics of Morals*.
36. Kant, *Critique of Pure Reason*.
37. Wogaman, *Christian Ethics*, 174.
38. Ibid., 171.
39. Clark, *Thales to Dewey*, 328–34.

good for the greatest number of people. Utilitarianism cannot answer two important questions. First, how are all various combinations and possibilities of potential good to be quantified accurately for all given both (a) that any quantification of present variables is open to subjective understandings and (b) the unknown status of the future? Secondly, while appealing to apparent democratic principles, it cannot establish why individuals should be concerned with the good of others (the greater good).[40]

Present understandings prevalent within science and the AI community also include acceptance that ethical theories are inherently just social constructs, lacking objective external metaphysical foundations. Ethical formulations simply are arranged through consensus, allowing societies to cooperate and determine jointly what is of value. This conception opens itself up to the claim of being pluralistic and relativistic, hence not necessarily comporting with rationality. Lacking a unity tied to objective requirements, such as rationality, all moral actions are tolerated. In essence, the ability ethically to distinguish wrong from right is subsumed and undermined. All are allowed to decide for themselves. Ultimately everything is simply personal preference and unstructured. In such a system, the power to persuade and reward people and groups provides sway to the ethical direction of the group. Existentialism argues that the self is created by action. Life is now, and what we experience is our existence, and whatever is happening to us personally is what is real. Existentialism believes that man has freedom whereby almost anything is possible and values are inconsequential to both choice and action. Unconstrained freedom of choice, the ability to choose differently at any particular moment makes life devoid of meaning. Unfettered choice means no information can be provided that tells one how to choose, making ethical understandings impossible.

It has been shown that theories of knowledge dependent solely upon logical reasoning (rationalism), sensory experience (empiricism), or combinations thereof are abject failures for a coherent and universal system of ethics. They are unable to provide an authoritative and normative code of ethics that is comprehensive and sufficient. One must either look for a theory of knowledge that does lead to an authoritative and normative code of ethics or one is left to recognize that upon mankind's own self-referencing efforts no unifying theory of knowledge provides a universal authority; ethics cannot be normative and must rather be relativistic. It is claimed that an authoritative and normative possibility exists from what has come to

---

40. Bentham, *Deontology*, parts 1 and 2.

mankind through the special revelation of Scripture by the God who has chosen to speak to mankind. It is claimed that anthropologically based metaethics are not comprehensively satisfactory to utilize within society itself and subsequently to be used to program ethical parameters into AI. This is because AI will simply exhibit these same characteristic ethics flaws as a result of nonuniversal authoritative and normative principles used in its programming instructions. Mankind should never assume that in his role of *Homo faber* he can relieve himself of the moral responsibility regarding any outcomes that derive from any technological systems that incorporate AI, since man maintains ultimate responsibility because he is its originating designer.[41]

If a rational agent attempts to employ the most efficient means to achieve its objectives, how are various situational aspects to be resolved? A reliance on the most favorable expected outcome prompts the question of by whom and how these expected outcomes are to be calculated and programmed since they may fail to take into account all the factors and weigh them properly because, by definition, the machine is only finite and thus not capable of an infinite and thus perfect perspective. How are these challenges to be faced? It will be subsequently argued that biblical ethics provides the best ethical framework for ASI.

A metaethic that takes seriously the biblical creation account provides a foundational baseline for understanding man's relationship to ethics (Gen 1–3). The cosmos is called into existence by a personal agent, the triune God of the Bible (Gen 1:1). Made in the *imago Dei*, mankind inherently possesses a moral nature that inaugurates a relationship that connects God and mankind throughout eternity (Gen 1:26–27; 2:7). This relational bond, endowed by his Creator, allows mankind the capacity to distinguish, recognize, and understand good and evil as it has been communicated by God through divine revelation.[42] Mankind can only know and understand divine revelation through faith given as a gift from God, a faith that precedes clarity and certainty of our intellectual understanding (Eph 2:8–9).[43]

---

41. For further discussion of this specific concept as it might apply to responsibility for AI and robots in military efforts, look at Lorkhorst and van den Hoven, "Responsibility for Military Robots," in Lin, Abney, and Bekey, *Robot Ethics*, 145–55.

42. Sire, *Universe Next Door*, 34–35.

43. Augustine's moral epistemology is reflected in his belief that faith seeks understanding. Man's faith is supplied by the Holy Spirit, which illuminates man's minds so that man's moral consciousness (*synderesis*) and reasoning (intellect) are able to recognize eternal realities (*sapientia*, wisdom). Augustine, *On the Trinity*, bk. 8, preface 4. See

This moral relationship is woven into the creation in physical ways through the laws of nature that God has established that give regulatory and boundary conditions to physical sciences such as physics, chemistry, and biology. Yet, this relationship is not simply physical, subject only to the laws of science and observation. It is also spiritual in nature and has been negatively impacted by the sin of man against his Creator (Gen 2:7; 3:1–24; Rom 8:22) and, as Sire claims, "makes human ethics transcendent and based on the character of God as good (holy and loving)."[44] Jesus Christ, the Son of God, is the good (perfect) man incarnate and his atoning death on the cross to pay the penalty for the sin of mankind against the Creator is an act of infinite love (Rom 5:7–8; 1 John 4:10).[45]

MAN

Human Exceptionalism

Evolutionary naturalism believes that biblical creationism suffers from a misapplied anthropomorphic principle of stating that the first cause is a personal being. Followers reject the claim that human exceptionalism is a reality as biblical creationists would claim, identifying the time that they believe that mankind has been in existence relative to the time of the Big Bang as evidence that mankind is nothing more than an evolved animal that has a particularly high intelligence relative to other living beings, which has provided it with a high level of survivability and thriving skills. This high intelligence level is seen in the way that mankind has utilized technology and, with the advent of ASI, the exponential growth in intelligence provides reason for the evolutionary naturalist to believe that the future is optimistically bright.

The Copernican revolution caused a significant shift in man's own understanding of his place in the cosmos. Broadly speaking, this movement is characterized by a shift from man's belief that, philosophically and physically, Earth is at the center of the universe to a recognition that, spatially, Earth is not so. The loss of spatial significance in the cosmos is claimed to show that man should not consider humans to be exceptional philosophically or biologically (physically, including the area of intelligence).

---

also Nash, *Light of the Mind*, 1–10.

44. Sire, *Universe Next Door*, 42–43.

45. Ibid.

The Creature—Man

Scientists are searching for extraterrestrial intelligence (SETI) in hopes of discovering and making contact with extraterrestrial life. SETI researchers largely believe that (1) humans do not possess a privileged place in the universe, (2) humans should expect alien intelligent life to be morally superior, and (3) aliens may help humans overcome our ethical deficiencies, which are usually couched in terms of the long-term survivability of the human species, not social and interpersonal interactions.[46] SETI scientists conjecture that because of the vast numbers of physical items observable in the cosmos and the seemingly endless possibilities, there must be something else out there and that something is very likely more advanced. Such thinking is an appeal to possibility of the form: X is possible; therefore, X is true. However, this commits a logical fallacy. The physical location of Earth within the cosmos has no direct bearing on the impact on human significance, just as living in either North America, Africa, or Asia makes no impact on one's value as a human.

Minsky, strongly opposing biblical creationism, believes that humanity's future is that of transhumanism or extropianism, whereby humans transform themselves by technological changes to their biology, including their minds.[47] He affirms that humans are not yet all they can be biologically and thus he concludes that more should be done immediately by mankind to advance the evolution of mankind swiftly. Minsky, a strict evolutionary determinist, states that humans' dignity derives not from a soul, spirit, or self, but rather from the diversity of ways that each human has existentially distinguished himself by dealing with different situations. He holds that this diversity provides us with dignity that is greater than that of both animals and machines that humans have created up to this point in time.

Minsky's view is entirely functionalistic; that is, dignity and value are dependent upon what one can do and the extent to which one can do so. Such thinking would mean that the young are inferior to the experienced, intelligent people are of greater value than mentally handicapped ones, and machines could be of greater value than humans if they could "outthink" the human. Minsky believes and hopes that there will soon be a day when everyone gives up on biblical creationism and the idea of a soul and instead understand humans simply as computers made of meat and machines able to feel and think.[48]

46. Rubin, *Eclipse of Man*, 54–56.
47. Minsky, *Emotion Machine*.
48. Minsky, *Society of Mind*; *Emotion Machine*.

Biblical creation articulates that humans are exceptional because they are people made in the *imago Dei* (Gen 1:26–27). Human exceptionalism places value on the incarnation of Jesus Christ because it demonstrates that God came into his creation as fully God and fully man, the same essence (*homoousia*) as the Father and the same individual (*hypostasis*). Man is exceptional not because he is a biological (material organism), social (relationships), and psychological (awareness) animal. He is exceptional because he is able to have a personal relationship with God and the quality of this relationship significantly impacts God, the individual, society, and the created natural realm. God has ordered it such that human beings are more important than any other earthly creature. This idea should lead not to human pride and the abuse of the rest of creation. It should be directed toward faithful stewardship, humility, and the imitation of Jesus Christ (Matt 5–7; 1 Cor 11:1).

Biological Machine vis-à-vis *Imago Dei*

Humans as Machines Only

Is intelligence just an evolutionary byproduct or is intelligence connected to the Creator of the cosmos? Are human intelligent agents and artificial agents morally equivalent or is there a relevant distinction to be made? How do the two different sides view these questions?

Evolutionary naturalists believe that man is nothing but a biological machine, maintaining that matter is all that exists and that the mind is connected to and is simply a part of the materiality of the body.[49] When the body biologically dies, the mind dies with it. They also claim that one of man's primary and key differences from other species of animals is his high level of intelligence; however, often they downplay this reality.

Scientism desires to assume control over nature, making nature conform itself to the image of man.[50] Evolutionary naturalists and neuropsychologists maintain the intelligence of the human mind is the result of ordered biology. Molecular biology rejects a spiritual dimension to reality, instead accepting only the physical realm. The human body is believed to

---

49. In philosophy this position is exemplified by Daniel Dennett and in AI by Bostrom, Kurzweil, and Minsky. Dennett, *Consciousness Explained*; *Darwin's Dangerous Idea*. Bostrom, "History of Transhumanist Thought." Kurzweil, *Age of Spiritual Machines*; *Singularity Is Near*; *How to Create a Mind*. Minsky, *Society of Mind*.

50. Gay, *Way of the (Modern) World*, 79–129.

be an evolved ordered biomass that operates as a machine with a set of encoded operating instructions based upon the physical laws of nature.[51] Believing it took hundreds of millions of years for the human mind to evolve and become "human," they endeavor to accelerate the evolutionary speed of change of the matter of the brain by employing technology.[52]

In this view the human body has ordered parts combined together—each working in cooperation to perform a specific function—that operate toward an end goal. They believe the body is a machine and nothing more. Such a conception opens up the potential for a future in which AI robots may be considered as worthy of moral status equivalent to or greater than that of humans because at some point in time they may be able to perform all the tasks and goals of which humans are capable.

Kurzweil believes humans and their brains are simply biological machines and rejects that they are anything other than a product of evolution.[53] He believes that the human brain observes the law of physics and that there is no supernatural element involved. He articulates that it is time for mankind to accept the fact that artificially intelligent entities, whether strictly man-made machines or a coupling of man and machine, are a future reality. It is the intelligence of these entities that will allow them to take control and direct the path of civilization.

As AI-enabled machines continue to advance and proliferate, their ethical programming requires further human solutions regarding decisions related to their autonomy and ethics. A potential question is, if AI robots can function as machines in a way equivalent to humans, should they not be granted the same privileges and rights as humans? Professor Amy DeBaets argues that AI robots that are embodied, sociable, and mirror humanity should be considered to be morally valuable in themselves.[54] However, the key concern prior to addressing any ethical issues for AI is to have a solid

---

51. Explanation for the original source of this order is a discussion of metaphysics. Biblical Christianity and evolutionary naturalism diverge on their metaphysical understandings. Biblical Christianity accepts that (1) there is a transcendent God outside his creation and that (2) the created realm that has been structured for humanity. Evolutionary naturalism rejects this concept and believes that everything is within one realm, the physical. Such a conception leads to all things being one and destroys distinctions. Jones, *One or Two*.

52. Moravec, *Robot*, 127–89.

53. Kurzweil, *Age of Spiritual Machines*, 5.

54. DeBaets, "Robot as Person."

grasp on what is proper for human ethics. This is requisite, since any AI ethics is ultimately derived from a human ethic.

Humans as Image-Bearers

Man's original commission in Genesis 1 states that mankind is created in the *imago Dei*. Mankind is thus an image-bearer of God. This image is wired into the humanity of every tribe, tongue, and nation. This means that the whole person, both one's body (material) and spirit (immaterial), have been created by God with a spiritual purpose in mind. Augustine said, "You have made us for yourself, O Lord, and our heart is restless until it rests in you."[55] One purpose for the creation of the cosmos is so that man may glorify God and enjoy him forever (1 Cor 10:31; 1 Pet 4:11).[56] Additionally, redemption is also a purpose of its creation (Rom 8:18–25).

Being an image-bearer should not be understood to mean that mankind is made with a direct physical resemblance to God. After all, God is spirit (John 4:24). In Genesis 1:27 God is said to have created two genders, male and female. In this manner, mankind is similar in nature to the created animals, which also (generally) have sexual distinctions. The Bible presents that at least one reason that God manifested distinctions in the sexes was to demonstrate and illustrate some of the truths of the relationship between Christ and his church (Eph 5:22–33). This truth means that created sexual distinctions do, in fact, analogically connect God and creature through a physically embodied picture of a spiritual reality. One issue that this raises is how physical sexual identity is to be understood in embodied AI entities. Western society is presently losing its grasp on sexual distinctions.[57] What happens as mankind programs himself and AI without regard for these

---

55. "Great are you, O Lord, and exceedingly worthy of praise; your power is immense, and your wisdom beyond reckoning." Augustine, *Confessions*, bk. 1.1.

56. For an excellent sermon on this topic consider Watson, "Man's Chief End Is to Glorify God."

57. The definition of marriage in Western society has been changed from one man and one woman to its present affirmation of homosexual marriage. The Bible condemns homosexual behavior as a sin and is thus not compatible with marriage. Additionally, the United States has moved towards the acceptance of transgender bathrooms, demonstrating a denial of biological function and reality. For more information on this societal transformation from a theological perspective, look at Allberry, *Is God Anti-Gay?*; Burk, *What Is the Meaning of Sex?*; Girgis, Anderson, and George, *What Is Marriage?*; Reilly, *Making Gay Okay*; Via and Gagnon, *Homosexuality and the Bible*.

physical and sexual distinctions? It is anticipated that as these lines continue to blur AI entities will take on physical embodiments that are both fluid and amorphous.

Christians hold that man is more than a biological machine and that he is unique from all other animals. As the pinnacle of God's creative activity, man is given dominion over all animal species (Gen 1:26–28). He is both a ruler and representative in nature on behalf of the Creator and Sustainer, made in the *imago Dei* (Gen 1:26–28; Ps 8:3–8).[58] The king-like authority given to Adam to rule and govern through the cultural mandate and dominion over the animal kingdom represents an analogical expression. Mankind is a physical representation of God within the created realm. Mankind is to exhibit kingly stewardship on behalf of the Creator as he proceeds with scientific investigation (Ps 8:6; 1 Cor 15:24–28; Eph 1:20–22; Heb 2:7–8).[59]

The *imago Dei* also means that life is a unique gift. It is understood to be holy and awesome and has inherent dignity because of the nature of its giver, the Creator. This is reflected in the prohibition to commit murder most notably specified in the Ten Commandments (Exod 20:13; Deut 5:17). The sacredness of life also means that any work that humans do has special value because it is an imitation of man's Creator, who has called mankind to work (Gen 2:15). Technology is one of the items that the work of humans produces. Additionally, the *imago Dei* mirrors distinctly personal manifestations of God's nature, including (1) intellect/reason, (2) free will, and (3) social relationality.[60]

Another implication is that mankind has moral attributes in a manner that reflects God's own nature. In addition to being an image-bearer, mankind is also a royal subject of a King. The Bible communicates this reality in Psalm 8, which may be seen as a commentary upon Genesis 1:26–28. God is identified as the Creator of the cosmos and desirous of praise from mankind, his special creation (Ps 8:1, 3). David, the writer of this psalm, rhetorically asks what it is about man that makes God care so deeply. David communicates that even though mankind is presently lower than the heavenly beings in the created order, mankind is crowned with glory and honor (Ps 8:5). This glory and honor details a personal and intimate connection in the relationship between God and mankind. The idea of a crown connects

---

58. Middleton, "Liberating Image?"; *Liberating Image*.
59. Poythress, *Redeeming Science*, 170, 232.
60. Hahn, "Creation and the Image of God."

God and mankind in a royal relationship. Mankind may be understood as vice-regents for God in his relationship with creation (Gen 1:26–30). David continues by acknowledging that mankind has been given stewardship over God's creation and specifically the animal kingdom.

One must not neglect to consider the eschatological implications involved in Psalm 8. Human nature is presently afflicted with sin and is fallen. Christians believe in the reality of the fall: that Satan, the demons, and mankind—literally and historically—rebelled morally against God, rather than properly submitting (Gen 3:5; Isa 14:14; Rom 5:12; 1 Tim 2:13–14). The fall of man is understood to mean that the *imago Dei* has been "frightfully deformed."[61]

The created order is never going to come completely upon its own into a position of submission. The corrupted human nature is in rebellion against the Creator. The crucifixion of Jesus Christ is the central point of created history, and its action and implications must always be placed at the center of any discussion on this topic (Gal 6:14).

Besides dominion over creation, as special creatures in the cosmos, image-bearers are to serve the King. That is, they must make a choice to serve God or idols (Exod 20:3; Deut 5:7). Image-bearers are to be priests and kings (Col 3:10). Unfortunately, the deformity of the image-bearer results in many worshipping false gods of this age. This includes the worship of both science and technology. This worship is a position that is to be reserved for the Creator. The human body, including the mind, was made to worship the Creator God. Image-bearers that do not worship the Creator, but rather science and technology, only view their minds as tools. The result is that love is degenerated.[62]

---

61. Calvin (1509–1564) states that "at the beginning the image of God was manifested by (1) light of intellect, (2) rectitude of heart, and (3) the soundness of every part" (*Institutes*, I.15.4). Mankind was originally created in God's image, which means "that man was blessed, not because of his own good actions, but by participation in God" (ibid., II.2.1). For Calvin, "The image of God is not to be understood only as a possession but a relationship—and 'participation in God' involves 'union with Christ.' Human sin means that the image of God cannot be understood solely in terms of creation or fall but in the true image of God restored in Jesus Christ. In other words, Calvin defines the image more in terms of redemption than creation. Regeneration is nothing else than the reformation of the image of God in the godly, but the second creation of the image in the restoration by Christ is a far more rich and powerful grace (Com. Eph 4:24). The grace of God exhibited in Christ exceeds all miracles. Indeed, the redemption that he has brought surpasses even the creation of the world (Com. Isa 9:6)." Partee, *Theology of John Calvin*, 86–7.

62. Naugle, *Reordered Love, Reordered Lives*.

Christians should properly affirm that scientism's explications are in fact reductionistic. Christian professor Kevin Staley of Southern Evangelical Seminary is correct in articulating that man is not simply a machine; he is a spiritual being for whom "communion with the Godhead in Christ is the potential which is uniquely proper to humanity," and such communion is not possible for AI (Ps 133:1; John 13:35; Acts 2:42; 4:32; Eph 4:1–16; Col 3:14; Heb 10:25).[63] Puritan Stephen Charnock (1628–1680), long before technology created AI, discussed the issue of mankind and machines. Charnock argued that Scripture taught that angels increased in knowledge every day. This increase in knowledge was of God himself. Neither sinners nor machines were capable of this increase in knowledge because they were like dead men and did not have the Holy Spirit drawing them. Charnock held that God can take any creation of his away at any time because it is by his power that he holds everything together (Ps 104:29; Dan 4:35). He concludes that the creature is always subject to a higher cause.[64] The biblical claim is that "God desires for mankind to be conformed to the image [*eikon*] of His Son Jesus Christ" (Rom 8:29; 2 Cor 3:18; Eph 3:19; 4:13–6; Col 1:28).[65]

Monism (Body Only) vis-à-vis Holistic Dualism (Body and Soul)

Scientific conceptions of AI rely exclusively on the physical realm. This worldview explicitly denies that anything spiritual exists. The mind is understood by naturalists as consisting of elements existing wholly in the natural, physical world. The brain is held to be an amalgamation of chemicals and electrical connections operating in response to the laws of nature. What understanding does this imply? Roboticist Rodney Brooks understands the resulting implications and states it explicitly:

---

63. Staley's focus is on man and machine relative to the issue of *imago Dei*. He concludes that "communion with the Godhead in Christ is the potential which is uniquely proper to humanity; therefore, since human beings are uniquely related to by God, one must be human in order to properly commune with God and other human beings." Staley, "Imago Dei in Machina?," 10. Staley maintains that humans are ethically accountable to Jesus Christ and the Word of God. See Staley, "Imago Dei in Machina?"; "Moral Perspectives for a Possible Posthuman Future"; Herzfeld, *In Our Image*.

64. Charnock, *Discourses upon the Existence and Attributes of God*, 336.

65. Kuruvilla, *Privilege the Text!*, 260–68.

> If we accept evolution as the mechanism that gave rise to us, we understand that we are nothing more than a highly ordered collection of biomolecules. There is an implicit rejection of mind-body dualism, and instead an implicit acceptance of the notion that mind is a product of the operation of the brain, itself made entirely of biomolecules.[66]

Rejection of mind/body dualism goes against the traditional thinking of Western societies where freedom, choice, and the soul have been generally recognized. Professor Edward Slingerland believes he has the answer for how this is to be resolved. He asserts that Darwinian evolution has made mankind such that mankind are embodied robota that have been designed not to believe that we are robots.[67] Slingerland's claim attempts to provide the acceptance of autonomous perspectives of subjectivity in a scheme that demands strict determinism, yet fails to account for how human minds rationally and subjectively understand themselves to believe they are not inherently strictly determined by physical laws. In essence, Slingerland wants to argue that humans are under an illusion.

Biblical creationists believe that man is more than a biological machine and that he is unique from the animals in that mankind was given dominion over them (Gen 1:26–28). Biblical creationists also believe that man is made in the image of God (*imago Dei*) (Gen 1:26–28). The Bible articulates a spiritual realm where there are intelligent entities that exist outside the physical realm and can casually act within the physical realm.[68] Both Jesus and the apostle Paul testify explicitly that this spiritual realm exists and that mankind has a soul (Matt 10:28; 22:23–33; Acts 23:6–10; 2 Cor 12:1–4).[69] Christianity affirms that man consists of more than the body. It understands the nature of man as anthropologically holistically dual, in the sense that man has a body and a soul united together while living (Gen 2:7). When a man biologically dies his spirit leaves his body (Eccl 12:7).

---

66. Brooks, *Flesh and Machines*, 172.
67. Slingerland, *What Science Offers the Humanities*, 250–96.
68. Cooper, *Body, Soul, and Life Everlasting*.
69. Theologian Joel Green, building upon Neo-orthodox understandings (including Barth, Brunner, and Bultmann), believes that Christianity should reject holistic dualism and argues for Christian physicalism. Similarly, philosopher Nancey Murphy believes the soul does not warrant consideration due to the principle of Occam's razor. John Cooper properly defends the understanding of holistic dualism presented. Green, *Body, Soul, and Human Life*; Murphy, *Bodies and Souls, or Spirited Bodies?*; Cooper, "Bible and Dualism Once Again"; "Current Body-Soul Debate."

However, the soul is also able theologically to ground personal identity beyond the grave, when the physical body is destroyed (Rom 7:20–25; 1 Cor 15:35–58; 2 Cor 5:1–5; Phil 1:21–23; 3:20–21; 2 Pet 1:13–14; 1 John 3:2–3).

If God, angels, demons, and mankind are understood to be real—a reality that physical monism rejects—then immaterial spirits have something in common with persons. J. P. Moreland and Scott Rae take the Christian conception of body and soul and emphasize that the distinctive issue to address is the understanding of personhood. They argue that what constitutes personhood is a "set of ultimate capabilities of thought, belief, sensation, emotion, volition, desire, intentionality, and so forth. None of the ultimate capacities is physical and, therefore, neither is personhood itself."[70] Roman philosopher Boëthius (c. 480–524) wrote, "Wherefore if Person belongs to substance alone, and these rational, and if every nature is a substance, existing not in universals but in individuals, we have found the definition of Person, viz: 'The individual substance of a rational creature.'"[71] Personhood and rationality (intelligence) are thus integrally connected and cannot be separated. Such a connection might lead one to believe that a claim that any AI, because it operates with rationality, could thus be categorized as a person. This issue will be put aside for the moment, but the understanding of the issue of the soul will at that time be of paramount importance.

The incarnation of Jesus Christ leads to the reality that mankind may receive salvation. It connects God with humanity and provides a better view of what God and humanity are really like. It takes seriously that mankind exists in a physical world, but also gives value and meaning to a spiritual realm that is connected to and part of the reality of the fabric of nature. Jesus Christ eliminated the possibility of mankind giving all thought only to the physical world and nature, while additionally it keeps mankind from contemplating its opposite error—thinking that idealism is correct. Jesus Christ connects the physical and spiritual realms, eliminating both monism and nonholistic dualism as valid conceptions. It articulates a holistic dualism whereby facts and values are brought together in the person of Jesus Christ.

---

70. Moreland and Rae, *Body & Soul*, 25.

71. Boëthius, *Against Eutyches and Nestorius*, ch. 3. Boëthius's definition of person (*persona*) was adopted by Thomas Aquinas (1225–1274). Aquinas, *Summa Theologica*, I.29.1.

Mind and Intelligence: The Impact of Sin

Is morality always to be considered rational? Any moral conceptions within ASI require it to be so by definition. If morality is not rational, then ASI cannot determine morality because it only arrives at solutions by applying rational approaches. What is the impact of divergent first principles regarding man's rationality as it pertains to morality?

Naturalism rejects the biblical claim regarding the reality of sin: that mankind, in his natural state, exists in a state of disobedience and alienation from God. Bostrom, Hawking, and Kurzweil are very intelligent and reject God.[72] The biblical claim is that death—characterized by the activity of physical separation from the living and spiritual separation from God—originated with man's decision to reject God (Gen 2:17; Rom 5:12–21; 8:6–7, 21–23; 1 Cor 15:21; Eph 2:5).

Bostrom, speaking of seed AI, maintains that it is like a *tabula rasa*, a blank slate with no previous noetic degradations.[73] Bostrom believes that man's reason is grounded and reigns supreme. He articulates a view of the human mind that conceives of it as immaterial. The human mind is only to be understood physically through its resultant knowledge and generated activity. AI is understood to be a replica of the human mind. It was previously mentioned that evolutionary naturalism fails to establish its own epistemic foundational grounding. Bostrom thereby improperly dismisses Christian understandings of the noetic effects of sin and neglects any accounting of it, declaring, "The point of Superintelligence is not to pander to human preconceptions but to make mincemeat of our ignorance and folly."[74]

ASI researchers generally focus on raw processing power. The brain is viewed simply as a processing machine and ASI capabilities to replicate the brain are always able to be enhanced as a result of more processing power.[75]

---

72. Stephen Hawking's physical body has amyotrophic lateral sclerosis (ALS), which is a disease that involves the death of his body's motor neurons. Hawking, no different from all other people, has a sin condition that needs remedy. Christians correctly understand all disease and death are an effect of human sin. Hawking's dream is not to acknowledge Jesus Christ but rather to know the mind of God. Hawking, *Brief History of Time*.

73. Bostrom, *Superintelligence*, 192.

74. Ibid., 225.

75. Del Monte, *Artificial Intelligence Revolution*, 43–44. Desired capabilities for ASI include reasoning, knowledge, planning, learning, language, movement, manipulation, vision, social intelligence and creativity. In 1999, Kurzweil stated that by 2020 that the

Assumed within this operating condition is the rationality of man's reason through supervenient materialism. Since man is viewed as being rational and ASI is created in the rational *imago Hominis*, ASI, by result, is rational. This perspective respects rationality as laudable, logical, and beneficial for achieving mankind's intended purposes. However, if the rationality of ASI, which derives from its creation by man, is built upon ungrounded rationality, then ASI itself cannot justify its rationality. Is there something better that can provide a basis for grounding man's intelligence?

Christianity affirms that because of the impact of sin on mankind the mind is negatively intellectually impacted such that apart from the operation of God's grace mankind cannot intellectually come to God (John 3:19–20; Rom 1:21–23, 28; Eph 4:17–19); thereby, Christianity holds that the noetic effects of sin in the spiritual realm adversely affect man's mental acumen.[76]

For the Christian, the highest form of knowledge is a saving personal relational knowledge of the person and work of Jesus Christ, the wisdom of God (Prov 8:12; 1 Cor 1:18–31). The Scriptures, and the revelation of God, are understood only from God working upon the hearts and minds of his people (Luke 24:45; John 20:9; 1 Cor 2:6–16). The Bible does not promote the idea that high intelligence, in the form of applied knowledge and skills, is the ultimate goal that God has for mankind because apart from God's spiritual and moral character, intelligence is futile because such wisdom is only from the created realm and not the Creator (Ps 110:10; Prov 9:10; Jas 3:13–18). Christians understand that God knows all of their thoughts and man cannot come to know the mind of God through human intelligence, but only by way of what has been revealed to him by God (Ps 94:11; 1 Cor 1:20–21; 2:11; Eph 1:17; Heb 4:12). Man's reliance upon his own intelligence cannot obtain godliness before God (Col 2:23). Man is under a misconception if he believes that his own intelligence matches God's omniscience (1 Cor 1:19). God's desire for all of mankind is that the human mind would be used to serve and glorify God (Jer 31:33; Mark 12:30; Rom 8:5–6; 12:2; 1 Cor 14:15; Eph 4:23; Phil 4:6–7; Col 3:2; Heb 10:16).

---

processing power of the human brain, which he stated to be on the order of 20 petaFLOPS (20 x 10^{15}), or 20 million billion floating-point operations per second (FLOPS), would be achieved on a computer. As of 2013, a supercomputer located in National Supercomputer Center in Guangzhou, China, named Tianhe-2 (aka TH-2; Tianhe means "Milky Way"), has achieved 33.86 petaFLOPS.

76. Poythress, *Redeeming Science*, 54ff.

It has been shown that one's worldview matters. Purely materialistic conceptions of mankind are in conflict with theistic conceptions as articulated by Scripture. One's understanding of the cause of the creation defines one's view of ASI and its ethical implications. Man is *Homo faber*, a creator of things, of which technology is one subset of this category. Man fashions technology in his own image but always does so in a context of understanding: as an imager of strictly himself (evolutionary naturalism) or of his Creator (theism). Ethical understandings are impacted by one's understanding of his expected behavior in various relationship and circumstances. Any ethics applied to ASI are determined based upon the initial ethical conceptions and framework that mankind takes and employs from the outset of the technology. It will be argued that man's relationship to God and God's revelation through Scripture is the better understanding from which to formulate any ASI ethics.

SUMMARY

Evolutionary naturalism and theism are at odds in their basic conceptions of anthropology. Evolutionary naturalism has no satisfactory explanation for the cause of man and his intelligence while theism relies on the authoritative witness of divine revelation. The ordering of the universe requires an explanation. Human intelligence demands a satisfactory answer in order to have proper grounding for ethical claims. Man develops technology in order to help him realize his aims. AI is an intelligence that is made in the image of man (*imago Hominis*). Those who hold to a Christian perspective see technology as an act of creation that is allowed by the freedom and creativity bestowed upon mankind as made in image of God (*imago Dei*).[77] The starting anthropological understandings of man will shape one's ethical understanding of ASI. It is best to understand man as

---

77. The concept of the image of God is divinely revealed in Gen 1:26-27; 5:1-3; 9:6; Refer also to Rom 8:29; 1 Cor 11:7; 2 Cor 3:18; 4:4-7; Col 1:13-15; Heb 1:3; Jas 3:9. Note in Gen 5:3 the Hebrew distinguishes that Seth, Adam's son, is born in the image of Adam. Image of God: Hebrew transliteration, *tzelem elohim*; Latin, *imago Dei*. *Tzelem* is an image representation that is both concrete and abstract. Freedman, *Anchor Bible Dictionary*, 3:390. The image of God may include concepts containing aspects such as (1) intelligence, (2) rationality, (3) spirituality, (4) personality, (5) morality, (6) authority, (7) self-transcendence, and (8) creativity but "which are expressions within a unified image." Clark, "Image of God."

more than a mere machine since a failure to do so is reductionistic in its philosophical understandings of creation and mankind.

Chapter 3

Intelligence

After looking at mankind as a creature it is now time to turn attention to the issue of intelligence as it pertains to humans, animals, and machines. The first order of business will be to look at the distinction to be drawn between natural, human, and animal, compared to artificial intelligence as exemplified in machines. From there the project will outline some of the notable categories that demand further discussion as the ethical implications of ASI are considered.

WHAT IS INTELLIGENCE?

How one defines intelligence is important. The history of thought has connected intelligence to different understandings of the mind, brain, soul, consciousness, and/or reason. As this issue is examined, it must be noted that evolutionary naturalists, who dominate the field of AI, largely look at intelligence as an action. Thus, understanding what it takes to make an action happen and also what is the ethical basis and implication of this action will be indicative of what will be explored in this project.

Azamat Abdoullaev, an ontologist and theoretical physicist specializing in computing machines, believes intelligence should be understood as "... the sum total of acts and actions related to knowledge processing such as perceiving, understanding, remembering, and thinking."[1] Physicist Louis Del Monte, a developer of microelectronics for leading technology firms, believes that raw processing power is sufficient in describing what

---

1. Abdoullaev, *Artificial Superintelligence*, 1.

a human brain is, the seat of human intelligence.[2] In essence, he believes that human intelligence is equivalent to computational power and that natural intelligence is not too differentiated from a computer's intelligence. John McCarthy, computer scientist at Stanford University and a recognized pioneer in the field of AI, believes "intelligence is the computational part of the ability to achieve goals in the world. Varying kinds and degrees of intelligence occur in people, many animals and some machines."[3]

Kurzweil believes that human intelligence is characterized by its great ability to recognize patterns.[4] He views human intelligence as an evolutionary self-organizing hierarchical system operating in the context of a biological pattern-recognition machine. Kurzweil also believes that the mind, the seat of human intelligence, is a ". . . system with qualia" and that the ". . . consciousness of the mind is an emergent property of a complex physical system."[5] He believes that by 2030 nonbiological machines will be able to function at a level where they appear to match or exceed the present level of human consciousness.[6]

Kurzweil adds additional constraints into his understanding of intelligence. He maintains that intelligence is "the ability to solve problems with limited resources, in which a key such resource is time."[7] Furthermore, any of the resultant "products of intelligence may be clever, ingenious, insightful, or elegant."[8] Kurzweil attributes to R. W. Young one of his favorite definitions of intelligence, "Intelligence is that faculty of mind by which order is perceived in a situation previously considered disordered," which Kurzweil considers to be an excellent definition.[9]

Intelligence thus requires a conceptual hierarchy of programming and language from within itself in order to be sustained. Memory and computational resources are required in order to be able to access, handle, manipulate, and process information. External and internal sensors are necessary in order to be able to absorb and compare information within

---

2. Del Monte, *Artificial Intelligence Revolution*, 41–49.

3. McCarthy, "What Is Artificial Intelligence?"

4. Kurzweil, *Singularity Is Near*, 25.

5. Kurzweil, *How to Create a Mind*, 199–207. Kurzweil is incorrect in this assessment. Only God can create intelligent conscious persons.

6. Ibid., 209–10.

7. Ibid., 277.

8. Kurzweil, *Age of Spiritual Machines*, 304.

9. As cited in ibid., 305. See Fatmi and Young, "Definition of Intelligence."

a context relative to information that already exists within the mind. The ultimate measure of an intelligence is its ability to act and respond appropriately to the situation. Machines are initially programmed with an initial starting point called a bootstrap. When machines are initially turned on, their inherent starting basis is their programmed instruction set that is downloaded to start and initiate all future processes. Through interaction and feedback, an intelligent system can reprogram itself to enable itself to achieve its goals. For Kurzweil, thinking is an ongoing and background scan performed by an intelligence.[10]

Christians should maintain a different and less reductionistic viewpoint. Christian philosopher William Dembski believes that both man's and God's intelligence may be identified as "creative intelligence."[11] Dembski properly points to the Christian God as the Creator of all things, including any and all intelligence that is manifested in the cosmos. Dembski goes on to take note that the "defining characteristic of intelligent agents," which Robertson defines as agents effected by teleological causes that act for an end or purpose, "is their ability to create and communicate information."[12]

NATURAL INTELLIGENCE

The term "natural intelligence" refers to intelligence that is present in the natural world as exemplified by living beings in biology. Since it resides within the natural world, intelligence is found and bound within a certain prescribed external environment, from which it receives a variety of sensory inputs. These inputs provide the informational content that must be processed in order for things such as learning and remembering to happen. The effectiveness of how this information is processed and analyzed is, in part, determined by inherent intelligence.[13] Higher levels of intelligence distinguish themselves by successfully receiving, processing, and transforming the processed information in innovative and creative ways in order to achieve goals.

---

10. Kurzweil, *How to Create a Mind*.

11. Dembski, *Being as Communion*, 48.

12. Robertson, "Algorithmic Information Theory, Free Will, and the Turing Test." Gathered through Dembski, *Being as Communion*, 48.

13. By inherent intelligence it is meant the total composite of the intelligence under consideration with respect to its essential and characteristic attributes.

Intelligence

It was Western philosophy by way of the Greeks that first took serious consideration and reflection onto the nature of being and reality. Plato (427–347 B.C.) postulated a world for forms (*morphe*) existing independent from matter (*hyle*) while his successor, Aristotle, believed that everything that has being (*ousia*) was composed of matter and form that existed in a unity together known as hylomorphism.[14] Aristotle conceived of intelligence (*nous*) as being the form required to be present in order to obtain understanding of what is the good (*agathon*), true (*alethes*), and beautiful (*kalon*), which provided the proper understanding of that which is reality.[15] Both of these philosophers stated that there were three distinct categories of living beings: (1) plants, (2) animals, and (3) human beings.[16] This categorization matches the creation accounts (Gen 1:12–13, 20–26).[17]

Aristotle proposed the soul principle for these hierarchies of life forms, attributing them as (1) vegetative or nutritive, meaning that it takes in food and/or has an appetite; (2) sensitive, meaning that it employs its senses and has a will; and (3) rational, meaning that it uses intelligence in order conform its beliefs and actions in the process of reasoning and thinking.[18] From the formulation of his theory of the forms, Plato maintained that the soul, and thus rationality and intelligence, could exist outside of and apart from matter. Aristotle's hylomorphic understanding of matter and form required them to be bound together into a unity. This means that, for Aristotle, when the body, composed of matter, dies, the soul dies with it. The result is that the form (*morphe*) of the body (soul) in which rationality and intelligence were considered to be is no longer in existence.

Aristotle's understanding of rationality, and, by implication, intelligence as the distinguishing characteristics of mankind is problematic for a proper understanding of intelligence because it implies that human intelligence is uniquely different from animal intelligence. If intelligence is what distinguishes humans from animals, what happens if it is possible to modify animals or machines so that they exhibit more rationality than a mentally challenged human being? It may be true that the human species is

---

14. Plato, *Phaedo*; *Republic*; Aristotle, *Metaphysics*.

15. Aristotle, *Aristotle's Metaphysics*.

16. Plato, "Republic"; Aristotle, *On the Soul (De Anima) and on Memory and Recollection (De Memoria Et Reminiscentia)*.

17. Day 3, 5, and 6, respectively.

18. Aristotle, *On the Soul (De Anima) and on Memory and Recollection (De Memoria Et Reminiscentia)*.

overall superior in its intelligence to any other species of animal that exists in nature, but is it not possible for an animal, or for that matter a machine, to actually exceed human capabilities in thinking and intelligence?

René Descartes (1596–1650) rejected the idea that matter and form were a unity and introduced into philosophy of mind the idea of dualism, whereby he asserted that the mind and body were two separate items.[19] Descartes believed that the mind, in which consciousness and self-awareness resided, was a nonmaterial entity that directed the physical body, which was subsequently required to observe the laws of nature. Descartes believed that the brain is to be considered the seat of intelligence and part of the physical body.[20] Descartes' proposal is not helpful from a Christian perspective because it improperly asserts a false distinction into what the Bible claims is a unified whole. Unfortunately, much of Western philosophy has been negatively impacted due to Descartes' epistemological turn with its overemphasis on subjectiveness.

Progress in science, through the age of Enlightenment, led to conceptions that the body is nothing more than a machine.[21] Evolutionary and material conceptions of biology fuel the belief that the human mind is an amalgamation of chemicals. Kurzweil understands the definition of a mind as entailing a brain that is conscious.[22] The brain, mind, and intelligence are considered to be mere results of time and chance and the products of evolutionary developments that have turned out, to date, to be fortunate to the human species, enabling it to survive and thrive, although not the result of divine creation. Bereft of purpose, an impersonal creation of mindless combinations of information and matter, intelligence is conceived by evolutionary naturalists to be a present reality without an initiating agent or cause. Kurzweil accepts Descartes' reality that a subjective experience is occurring to the subject, thereby leading the subject to conclude that he exists. However, he goes farther and believes that Western Cartesian rationality must be buttressed with the Eastern perspective that consciousness

---

19. Descartes, *Discourse on Method and Meditations on First Philosophy*.

20. Mistakenly, Descartes believed the pineal gland within the brain was the connection point between mind and body, allowing them to causally interact.

21. Roughly equivalent to the time period corresponding to the beginning of Descartes' writings through the French Revolution (1620–1789).

22. Kurzweil understands "conscious" to mean to be capable of having subjective experience of another object. Kurzweil, *How to Create a Mind*, 205. See also Kurzweil, *Age of Spiritual Machines*; *Singularity Is Near*.

is "fundamental and represents the only reality that is truly important."[23] Kurzweil believes that evolution "can be viewed as a spiritual process in that it creates spiritual beings, that is, entities that are conscious."[24] Kurzweil maintains that there is no distinction to be made between that which is spiritual and that which is conscious.[25]

The history of humanity points out that people indeed act with a purpose: a series of goals for which they aim. Biological evolutionary theory maintains that the primary purposes that humans direct their actions to are toward happiness and pleasure and away from pain. Whether it is happiness stemming from the pleasures of the body through sensual, self-gratification or happiness in the pleasures of the mind such as through one's moral self or self-sufficiency, both methods are disavowed by the Bible (Acts 17:18).[26]

Kurzweil himself believes that the best starting place for ASI ethics is the golden rule (Matt 7:12; Luke 6:31).[27] It is unclear what baseline between the self and the world Kurzweil uses to adjudicate ethical claims that may be hard and difficult to calculate based upon incomplete or indeterminable information. Ultimately, it would appear that the self is the final arbiter. Unfortunately, this is an unsatisfactory ethical starting point since selves might come into conflicting claims. Kurzweil thus is suggesting a starting point for ASI ethics that he neither believes is an ultimate truth nor follows personally. For Christians, Kurzweil's ethical proposal must therefore be rejected. Although it has ties to the Bible, it is insufficient since it cannot fully arbitrate conflicting claims of mankind. There is no final absolute method to resolve potential ethical conflicts.

Increasing Natural Intelligence

David Chalmers, philosopher and cognitive scientist, argues that, as biological machines, natural human sexual reproduction will not achieve significant gains in human intelligence without the addition of genetic engineering.[28] For evolutionary naturalists such as Kurzweil and Chalmers,

---

23. Kurzweil, *How to Create a Mind*, 222.
24. Ibid., 223.
25. Ibid.
26. Charnock, *Discourses upon the Existence and Attributes of God*, 1:165.
27. Kurzweil, *How to Create a Mind*, 178.
28. Kurzweil, *Singularity Is Near*, 11–12.

the pursuit of a more intelligent biological machine is a great possibility and genetic engineering should be pursued.

Bostrom, in discussing human biological cognition, speculates that the functioning of human brains might be improved through genetic selection or genetic engineering so that over several generations a perceivable increase in human intelligence could possibly be achieved. Members of such a society could band together collectively to pool their human intelligence in order to potentially realize new and exciting breakthroughs, further accelerating the process or raising the ceiling.[29]

Kurzweil articulates that human brains are very slow when compared to the speed at which electronic computers can process. Despite the human brain's inherent ability to parallel process vast amounts of information, Kurzweil believes that the increasing computational speed of digital computers will far outstrip the ability of the human brain. Kurzweil believes that if scientists can learn how the brain takes chaotic and complex activity and organizes it for understanding, this will lead to breakthroughs in computer processing that will far outpace any biological improvements that might result in increased human intelligence. Kurzweil believes that understanding the mechanisms behind the internal programming of the brain will yield more improvements in the area of AI than for human intelligence.[30]

The Bible on Intelligence

Evolutionary accounts of intelligence are, however, problematic because they provide no foundational support for logic, objective truth, and rationality. It is best to understand logic as a manifestation in the way that God thinks. Truth has more than just instrumental value; it supervenes on being through states of affairs that act as truth-makers.[31]

The Bible's account of intelligence rejects it as being something that has come into existence through a process of evolution as it claims from the outset man was naturally bestowed with this attribute as a gift from God (Gen 4:19–22). It is through mankind's resemblance to God, by way of the

---

29. Bostrom, *Superintelligence*, 37–44.
30. Kurzweil, *Singularity Is Near*, 111–53.
31. Alston, *Realist Conception of Truth*. See also Armstrong, *Truth and Truthmakers*; Fumerton, *Realism and the Correspondence Theory of Truth*. "Truth is what God thinks and knows. A proposition is true because God thinks it is so." Clark, *Introduction to Christian Philosophy*, 66.

imago Dei, that man has obtained his unique intelligence.[32] The Bible claims that God, in whom is found life, created life in the beginning (Gen 1:12–13, 20–26; John 14:6). He gave life to plants, animals, and to mankind life as his image-bearer (Gen 1:26–28). Man is a spiritual being who received the breath of life (*nishmat chayyim*, Gen 2:7). Man owes worship back to God who has given him his image and all things (Acts 17:25, 28).

The Bible sees natural intelligence as being the ability to obtain knowledge and to employ skills that result from learning (Prov 1:5; 9:9; 18:15). Left to its own devices, mankind's natural intelligence is insufficient to guide him to an understanding of his Creator. As a result of the fall, man's intelligence and reason have become distorted and are unable to provide him with the spiritual and moral knowledge that man needs to understand himself relative to the creation (Job 28:28; Ps 94:11; 111:10; Prov 9:10; Eccl 9:11; 12:12; Dan 12:4; John 5:39–40; Acts 17:21; 1 Cor 1:20–21; 3:20; 8:1–2; Jas 3:1–16).[33] Natural intelligence is one method by which humans can worship and glorify God regardless of their specific levels of intelligence, because the mind is to be given over to the understanding of who God is (Deut 6:5; Matt 22:37; Mark 12:30; Luke 10:27; 1 Cor 7:37; 14:15–18). The Bible acknowledges that man is capable of creating wonderful things, including powerfully smart machines. Human intelligence can build machines that do many things that human intelligence cannot do naturally.

The Bible contends that intelligence without renewal of the mind, through belief and faith in the person and work of Jesus Christ, will lead to separation of relationship with God for eternity (Jer 31:33; Rom 8:5–6; 12:2; Eph 4:23; Phil 4:6–7; Col 3:2; Heb 10:16). God will judge each and every individual for their rebellion against his rule. Man's overall spiritual condition is that of total depravity, making it so that his own mind and intelligence is unable to lead him to God. Through the divine revelation of God's will and plan for humanity God revealed that he sent his Son Jesus Christ to die as the atoning sacrifice for our rebellion against him (Eph 5:2; Heb 10:21). God provides mankind with grace through the power of the Holy Spirit to repent of our rebellion and believe in his Son, Jesus Christ, as the means for eternal life reconciled to God (Rom 5:10; 2 Cor 5:18–20; Col 1:22). French Reformer and theologian John Calvin, commenting on Luke 24, stated that "True discrimination between right and wrong does not then depend on the acuteness of our intelligence, but rather on the

---

32. Clark. "Image of God in Man."
33. Kilner, *Dignity and Destiny*, 228.

wisdom of the Spirit," and that "There is no worse screen to block out the Spirit than confidence in our own intelligence."[34]

The degree of natural intelligence that a person has is a very good gift of God that is provided to mankind within his biological life. Each individual's intelligence is a personal attribute, bestowed by God, that helps mankind connect and reflect the *imago Dei* (Gen 1:27; 2:7; Ps 8:4–5).[35] Scientists who claim they are concerned with intelligence are, by implication, making a claim that attaches and connects some sort of importance between life itself and intelligence. Life is a gift from God (Gen 1–2). Being made in the *imago Dei* is not anything that AI scientists seem to address or be concerned with. Yet the Bible claims that ultimately life, both biological and spiritual, as well as the attribute of intelligence, is a direct result of mankind being made in the *imago Dei*.

ARTIFICIAL INTELLIGENCE

If natural intelligence is understood to be biological in nature, artificial intelligence is thought to be artificial in that the "life" given to it is not biological but is rather provided by the initial design of a creating agent, such as a human being. German writer Johann von Goethe (1749–1832) captured this concept long ago in his work on Faust, where he proclaimed:

> Great plans seem mad at first. But one day we
> Shall laugh at what is bred haphazardly;
> And one day, too, some great brain will create
> A brain designed to think and celebrate![36]

Artificial intelligence is intelligence that has a creator, a designer. By this definition, all AI is intelligently designed. Since AI is what leads to ASI, the implication is that ASI is inherently intelligently designed superintelligence.

In 1950 British scientist and mathematician Alan Turing (1912–1954) proposed to answer the question as to whether machines could "think" by stating that if a machine can be interrogated by a person in such a manner that the interrogator does not realize a machine is responding, then the machine may be considered to be "thinking." Machines that are able to do so are able to pass what has come to known as the Turing test. For many AI

34. Calvin, *Commentary*, on Luke 24:16 and Luke 24:45, respectively.
35. Kilner, *Dignity and Destiny*.
36. Goethe, *Faust*, part 2.

scientists passing the Turing test is a sign that a thinking machine might be thought of as having attributes of intelligence that are required for it to be recognized as something more than just a machine, even if not necessarily provided with the same status as persons.[37] However, the Turing test sets the bar much too low. It fails to properly distinguish between the illusion of strong AI and actual AI. The Turing test is an unsatisfactory tool to ascertain intelligence.[38]

The Pursuit of Artificial Intelligence

The idea of artificial intelligence was first actively pursued at Dartmouth College in the mid-1950s. The work was undertaken on the basis of a belief that machines could be designed to emulate human intelligence.

> The study is to proceed on the basis of the conjecture that every aspect of learning or any other feature of intelligence can in principle be so precisely described that a machine can be made to simulate it. An attempt will be made to find how to make machines use language, form abstractions and concepts, solve kinds of problems now reserved for humans, and improve themselves.[39]

The result from this summer of research was that the field of artificial intelligence was born. Just four years later one of the participants of the Dartmouth project, American psychologist and computer scientist J. C. R. Licklider (1915–1990), envisioned humans working in close relationships with machines.

> It seems reasonable to envision, for a time 10 or 15 years hence, a 'thinking center' that will incorporate the functions of present-day libraries together with anticipated advances in information storage and retrieval. The picture readily enlarges itself into a network of such centers, connected to one another by wide-band communication lines and to individual users by leased-wire services. In such a system, the speed of the computers would be balanced, and

---

37. Turing, "Computing Machinery and Intelligence."

38. Dixon, "What Does It Mean to Be Intelligent?"; Larson, "Transhumanist Claims Aside"; "Group Delusions Aside."

39. McCarthy et al., "Proposal for the Dartmouth Summer Research Project on Artificial Intelligence."

the cost of the gigantic memories and the sophisticated programs would be divided by the number of users.[40]

Licklider was able to look forward in time and extrapolate to predict, based upon the future processing power of machines, the possibility that ultimately came to full-fledged reality in the Internet (World Wide Web).

The Possibility of Artificial Superintelligence

British mathematician Irving Good (1916–2009) was one of the first to see and to realize the possibilities that eventually AI would inevitably lead to ASI and that the rise of ASI would develop the certain issue of whether man could maintain sufficient control in order to ensure he was not harmed by ASI.

> Let an ultraintelligent machine be defined as a machine that can far surpass all the intellectual activities of any man however clever. Since the design of machines is one of these intellectual activities, an ultraintelligent machine could design even better machines; there would then unquestionably be an 'intelligence explosion,' and the intelligence of man would be left far behind. Thus the first ultraintelligent machine is the last invention that man need ever make, provided that the machine is docile enough to tell us how to keep it under control.[41]

Assuming naturalistic evolutionary understandings and applying them to machines leads many scientists to speculate that, due to the absence of biological limitations, the increase in intelligence for machines will be exponentially faster in growth than that of natural intelligences. The corresponding exponential growth in electronics in terms of computational speeds and decreasing physical densities is apparently proof to many cognitive scientists, philosophers, and artificial intelligence researchers that ASI will come to reality.

Weak and Strong

John Searle proposed a distinction in the classification of AI. He argued that there were two major types of AI: weak and strong. Weak AI he declared is

40. Licklider, "Man-Computer Symbiosis."
41. Good, "Speculations Concerning the First Ultraintelligent Machine."

primarily a sophisticated computing tool that is useful for humans, while strong AI is a mind. His Chinese room argument took issue with the claim of strong AI and the reality of a machine that could be considered to think for itself. He argued that thought requires internal causal powers equivalent at least to a properly functioning human brain. Since machines run on programs and are not based upon their own internal causal powers, he doubted the claim that machines could be considered able to obtain strong AI, the ability to think in the manner on a par with or greater than that of a human mind.[42]

Kurzweil believes that Searle's objections are overstated. Kurzweil responds to Searle's claims by articulating that in the future machines will be able to self-organize from what starts as chaotic systems due to the reverse engineering of the brain and the employment of technological developments that allow machines to simulate the neurons in the brain. Thus, Kurzweil believes that evolutions in technological development will provide the ability for machines to be conscious as a result of "emergent properties of complex distributed patterns."[43]

Human beings are able to apply their intelligence to solve problems across large contexts.[44] Does the potential for ASI and "intelligence unbounded" mean that these machines will be able to see their way through all the problems associated with complicated and changing contexts?[45]

If Searle's argument against strong AI holds—as many evolutionary naturalists may grant, but Christians should not—then machines may be able to achieve results that rival and surpass humans, but such a machine's accomplishment is actually achieved due to its excellent weak AI

---

42. The argument goes something as follows: Imagine a human being locked in a Chinese room that is required to simulate the Turing test by producing Chinese language propositions. The human in the room understands the English language but not the Chinese language. All the instructions the human receives are in English. The human follows these English instructions and is able to follow the program instructions such that he is able to successfully produce the Chinese language. The human appears to understand what he is accomplishing but in point of fact he does not understand the output. It is argued that computers thus do not understand the output; they only follow the program and by implication do not exhibit strong AI. Searle, "Minds, Brains, and Programs." As mentioned previously, Christians should consider the Turing test as insufficient. Dixon, "What Does It Mean to Be Intelligent?"; Larson, "Group Delusions Aside"; Richards, ed. *Are We Spiritual Machines?*

43. Kurzweil, *Age of Spiritual Machines*, 191; *Singularity Is Near*, 458–68.

44. Bostrom and Yudkowsky, "Ethics of Artificial Intelligence," 320.

45. Blackford and Broderick, *Intelligence Unbound*.

performance. It is reductionistic to natural human intelligence to claim that AI is of higher intelligence because AI is able to achieve a similar, better, or faster result than human intelligence. If strong AI, characterized by the ability to supply internal causality into any action of knowledge processing, is lacking from a machine's capabilities but present within human capacities due to mankind being made in the *imago Dei*, this would be a basis for claiming that machines cannot have a stronger intelligence than mankind even if machines' processing capabilities far outreached that of humans.

Perhaps what is most important and relevant to the discussion of natural intelligence versus artificial intelligence is not that of memory, processing power, or the size and power of the brain and/or computer (that is reflective of the concept of a mind). One may ask whether, as created ontological entities, humans and machines exist within a different relationship due to who or how they were initially created. Humans create intelligent machines with the purpose of assisting mankind. AI scientists claim mankind was not created with a purpose.

The Bible claims mankind was created with a purpose: to glorify God and enjoy him forever (1 Chr 16:29; Isa 48:11; Acts 7:2; 1 Cor 6:20; 10:31; Phil 1:20; 1 Pet 4:11).[46] The view one maintains regarding the "original" programmer provides an important distinction that will impact how one understands intelligence, natural and artificial.

EPISTEMOLOGY

Discussions on intelligence require clarification on epistemology. Epistemology is the study of knowledge and understanding.[47] In both human and machine terms, "epistemology" is often replaced with the word "cognition." For both humans and machines, one must take into consideration not only the content of the information they acquire but also how they process this information.

Christians should all employ proper prolegomena to their epistemology. The Bible, claims historian Herbert Schlossberg, says that "God is *totaliter oliter*, wholly other than the universe. Being free of the universe,

---

46. See also the Westminster Shorter Confession: man's chief end is to glorify God and to enjoy him forever (Ps 73:25–26; 1 Cor 10:31). Orthodox Presbyterian Church, *Westminster Confession of Faith and Catechisms*.

47. Greek: *epistēmē*, knowledge; *epistanai*: to understand, know, from *epi-+ histanai*, to cause to stand. Bibleworks, version 10.

He is free, and those who are created in His image are also free."[48] By this, Schlossberg means that God is a reality that is not bound or contained within a closed system that evolutionary naturalists take as a starting point.

In contrast to the scientific method, which dominates the study of ASI, Christian epistemology allows an additional source of knowledge besides that obtained through empirical and rational methods. It allows God to communicate to mankind. It acknowledges the historical, empirical, and rational reality of God's communication to man both in Scripture and in becoming human by way of the incarnation (Isa 9:6; Matt 1:18; Luke 1:35; John 1:9, 14; 8:56; 14:9; Rom 1:4; Col 1:15; 1 Tim 3:16; 1 John 1:1–2; 4:2).

Evangelical theologian Carl F. H. Henry (1913–2003) maintains that Christian epistemology should be based upon scriptural revelation and the authority of God.[49] It is God who has spoken and communicated to mankind, including his speaking directly to Moses (Exod 33:11).[50]

There is a spectrum of available philosophical positions regarding epistemology. Idealism holds that fundamental reality consists of nonmaterial mental thoughts and ideas. On the opposite side is materialism, which believes that all reality is essentially physical matter. Mental thoughts and ideas are conceived to be the result of material interactions that produce effects upon the body. The brain is part of the physical body. The mind is considered to be nonmaterial and thus different and distinct from the brain. How the brain and mind work in concert must be explained. Idealism is characterized by its strong reliance on rationalism, the belief that reason is the main way that one comes to obtain knowledge. It believes that the structure of reality is able to be deduced through the workings of intelligence.

The field of ASI is largely characterized by scientists holding on to scientism, which is the idolization that scientific methods are the only way to achieve knowledge and truth. Atheist philosopher Thomas Nagel correctly points out that scientism should be considered to be an improper employment of idealism. He articulates this view because he sees scientism

---

48. *Totaliter oliter*: meaning that God is transcendent, existing beyond the created universe (Gen 1:1; Ps 113:4–5). Schlossberg, *Idols for Destruction*, 175.

49. Christians should properly take Scripture as cognitive propositional revelation. Clark, *Christian Philosophy*; "Nature of Truth"; Henry, *God, Revelation, and Authority*.

50. Moses is the author of the first five books of the Bible, often called the Torah or Pentateuch. These include Genesis, Exodus, Leviticus, Numbers, and Deuteronomy (Exod 17:14; 24:4; 33:11; 34:27; Num 33:1–2; Deut 31:9–11; Matt 19:8; Mark 12:26; John 5:45–47; 7:19; Acts 3:22; Rom 10:5).

as being guilty of cutting out others' sources of knowledge without prior scientific evidence that conclusively proves knowledge and truth may not be obtained via methods that are not based upon empirical inductive reasoning to principles based upon testing.[51]

Contra idealism is the philosophy of physicalism (materialism). It claims that reality is comprised of matter and physical entities. To the physicalist, this means that the cosmos is a closed system and thereby considerations of God are excluded. This philosophy believes that only what can be sensed and experienced is real. Any phenomenon, such as mathematics, thinking, and vision, is the result of the interactions of physics, biology, and chemistry but is not to be considered as dependent upon a nonmaterial reality.[52] This epistemology is characterized by its adherence to the understanding that knowledge primarily is a result of what comes to the intelligence from external sensory experience, and allows for significant knowledge to be obtained by way of inductive reasoning. Both idealism and physicalism/materialism take the position that knowledge requires "justified true belief" (JTB). Philosopher Alvin Plantinga has successfully taken aim at this position and dealt it a serious blow, meaning this simple definition may require further nuancing, to which Plantinga has suggested that warrant is the connection point between knowledge and JTB.[53]

Yet this specific understanding is the prevailing epistemology in the field of AI. The human body is conceived as being entirely physical and thus the body is a machine. Both human (and animal) bodies and machines can be conceived to do the same things simply if the programming and capabilities are within the capacity of the body/machine. Since humans can make machines, it is the perspective of this line of thinking that machines can be replicated to yield the intelligence that is demonstrated in human beings.

---

51. For example, by way of special revelation, an example of which would be the Bible. Nagel, *View from Nowhere*.

52. "If we accept evolution as the mechanism that give rise to us, we understand that we are nothing more than a highly ordered collection of bio-molecules.... A central tenet of molecular biology is that *that is all there is*. There is an implicit rejection of mind-body dualism, and instead an implicit acceptance of the notion that mind is a product of the operation of the brain, itself made entirely of biomolecules." Brooks, *Flesh and Machines*, 172.

53. This theory of knowledge is known as internalism and requires that intelligence must be certain of how he knows that what he believes is true. It is unable to account for the Gettier problem. Philosophically it leads to skepticism. See Gettier, "Is Justified True Belief Knowledge?"; Plantinga, *Warrant and Proper Function*; *Warrant*; *Warranted Christian Belief*.

Given time and increases in technology, everything can be programmed such that ASI arrives.

A third major position is that of realism. Realism articulates a position that there are objective realities that exist ontologically independent from perception. Christianity holds to a form of realism, maintaining that God is transcendent and exists independently of both material and nonmaterial entities.

All statements of ethics and morality ultimately go back to being able to make statements of value. In order to be understood and to have meaning, any statement of value must be an attempt to correspond to truth.[54] All idealism inevitably leads to philosophical skepticism, the position that one cannot really know anything. This is because there is no anchoring point for truth claims because there is no clear path for how to make predicative statements eventual reality.

All knowing and understanding must result in action. Without action, neither humans or machines are able to accomplish their desired/aimed ends (*telos*). Computer scientists John McCarthy (1927–2011) and Patrick Hayes identify the frame problem as being a key consideration that must always be initially addressed when dealing with AI. The frame problem states that AI must first be loaded with all stable first-order logic (FOL) that defines its starting first principles. These principles are a framework (starting presuppositions) from which the machine will view the outside world. If the frame changes, for any reason, then the outputs that the machine makes in an attempt to achieve its programmed goals will also change.[55]

---

54. This fact comes from the basic law of noncontradiction. The principle of noncontradiction states that A cannot equal A and also equal non-A. In language, this means that rationality requires communication where the communicator is not asserting and denying the predicate at the same instance. Aristotle, *Aristotle's Metaphysics*, bk. 4 (Γ).

55. McCarthy and Hayes, "Some Philosophical Problems from the Standpoint of Artificial Intelligence." The frame problem is extremely problematic for AI as it identifies the problems that AI has with having a grounding for *a priori* knowledge and thus cannot establish its own starting presuppositions. In contrast, the Christian identifies the Word of God (the Bible) as establishing knowledge regarding first principles. Dixon, "What Does It Mean to Be Intelligent?"; Larson, "Group Delusions Aside"; Richards, ed. *Are We Spiritual Machines?*

COGNITION

In both human and machine terms, epistemology is often associated with the word cognition.[56] It is necessary to ensure that the proper distinctions between these two words are defined. Whereas epistemology is concerned with the philosophical understanding of how knowledge is obtained, cognition is usually defined as focusing on the empirical aspects of how knowledge is obtained. Cognition may then be stated as "empirical epistemology." Aspects of cognition may include empirical factors such as reliability, power, and speed that influence and impact how understanding happens in intelligent systems (human, animal, and/or machine). In essence, this is a distinction between the epistemological process and method of understanding and knowledge as unique and different from that of cognition, which is understood as the physical and psychological aspects involved with intelligence, such as the size of the human brain, whether the brain is fully developed physically, whether the brain is operating under the influence of some drug, the processing speed of the machine, the memory capacity, etc. Brain-computer interfaces, mind networking, and genetic selection and alteration are possible ways that humans may potentially increase cognitive capabilities and achieve ASI.[57]

Alvin Plantinga equates cognitive facilities with mankind's "belief-producing faculties aimed at truth."[58] Plantinga contends that it is irrational to accept naturalism because it does not provide proper warrant, which is best thought of as proper function.[59] Naturalism is irrational. By Plantinga's definition, "A belief has warrant, for a person (conceivably a machine) if it is produced by their cognitive faculties functioning properly in a congenial epistemic environment according to a design plan successfully aimed at the production of true or verisimilitudinous (appearing to be true) belief."[60]

The Bible claims that God is the Creator of man. The Bible articulates that "man desired to be both his own ruler and his own end" (Gen 3).[61] The biblical account of the fall of man takes as real that man was negatively

---

56. Cognition is derived from the Latin verb *cognosco* (*con*: with + gnōscō: know), a cognate of the Greek verb γι(γ)νώσκω *gi(g)nósko*: I know. For more on cognition look at Franchi and Bianchini, *Search for a Theory of Cognition*.

57. Bostrom, *Superintelligence*, 37–51.

58. Plantinga, *Warrant and Proper Function*, 216–17.

59. Ibid., 216–37.

60. Ibid., 237. See also Plantinga, *Warrant*; *Warranted Christian Belief*.

61. Charnock, *Discourses upon the Existence of God*, 1:174.

and permanently impacted within his total being (Jer 17:9; Rom 3:10, 23; 6:23). The fall's impact was to create distortion, confusion, and damage in the cognitive, affective, and conative portions of man's being (Gen 3:6–7). Jon Kilner takes note of the significant impact that the fall has had upon distorting man's reasoning:

> By creating humanity in God's image, God has created an unbreakable connection with humanity, with the intention that humanity would live with rational and spiritual attributes that in some small but wonderful way reflect God's own. Reason, then, is one of the human attributes that ought to flow from being in the image of God—it is not, in itself, what constitutes being in God's image. It is a particularly strategic capacity since it is a prerequisite for other human attributes that flow from being in God's image such as rulership and relationship. Because of sin, reason has not developed as God intended. This does not mean that people are devoid of reason. Rather it means that people's reason is distorted until Jesus Christ breaks the power of sin to allow reason to develop and function as God intended.[62]

Mankind was now stained with sin and needed spiritual healing (Gen 3:17). God provided their spiritual healing by clothing them in garments of skin and in his provision of his Son (Gen 3:15, 21; Heb 7:20–28; 10:10–14).

Now that man has gone on to create machines with AI with the potential to be eventually an ASI, a further look at the impact of the distorting effects that sin has upon mankind's cognitive, affective, and conative capabilities is warranted. Doing so will help assist people to understand what ethical implications there are for ASI created by humans.

One way that man's cognitive capabilities have been negatively impacted is in his inability fully to understand his own mental state as well as another person's mental state. When a person expresses his perception of his own mental state through his own language, he is declaring a propositional attitude. This propositional attitude is a feeling that the subject is expressing about his mental state. It creates a relationship between the thought contained in the language expressed (proposition) and the person.

It is possible to express a propositional attitude in one way yet for the mental position behind the proposition to change over time. Because the subject can express different mental propositions with the same proposition, the issue of intention becomes relevant. Anyone listening to the

---

62. Kilner, *Dignity and Destiny*, 208.

expressed propositional attitude by the subject would have to understand the subject's intention in making the propositional expression in this way. The implication of this is that, from a biblical perspective, the fall has made man cognitively impaired so that he has difficulty in grasping the communication his Creator actively communicates to him.

The mind of man has affections, meaning he has feelings, emotions, and moods. Man's affections are connected to his reasoning and thinking capabilities and "emotions are a type of value cognition."[63] Mankind desires to make it so that machines utilizing AI and ASI also have this human capacity. Philosophers of mind debate whether empirical sensations, known as qualia, can be said really to exist or are simply appearances.[64] Regardless, an understanding of how humans can intelligently program ASI with affective capabilities has ethical implications. If there is not an agreed-upon methodology of how affective elements should be universally programmed into ASI, various outcomes that humans may desire ASI to have, such as love, pity, mercy, and compassion, will have a hard time being programmed into the machine.

The mind has a conative orientation that propels and directs it towards goals. In human terms, these have been discussed historically under philosophical terms including (a) will, (b) freedom, (c) determinism, and (d) action.

LANGUAGE

Discussions about the nature of intelligence lead naturally to looking further into the methods and manner whereby processed information is communicated both internally and externally to the intelligence. This field is called language or linguistics. Language is viewed in philosophy as a substudy of the mind.[65]

Humans use what is called natural language. According to W. Bernard Carlson, natural language, like technology, is something that is naturally

---

63. Achtenberg, *Cognition of Value in Aristotle's Ethics*, 44. Aristotle, *Nicomachean Ethics*.

64. For two differing perspectives on qualia consider looking at Chalmers, "Absent Qualia, Fading Qualia, Dancing Qualia," arguing for its affirmation; and Dennett, *Consciousness Explained*, which rejects it.

65. Philosophy of mind is related to the discipline of metaphysics. Analytic philosophy's "cognitive turn" identifies philosophy of mind as the foundational proposition to understand within philosophy. For more on this refer to Pinker, *Blank Slate*.

characteristic of the human race.⁶⁶ Human intellectual and technological capabilities are supported by their sophisticated communication abilities.

Language is employed by using complex symbols that are perceivable to the senses. Notable human examples include speech (hearing), written or sign language (visual), and physical contacts such as handshakes and hugs (touch). Kurzweil's commitment to the theory of evolution makes him believe that human language was the first invention of mankind.⁶⁷ Language is a way that humans are able to work together and build a society, have culture, and create technology.

All intelligences manipulating communication require a method to structure language. Grammar, syntax, and discourse provide structure to a language so that its constituent components may be properly understood and interpreted.⁶⁸ Postman believes that language is "pure ideology" and should be viewed as an "invisible technology."⁶⁹ By this, Postman means that language is not neutral. It is a reflection of the starting assumptions and its use frames the entire informational content that intelligence utilizes.⁷⁰

Interpretation is the art of properly receiving communication and processing it in the manner that was intended by the communicator. The circumstances surrounding the specific grammar, syntax, and discourse employed are called the context. It provides the external and internal environment into which the information is being processed. The context that language finds itself in is a critical key in ascertaining what a communication means from the perspective of the communicator's intention. Because the intention of the communicator matters to the context, the issue of agency that was discussed previously is brought to bear. If intention is

---

66. Carlson, *Technology in World History*.

67. Kurzweil, *How to Create a Mind*, 3.

68. Köstenberger and Patterson define grammar as a specific feature of syntax that yields a range of meaning. Syntax is understood to be the relationship between individual words. Semantics is the understanding of the meaning of individual words. Discourse is a coherent and intelligible sequence of phrases of sentences. Köstenberger and Patterson, *For the Love of God's Word*, 305–50, esp. 306.

69. Postman, *Technopoly*, 84–85.

70. For a further look at important theories regarding specific issues in the field of language consider Austin, *How to Do Things with Words*; Ayer, *Language, Truth, and Logic*; Clark, *Philosophy of Science and Belief in God*; Davidson, *Essential Davidson*; Fodor, *Language of Thought*; Grice, "Logic and Conversation"; Kripke, *Naming and Necessity*; Locke, *Essay Concerning Human Understanding*; Mill, *System of Logic*; Putnam, "Meaning of 'Meaning'"; Quine, "Main Trends in Recent Philosophy"; Russell, "On Denoting"; Wittgenstein, *Philosophical Investigations*; *Tractatus Logico-Philosophicus*.

not part of the communicated message, then whatever is communicated cannot produce meaningful action since it will have only been derived from an original set of happenstance, from which it is not possible to assert meaning.

Humans are able to create and utilize symbols to express themselves in new and unique ways without limitation. A human can cry in pain, read Shakespeare, or sing an opera. These symbols come to have meaning as a result of social interaction and agreement. Because human language is based upon social meaning, it allows both change over time and unlimited variety as society develops new symbols to communicate what people experience.

Besides natural human language, other life forms are able to communicate in a manner that is natural yet distinct and different from human language. It is generally a form of signaling understood within the species but does not involve the manipulation of symbols and creative thought. For example, a dog may bark and provide information to other dogs that is capable of being received and understood by others of its own species in a manner that humans cannot understand, except in generalities. Animals may also use other ways to communicate that are not inherently understandable to mankind at initial glance, such as the abilities of bees to do a dance that indicates the direction to fly in order to obtain pollen for the hive. Scientists recognize that even though animals may communicate with other animals of their species, there is no animal, including apes and chimpanzees, that can manipulate signs and symbols to the degree that mankind can.[71] Animals only work and communicate regarding particular contexts and do not communicate regarding universal or abstract relationships.

Evolutionary naturalists contend that it is the evolved intelligence of man that has allowed him to master spoken and written language relative to other animals such as apes. The biblical account is different. The Bible states that man's ability to communicate personally is an attribute of God.[72] As an

---

71. Hockett believes human language means it has design. Evolutionary naturalism rejects design and thereby proposes other accounts for the basis of human language. Hockett, *Logical Considerations in the Study of Animal Communication*.

72. Poythress sees a reflection of the Trinity imaged in all language and communication. The Father is like a speaker who provides both authority and meaning by way of omniscience. The Spirit is a breath and hearer, which would represent the audience. The Spirit ministers by its presence reflected in its omnipresence. The Son (Jesus Christ) is the speech (Word), which represents God's control through his omnipotence. Poythress, *In the Beginning Was the Word*.

attribute of God, he has seen fit to pass it on to mankind in order to be able to have bilateral communication with mankind. Christian theologian and professor of philosophy Ronald Nash (1936–2006) believes this idea of creative communication is vitally important for any proper understanding as it provides a bridge to connect God and man. Nash states, "Communication is possible because the human creatures using language are enlightened by the divine *Logos*, are in possession of certain innate ideas."[73] Carl F. H. Henry believed that the purpose of human language is so man can know and have knowledge of the Holy One (God).[74] The Bible states that God has provided man with the ability to speak with him through prayer, a mental communication with the transcendent Creator (Ps 116:4; Matt 6:9; John 14:14; 1 Cor 1:2). "Prayer is God's idea. Man's need to communicate with God is a result of God creating that need in man."[75]

God first expresses himself when he called light into existence (Gen 1:3). He would go on to communicate his creative will and speak all of the cosmos into existence (Gen 1:3–31). God spoke to man from the very beginning, giving Adam special instructions for his well-being (Gen 2:16–17). Adam used his language ability in his first action of naming all the animals

---

73. Nash, *Life's Ultimate Questions*, 269; *Word of God and the Mind of Man*.

74. White, "Word and Spirit in the Theological Method of Carl Henry." The following will be a short but specific outline regarding Henry's biblical and theological basis. Henry took *a priori* the theological transcendent. Henry took as his first principle God in His revelation. This first principle would be expounded all through *God, Revelation, and Authority*. Henry's theological method was influenced tremendously by Gordon Haddon Clark (1902–1985). It was an apagogic method whereby one proves things indirectly by showing the absurdity or impossibility of the contrary. Henry took the source of truth as coming from transcendent divine revelation. The instrument for recognizing truth was reason, which came from human epistemic structures given on the basis of creation, the *imago Dei*. The verifying principle for truth was to be Scripture. The negative test for truth was logical consistency. For Henry, logical consistency would demonstrate coherence. Karl Barth (1886–1968), in contrast, held to a correspondence (representational) theory of truth. The logical process to be employed to reason was that of deduction. Henry believed in metaphysics. Metaphysical reality was known once one had taken a proper epistemic position. Henry took the one living triune God as the ultimate metaphysical reality. Henry held that the intelligibility or *Logos* of God was possible because the *Logos* was rational (John 1). Barth did not see it this way. Barth saw that the intelligibility of the *Logos* was paradoxical or dialectical. For Henry, the *Logos* was the Word. Henry viewed language as univocal. Clark, John Duns Scotus (1265–1308), and Norman Geisler are theologians and apologists that would hold a similar view. Henry took exception to the analogical understanding of language held by such prominent theologians as Cornelius Van Til (1895–1987) and Thomas Aquinas.

75. Crawford, *Giving Ourselves to Prayer*, 7.

(Gen 2:19–20). It is significant to note that mankind was created on the same day as the animals but was given this special assignment of naming based upon being created in the *imago Dei* (Gen 1:26–27). Mankind called upon the name of the Lord (*Yahweh*), indicating that communication between mankind and the Lord was not limited to the garden of Eden and the time of initial creation (Gen 4:26; Rom 10:13). The Lord also spoke to Noah, telling him of his plans to destroy life across the world through a great flood (Gen 6:14—7:5) Despite the restart of humans with the family of Noah, man continued to sin against God. At this time, the whole Earth spoke one language (Gen 11:1). The sin of man led him to be arrogant toward God and decide to build a tower to the heavens in Shinar (Gen 11:2–4). God rejected this action of mankind and confused their language and scattered them abroad across the Earth (Gen 11:6–8). The Lord categorically states that it is he who has confused the language of man across the Earth (Gen 11:9).[76]

The Bible also testifies that God controls the ability to unconfuse language. After the resurrection and ascension of Jesus into the heavens, the Day of Pentecost produced the filling of the apostles with the Holy Spirit so that they were able to speak words clearly and effectively to communicate the truths of the gospel, such that about three thousand people became believers in the person and work of Jesus Christ (Acts 1:8; 2:1–41). The implication is that language is not a characteristic that man has obtained through a long and slow process. It has not come through a series of gradual and continued increases of chaotic random events that led to mankind having greater intelligence than animals and the ability to utilize language. Man's unique language abilities come from God, his Creator.

In contrast, AI does not use human language. All AI utilizes some sort of programming, which enables it to receive information, compute, and act in an attempt to make sense of what it is experiencing. Humans have created these machines and programming languages in order to be able to participate in what the machine is capable of doing. In this way, humans are like the Creator God in that humans have enabled a creation to have some ability to communicate.

---

76. In December 2015, Southern Evangelical Seminary President Richard Land stated that he believed that attempts to modify human intelligence, such as conceived in transhumanism, may be considered presumptuous and a result of human pride and on accord with the actions of the tower of Babel. Mitchell, "Christian Leader Warns of 'Frankenstein Monsters.'"

These languages follow a specific set of rules that have been agreed upon by social and largely scientific convention.[77] Because of the general desire to be utilized universally, they are most frequently constructed with formality; that is, there is a universally agreed-upon method to the logic contained within the artificial language. Artificial languages (machine code or code) can be set up to perform certain predefined tasks. Programming is the art and science of writing machine code. It is performed by manipulating the functionally equivalent elements found in human language: grammar, syntax, semantics, and discourse. Programming is initially set up by humans but can be assigned to be done by machines (robots/computers) after initial setup. An algorithm is a set of instructions that have been formatted and arranged to achieve a certain function. Programming code is generally broken down into a long series of discrete binary digital signals. These signals, representing specific ON and OFF sequences, are then stored, analyzed, and processed in conjunction with the available intelligence of the machine. All AI programming is based upon human conceptions of structure. AI semantics and syntax thus function in a manner that emulates humans rather than, for instance, another species like apes, dolphins, or rats. The implication is that any ethical decisions that machines make ultimately have been "coded" into their system DNA by their creator; that is, it is a reflection of mankind's approach to processing and analyzing the information. This is the result regardless of whether the machine is operating as ASI or AI.

IDENTITY

Identity is the characteristic that differentiates a particular object from another. Human intelligence, assuming it is properly functioning, is naturally able to understand that it is a "self," an object that possesses a mind that is different and unique and apart from other humans. Should humans consider themselves to be the same person yesterday, today, and into the future? Is anyone aware of one's identity after the physical body perishes or does one cease to have any mental awareness that he or she ever existed? What, if anything, distinguishes the physical brain and the mental mind? Can intelligence be designed into machines so that, with ASI, they have humanlike understanding of their own identity?

---

77. Trudgill, *Sociolinguistics*; Wardhaugh and Fuller, *Introduction to Sociolinguistics*.

Humans are understood to be conscious and aware of themselves relative to their surroundings. The human body, with its potential for intelligent thought and action, helps to comprise what is known by the term humanity. Humankind is said to exhibit consciousness, which includes phenomenal perceptions such as (a) awareness, (b) being awake versus asleep, (c) the ability to reflect, (d) the ability to focus the attention of the mind upon an object, and (e) knowledge as well as psychological perceptions such as intentions and thoughts.[78]

Up until the seventeenth century, much of Western civilization's thought on personal identity was focused on what happens to one's identity upon one's death. Plato believed that man is composed of two substances (substance dualism) that separate from each other upon death of the body. The soul was believed to live on in a perfect state while the body decays. Aristotle believed that humankind maintains the ability to reason even after the death of the body (psychosomatic dualism). Christian theologians Augustine and Thomas Aquinas believed that identity continues on even after the body dies. John Locke (1632–1704) introduced a new philosophical perspective, that of internalism. He argued that identity depends on the physical and psychological relations between a person at one point in time and the person at another point in time. Locke thought that consciousness and memory are essential aspects of personhood.[79] This perspective is in contrast to the Greek and Christian view of the previous two millennia, a view known as externalism. Locke believed that identity is only a relationship of the self to the self over a continuum of time, whereas externalism holds that the self has a relationship to the rest of the world that presents itself to the self in time through events (history) and facts (reality).

Identity is also concerned with sentience, which is the ability to feel and perceive. Sentience is a reality for both humans and animals. Many evolutionary naturalists believe it is logical to assume that ASI will achieve sentience.

Kurzweil believes that continuity is the key to identity. "Identity is preserved through continuity of the pattern of information that makes us us. Biological substrates are okay, but there is better."[80] Transhumanist Max

---

78. Dennett, an avowed atheist and evolutionary naturalist philosopher, believes that consciousness is an internal story of the mind that is assembled by the physical brain processing various sensory experiences and collections from memory in parallel. Dennett, *Consciousness Explained*.

79. Locke, *Essay Concerning Human Understanding*, bk. 2, ch. 10.

80. Kurzweil, *How to Create a Mind*, 247.

More, drawing on the personal identity work of philosopher Derek Parfit, believes that mankind should work to change the self over long periods of time.[81] More argues that mankind should utilize technology to transform himself in order to work towards extending the continuity of the self. He contends that too much consideration is given to people's memory of the past and of themselves, causing them to be improperly focused on achieving ongoing continuity of the self.[82] It is this type of vision that propels transhumanists and many ASI advocates to desire going beyond the limitations of the biological human body and transcend it via the employment of technological means and assistance.

Czech politician, philosopher, and writer Václav Havel (1936–2011) believed that responsibility is the key to human identity.[83] He maintained that humans have an identity because we are responsible creatures.[84] Havel observed that a focus on personal identity leads to an overemphasis on the body (secular, material) or the mind. Havel suggested that mankind should not concern himself with being "constrained to be" but should instead focus on what he is "called to be" in both freedom and the future.[85] Like Augustine, Havel claimed that it was God who understood who he was when he stated, "Whoever I am, thou knowest, O God, I am thine."[86]

After reflection upon the *imago Dei* and the relationship that human beings have as stewards over creation, the Vatican issued a statement in 2002 that affirmed its commitment to the position regarding the responsibility for the biological integrity of the human. Named *Communion and Stewardship*, it states that "Changing the genetic identity of man as a human person through the production of an infrahuman being is radically immoral."[87] The same statement also argues that the creation of a superhuman or spiritually superior being is "unthinkable," since true improvement can come only through religious experience. Such a definition would encompass changing people biologically so that they are capable of ASI.[88]

81. Parfit, *Reasons and Persons*.
82. More, "Diachronic Self."
83. Havel, *Letters to Olga*, 18.
84. Ibid., 19.
85. Ibid., 23–24.
86. Ibid., 26. Augustine, *Confessions*.
87. International Theological Commission, *Communion and Stewardship*, para. 91.
88. Ibid.

AGENCY

Agency is concerned with the understanding of intentional action performed in a given environment. Intentionality concerns the "of-ness" (which means generalness) or "about-ness" (which means specificness) of one's thoughts.[89] Agency has historically been considered to be part of what in philosophy has been called the will.

Aquinas argued that the will is a conative part of the human soul, which interacts with the intellect (cognitive). Aquinas's conception of agency was that the intellect determines a particular end goal of which the will either approves or rejects. If approved, the intellect ascertains whether the agent has the necessary resources to have reasonable certainty of success. The will expresses itself as an intention to move toward the success of that end. The intellect then weighs the various options it has at its disposal to achieve these ends and the will gives approval to the method that is determined to be the best and a choice is made to proceed in that direction.[90]

The general position of evolutionary naturalists working on the development of ASI, as noted earlier, is focused on creating desired actions that result in maximizing happiness and pleasure and minimizing pain. In contemporary philosophy of mind, intentionality is viewed in two different ways: internalism and externalism. Austrian philosopher and psychologist

---

89. Searle, *Intentionality*.

90. Stump, *Aquinas*. Choice implies the freedom and power to choose to do otherwise. The intellect in cooperation with the will moves to have the body respond accordingly. "Man has free-will: otherwise counsels, exhortations, commands, prohibitions, rewards, and punishments would be in vain. In order to make this evident, we must observe that some things act without judgment; as a stone moves downwards; and in like manner all things which lack knowledge. And some act from judgment, but not a free judgment; as brute animals. For the sheep, seeing the wolf, judges it a thing to be shunned, from a natural ant not a free judgment, because it judges, not from reason, but from natural instinct. And the same thing is to be said of any judgment of brute animals. But man acts from judgment, because by his apprehensive power he judges that something should be avoided or sought. But because this judgment, in the case of some particular act, is not from a natural instinct, but from some act of comparison in the reason, therefore he acts from free judgment and retains the power of being inclined to various things. For reason in contingent matters may follow opposite courses, as we see in dialectic syllogisms and rhetorical arguments. Now particular operations are contingent, and therefore in such matters the judgment of reason may follow opposite courses, and is not determinate to one. And forasmuch as man is rational is it necessary that man have a free-will." Aquinas, *Summa Theologica*, I.83.1. In the case of salvation (soteriology), man in his own strength is unable to convert himself. He is totally dependent upon the prior decision of God to translate him into the state of grace and free him from his depraved nature.

Franz Brentano (1838–1917) provided significant contributions to the field of intentionality. His views drew heavily from Aristotelian conceptions.[91] Aristotle provides useful insight into developing a theory of action.[92]

Philosopher Elizabeth Anscombe (1919–2001) wrote extensively on philosophy of mind and action, stating that the human intention is displayed when events are directed towards action.[93] If an event is understood to be something that happens at a specific time and place, they it may be understood as being either intended or unintended. If events happen without intention, these may be called happenstance. Things that have the capacity to drive towards action with intentions are called agents. This classification definitely includes humans and could include ASI. Actions are those things that happen with both an event and agency.

A key takeaway from this discussion is the issue of agency, something that will be covered in further detail. It has been shown that for one to discuss intelligent systems further dialogues are warranted regarding the issues of human and machine agency. If agency is neglected or ignored, what is being discussed is not action but rather happenstance. Evolutionary naturalism believes human intelligence arose from happenstance; that is to say it emerged from chaos.[94] However, anyone beholden to that opinion must first be held accountable to explain whether she personally has agency and whether agency is something that she desires as a goal for any ASI system she would create.

Discussions pertaining to agency lead to the question of moral agency. Is a being ethical responsible for it's action because it freely forms intentions that drive it to complete actions?

The Bible contends that humans are not able to act in a manner that is pleasing to God (Isa 64:6; Rom 3:10–12, 23; 1 John 1:8; 5:3). With this as a starting point, Christians believe that without divine assistance, in the

---

91. Brentano, *Psychology from an Empirical Standpoint*.

92. Aristotle, *Nicomachean Ethics*, bk. 3.

93. Anscombe, *Intention*.

94. Minsky believes that nervous systems work like swarm intelligence through emergence. He contends that this emergence leads to properties identified as sentience, identity, and intelligence. Minsky concludes that human planning for machines should be to build large swarms of neuron-like connections and let them interact and allow intelligence to emerge through random evolution. Evolutionary naturalists who maintain this line of thinking suggest that a good can come for mankind by having the human race connect their brains together through technology to form one emergent ASI. Minsky, *Society of Mind*.

form of Jesus Christ, any creation that humans make, including ASI, will be tainted by this inability to conform to what is pleasing to God.

IMAGING

Any creation is a partial reflection or image of its creator. Evolutionary naturalists and Christians differ on how man was created, with evolutionary naturalists believing man was created without agency by chance over extended periods of time while Christians affirm that God acted from the beginning to create man in his image (Gen 1:26–27; 9:6). Because evolutionary naturalists reject God, any ASI that is created is from their perspective created without reference to God. The ASI is created in the image of man (*imago Hominis*). Moral accountability and control are suspect in this articulation because mankind does not maintain or acknowledge absolute moral laws. Evolutionary naturalists are subject to believing that ethical injunctions are not fixed but are fluid and subject to evolutionary processes. The net result is moral relativism. Created in the image of man without any reference to an external absolute moral compass, ASI programming can never be absolute and universal. The net result is that whatever guidelines the machine is initially programmed with become a limitation on what types of outputs it ultimately generates, regardless of calculating power, speed, or time. Of themselves machines are not moral agents. Christians affirm that only God can create intelligent conscious persons morally responsible for choices. Machines can be programmed to imitate certain functions of human intelligence—like beating humans at chess and even learning new things within a certain framework established by programmers—but these devices will always remain capable of only "artificial intelligence," rather than personal conscious intelligence that carries moral responsibility.

Kilner argues that being made in the *imago Dei* makes people morally accountable to God because "people exist for the glory of God to participate in bringing the glory of God about."[95] All people will thus be evaluated based upon how they utilized the gift of their life from God (John 5:24; Rom 8:1; 1 Cor 3:10–15; 2 Cor 5:10; Rev 20:11–15). Jesus Christ is the exact imprint of God and, in being so, is a connection point and the exemplar of

---

95. Kilner, *Dignity and Destiny*, 208.

humanity (Col 1:15).[96] The *imago Dei* provides both a connection point and reflection of what God intends for humans to be, argues Kilner.[97]

ASI created in the *imago Hominis* has nothing to say to Christlike imaging. Programmed for maximizing the utilitarian output for the contextual situation being encountered, issues of reflection of the biblical Creator God are ignored. Any concern with the prophetic function of ASI is devoid of absolute truth. The Word of God and declaration of the gospel message are viewed as irrelevant by evolutionary naturalists involved in ASI projects. ASI will not function in a priestly role as it sees no connection between God and mankind. Left to its own devices, ASI may in fact work to take on the role of God because its intelligence will mislead it to believe that being more intelligent than its human programmers it should in fact fulfill the relationship void. Robert Geraci states that "intelligent robots are akin to the Holy," implying that their superior intelligence creates in humans an awe that may be considered transcendent.[98] Besides this perception by humans, it may be possible for the ASI to believe that relative to humans it is god-like, and thus to assume this position and take action from the perspective that its intelligence is transcendent to mankind's intelligence.

SUMMARY

Christians maintain that mankind is an image-bearer. Image-bearers are created with intelligence. An understanding of natural intelligence is a

---

96. Jesus Christ as exemplar was and is a prophet, priest, and king. As a prophet, he is concerned with the truth (John 14:6). He was and is the Word of God who declares the gospel message (Mark 16:15; Luke 4:18, 43; John 1:1, 14). As a priest, Christ pointed all humanity toward worship of God (Deut 6:13; Matt 4:10). Jesus focused on his relationship to God and humanity (Luke 2:52; 23:52; John 5:18–20; 8:29; 10:15; 14:11; 17:7, 26). As a servant, he is our example of perfect obedience to the will of God (Matt 5:17–18; 17:24–27; 19:17; 22:16–21, 37–40; 26:39; Mark 14:36; Luke 2:51; 22:42; John 4:34; Rom 1:5; 5:18–19; 2 John 1:6). Jesus Christ is also biblically identified as a king and ruler that has dominion over creation and mankind (Ps 2:7–9; Matt 1:1; 21:1–9; 27:27–30; Mark 15:9, 12–13; Luke 23:2–3, 42–43; John 1:49; 7:42; 18:36–37; 19:19–22; Heb 1:3; Rev 1:5; 11:15). In this capacity, he provides leadership, provision, and protection. Mankind is to be united with Jesus Christ and grow deeper in his connection and relationship with him. In this ongoing process of sanctification, man more intensely reflects the *imago Dei* and thereby brings glory to God (1 Cor 10:31).

97. Kilner, *Dignity and Destiny*, 116–33.

98. Geraci, "Robots and the Sacred in Science and Science Fiction"; *Apocalyptic AI*, 51.

necessary prerequisite for understanding artificial intelligence. Natural intelligence can be increased through slow adaptation in biology or conceivably through biological manipulations made in an endeavor to dramatically increase human intelligence. Evolutionary naturalists largely conceive of intelligence as practical computing power, thereby reductionistically conceiving of intelligence as an all-natural process that can be emulated by machines. The Bible states that intelligence includes concepts that are not entirely naturalistic, such as logic, truth, and rationality. It identifies the God-man Jesus Christ as the exemplar of intelligence. AI and its possibilities have been pursued over the past several decades with significant progress made in its capabilities but with zero progress in terms of machines being moral agents since they are not intelligent conscious persons. Intelligence was looked at from several angles, including (a) epistemology, (b) language, (c) identity, (d) agency, (e) cognition, and (f) imaging, in order to identify particular distinctions between evolutionary naturalism and biblical creationist understandings. Evolutionary naturalism requires biological determinism. Biological determinism is to be rejected by Christians who accept that the human conscience can be impacted supernaturally by the Holy Spirit, allowing human beings to have some degree of self-determination that stems from the holistic unity of their body and soul, of which their intelligence is part of assessing and weighing possible actions that the self can take under its own initiative.

Chapter 4

Singularity

The power of ASI is said to be extremely large due to its potential to continue with unlimited exponential growth resulting in a point that asymptotically goes off the charts. "The singularity" has been used to describe such monumental inflection points. Vernor Vinge coined the term "singularity" in his 1993 essay in which he proposed the thesis that because technological progress marks the past several generations ". . . we are on the verge of change comparable to the rise of human life on Earth. The precise cause of this change is the imminent creation by technology of entities with greater than human intelligence."[1]

For instance, "singularity" has been used to refer to the first instance in which time, space, and matter (cosmology) came into existence, at the moment of the supposed Big Bang. It is a moment when things take a dramatic and sudden change due to something reaching a point from which there is no turning back and only an exponential function increase occurring prior that is impossible to stop. It is similar to what happens when one overcomes the obstacles inherent in creating an atomic bomb explosion and reaches that point where the gain of the system goes into runaway build-up.

In the field of AI, exponential growths in technology may lead to such large gains that ASI becomes a reality. The realization of ASI would mark a point in human history that Kurzweil and others have described as the "technological singularity." Such a conception of a technological singularity is considered to represent an inflection point where technology has so impacted humanity that man can no longer understand himself from his past

---

1. Vinge, "Coming Technological Singularity," 12.

because he has so quickly and rapidly been moving forward.[2] Movement toward a technological singularity achieved with ASI offers great potential for human improvements but comes with existential risks.

The path to such a singularity may come in one of several manners. Biological enhancement coupled with the extension of biological life are important issues of discussion in this matter.[3] Among many possibilities of biological enhancements are making humans (or human-machines) more intelligent, qualitatively better in certain capabilities, feeling better physically, emotionally, and psychologically, living longer, and becoming physically stronger.[4]

THE POTENTIAL OF ARTIFICIAL SUPERINTELLIGENCE

Technological Advancement

ASI offers the promise of great potential. This is because ASI may produce pragmatic results that humanity can use to flourish providing potentially beneficial impact upon societies. Because of the potential promise of AI, many scientists want greater expenditures allocated for investigating human and machine cognitive improvements.

The first thing that comes inevitably with any movement toward an ASI is technological advancement. This is evident because realized technological improvements naturally are built upon to generate new technological improvements. This exponentially increasing function has been empirically demonstrated throughout the history of man. An advance in technology propels new ideas and thinking for ways to realize further gains.

---

2. Kurzweil, *Singularity Is Near*; *How to Create a Mind*; Von Neumann and Kurzweil, *Computer & the Brain*. In 2002 the Vatican issued a statement called *Communion and Stewardship: Human Persons Created in the Image of God*, in which it is stated that the "creation of a superhuman or spiritually superior being is 'unthinkable,' since true improvement can come only through religious experience." International Theological Commission, *Communion and Stewardship*, para. 91. For a good introduction to the concept of a technological singularity and its implications for ASI see Eden et al., *Singularity Hypotheses*. Eden et al. characterize the technological singularity as manifesting "a combination of acceleration and discontinuity." Ibid., 5.

3. For a look at some of the concepts of enhancement see also Bostrom, "Dignity and Enhancement."; DeBaets, "Enhancement for All?"; Hauskeller, *Better Humans?*; Mercer, *Religion and Transhumanism*; Miller and Wilsdon, *Better Humans?*; Persson and Savulescu; Savulescu and Bostrom; Schneider, "Future Minds"; Sparrow, "Beyond Humanity?"

4. Hauskeller, *Better Humans?*

Pursuit of Perfection

Steps taken toward a technological singularity have another implication, that of the relentless pursuit of perfection.[5] It is natural for man to focus his attention on things he believes need improvement, and then attempt to make them better. In and of itself, the pursuit of perfection is reasonable. AI is presently utilized to assist mankind with achieving better outcomes and results for a myriad of activities and processes. Inevitably, ASI will be subject to the same aims as current AI. However, any and all pursuits of perfection call for and demand ethical consideration. The criteria upon which this moral decision-making will be made is extremely crucial for the development of this technology.

Evolutionary naturalists believe everything can benefit from further adjustment because their worldview sees everything as part of a Hegelian-like process headed toward either improvement or extinction. Technology provides resources available for man's use; it is therefore a cultural adjustment to employ the materials available with knowledge and skill of society. For evolutionary naturalists, pragmatic considerations thus call for improvements to be done where there is an associated return on investment (ROI) that makes it seem logical and compelling to utilize the consumption of what are always finite resources to achieve an end. Nature is valuable in the context of its usefulness for mankind's purposes. Since man is a part of nature, even his life and body are subject to these considerations. Failing to account that life has dualistic reality to it consisting of both a material and spiritual aspect, evolutionary naturalists fail to have any proper grounding for a transcendent purpose.

Humanity is not just superior to animals because of supposed evolution or because mankind was more fortunate than other species and received more degrees of intelligence than apes, dogs, or worms. Man is a spiritual being made in the *imago Dei* (Gen 1:26–28; 2:7). Man's spiritual nature pulls all mankind toward a pursuit of transcendence. At his core, man is a worshipper (*Homo adorans*). This may be worship of himself, nature, idols, or the true Creator, the God of the Bible.

As technology increases, pragmatic considerations will inevitably lead mankind to look for ways he can further transform nature and his own biology to further his objectives, while simultaneously discounting the

---

5. Acknowledgement of this phrase to the Lexus marketing campaign slogan. Dawson, *Lexus*.

value of items that he does not consider as useful at this particular point in time. Mankind will thus be led to acquire only things that are pragmatically useful and give low consideration to things that are not. If man takes such actions upon his own biology in order to increase his intelligence, integrate AI, or achieve ASI, he exposes himself to a reduction of his existing nature.

When applied to ethical considerations for humanity, evolutionary naturalists, as materialists and determinists, are only able to reflect upon some form of consequential ethics.[6] Such an ethic may be charged with suffering from several weaknesses. The first is that it is entirely dependent upon a utilitarian calculus that is always open for debate since it has no foundational universal starting point to which to stake its mathematical claims for ordering.[7]

Additionally, it suffers from the inability to see accurately into the future in order to determine the impact and effect of resultant consequences. AI is presently employed to run "what if" and future simulations. An example from current culture is that predictions of who will win the Super Bowl and what the final score will be are made by feeding data into the AI to run multiple simulations in order to attempt to assess the final result. Ultimately, the AI yields a predicted value but this predicted value is nothing more than a statistical prediction that indicates something akin to a mean or average. The actual realities and results of the game are never subject to the AI's prediction. Such simulations can provide some level of probability but do not necessarily mean that the reality will match. Thus, some sort of inability to accurately obtain all the requisite information of the costs and benefits of each and every conceivable action applies to all consequentialist ethics.

Finally, such an approach does not take into account the reality that man is made in the *imago Dei*.[8] The *imago Dei*, among many things, provides an understanding of man's unique dignity and destiny (Gen 1:26–28).[9] Because man is made in the *imago Dei*, consequentialist ethics fail to take into account the reality of a transcendent God being imaged through his creation in the species of humankind.

---

6. Meaning one that is entirely ends based, due to its reliance upon the pursuit of perfection or otherwise extinction.
7. See Bentham, *Deontology*; Mill, *On Liberty*.
8. Jones, *Introduction to Biblical Ethics*, 11.
9. Kilner and Mitchell, *Does God Need Our Help?*

In contrast to evolutionary naturalists and their consequentialist approaches to ethics, Christians believe that sin has wreaked havoc upon God's good creation and that the entire cosmos is in need of redemption (Gen 1:31; 3:1–24; Rom 8:22–23). The *imago Dei* provides a grounding for a relational aspect between man and his Creator that leads to the understanding that God requires moral perfection from man in order to maintain that relationship, because God is morally perfect (Deut 32:4; Job 37:16; Ps 25:8; 92:15; Matt 5:48; Rom 12:2; Heb 7:26, 28).

Could it be that man's progress towards perfection through ASI is nothing more than the attempt for man to redeem himself through technology instead of through repentance and salvation in the God-man, Jesus Christ? Christian author Lawrence Terlizzese specializes in the ethical implications of technology. He points to Aldous Huxley's (1894–1963) *Brave New World* (1932) as an attempt to articulate a negative utopia, a place that is not heaven on Earth, painting a frightening vision of the future that comes through technological means.[10] In *Brave New World* it is not ASI that brings about man's "redemption" from the chaotic results of evolution but rather genetic engineering, pharmaceutical drugs, and propaganda. In Huxley's vision, man is perfected by his body and mind being brought into altered states distinct from their natural state.

Decision-Making

Any arrival of ASI likely means that AI has developed the ability to employ deep learning, a skill whereby myriads of individual neural networks within the system are able to respond to what initially enters the AI as abstract characteristics from which complex and usable meaning must be extracted. AI researchers are currently investing much effort into understanding how to make AI improve its deep learning capabilities. Deep learning requires making the different areas of perception, cognition, and language work harmoniously together. It is possible that AI will allow for robots and autonomous vehicles to make decisions utilizing sensors and data and with a speed that is outside the natural boundaries of humans. This does not mean that AI will make better decisions than humans. It only means that it will be making decisions in a different manner, yet these decisions are still based upon how the machine has been created and made to process information.

---

10. Huxley, *Brave New World*; *Brave New World Revisited*; Terlizzese, *Trajectory of the 21st Century*.

Fighter pilots today are surrounded with a full complement of computers and artificial intelligence that assists them with flying one of the highest performance vehicles man is presently capable of designing. Such technology may be viewed as Advanced Driver Assistance Systems (ADAS). AI is largely in control of the particulars of the plane with the pilot being in the position of the ultimate and overriding control agent, allowing him to adapt and take over control as needed. In the future, the continuing development in electronics and AI technology portends for more common items such as automobiles to have many similarities regarding the overall agency control of the vehicle.

Presently, many electronic technology companies that support the automotive industry are squarely focused on addressing the technical needs of ADAS by developing both adaptive and predictive systems and components that will allow for better and safer driving. ADAS assists the agents in charge of the vehicle by providing warnings or taking actions to reduce risk or through the automation of some portion of the control task of operating the vehicle so that safety and performance are improved. The current state of ADAS is largely cooperative with the driver; that is, the human-machine interface in ADAS functions as part of the overall agent control of the vehicle with the human still maintaining overall responsibility for the vehicle. It is expected that over time developments in technology will be successful in having more and more agency and control of the vehicle moved to the ADAS. It is anticipated that ADAS may ultimately develop further into autonomous systems that will offer a superior level of intelligence and the ability to respond quicker and with greater beneficial results than when a human agent is the controlling driver.[11]

It is the dream of many that future technological advancements will allow for completely autonomous vehicles to dominate the roadways of the world. These autonomous vehicles would be programmed to avoid accidents and damage to passengers as well as collateral damage, while simultaneously being programmed to optimize efficiencies in travel by optimizing various performance factors of the vehicle on the go so as to minimize expenses and maximize the functional utility of the vehicle.

There is no doubt that everyone desires vehicles to operate safely and efficiently for all concerned. In operating a vehicle upon today's roadways, the laws currently on the books place the responsibility squarely on the

---

11. Golata, "Ethics of Autonomous Vehicles."

human driver to ensure that everyone's well-being, both inside and outside the vehicle, are protected and that harm does not come to oneself or others.

It is possible to conceive of an automobile as a tool whose primary function is to get people from point A to point B safely and efficiently. However, there is little doubt that a vehicle can also be operated by an agent and used for vicious purposes, such as a murder weapon, where it can be used to run down people as they attempt to cross the street.

Besides autonomous vehicles, there is a host of other applications that might benefit from better decision-making than is now possible through human intelligence. The ethics of such decision-making by any AI must be well conceived prior to proceeding.

Safety, Defense, and Crime

What if AI were applied to other areas of personal and societal safety besides autonomous transportation? Currently, the militaries of the United States (US) and other countries employ unmanned aerial vehicles (UAV), also referred to as drones. They are used to provide different levels of support on the battlefield. The US military recognizes ten different categorical levels of UAVs' degrees of autonomy, with level 10 being fully autonomous vehicles controlled by the computer because it is understood to be cognizant of the battle space, able to coordinate as necessary with other military assets, and can operate independently without supervising oversight.[12] US military capabilities are closely guarded secrets, but are thought to contain level 8 potential.

AI and the coming Internet of Things (IoT) will provide levels of data and information that AI could use for the safety and defense of individuals and groups. IoT is about interconnecting embedded systems. "It brings together two evolving technologies: wireless connectivity and smart sensors. Combined with recent advances in low power microcontrollers, these new 'things' are being connected to the internet easily and inexpensively, ushering in a second industrial revolution."[13] Camera and video surveillance are commonly employed today, but tomorrow's AI may have the vision-sensing capabilities to perform full facial recognition and obtain other personal details that are available and yet controllable by the constant exchange of information between people and AI systems. Television shows such as

12. NIST, "Special Publication 1011-II-1.0."
13. Giovino, "Internet of Things."

Person of Interest conceive of a possible future where the ASI determines and warns about violent crimes that are yet to be committed based upon machines forecasting and anticipating where prior events coupled with people's expressed motivations will lead.[14]

Medicine

Since taking on and winning at Jeopardy in 2011, IBM's supercomputer Watson has moved on to other things. One of the primary areas it has been working on is the field of medicine. Presently medicine is the domain of highly specialized human experts who subject themselves to years of training and then first-hand experience in order to be able to diagnose, treat, and prevent biological problems associated with the human body and its ability to function properly. The designers of Watson wanted to see what would happen if AI were programmed to be able to perform in the manner of a physician.

> To continue Watson's advancement, IBM has created two business units: Watson, established for the development and commercialization of cloud-delivered cognitive computing technologies and Watson Health dedicated to improving the ability of doctors, researchers and insurers to surface new insights from the massive amount of personal health data being created daily to deliver personalized healthcare.[15]

IBM has bought or made announcements to buy four firms worth more than $4 billion, including Truven Healthcare ($2.6b), Phytel, Merge Healthcare ($1b), and Explorys. IBM intends to leverage the purchase of these companies in order to supply Watson with big data obtained from the records of millions and millions of people and their related medical data. This data will be processed in a variety of ways, but a key focus will be to take the digitalized data of the patients and the resulting diagnosis, treatments, and subsequent health of the patient through a deep learning process so that Watson can become the world's most successful cognitive computing physician, and exceed the performance of the medical industry as a whole. Watson is indicative of the types of machines that are striving

---

14. The American television series *Person of Interest* plays off of these themes with two AI machines fighting for control against each other, and the AI being referenced within the dialogue by various characters as "god" and "gods".

15. IBM, "IBM Watson."

for ASI and its programming and structure requires a proper assessment of its ethical decision-making basis.

Biological Enhancement

If AI and ASI can lead to improvements in how patients are medically cared for, how can this be utilized to make human biology even better? Almost a century ago, scientist, humanist, and atheist J. B. S. Haldane (1892–1964) proposed that the future of technology provided the belief that a new relationship may exist between man and different types of human beings. He believed that ultimately a scientist, a Prometheus of his time, would invent a change in the understanding of biology that would lead to a new conception of man because of his ability to take control and charge over his own biology. Haldane claimed that at first this conception would be conceived of a perversion, but over time it would be accepted after sufficient time to overcome the previous beliefs and prejudices of other men. Over time, it is just a matter of moving from the control of bacteria to contain disease to the enhancement of human biology to improve man himself.[16]

If man is the result of evolutionary forces rather than being made in the *imago Dei*, he should quintessentially be considered to be a machine so that it is natural to consider playing with both the hardware (body) and software (mind). J. Craig Venter, one of the mappers of the human genome, claims, "We're going to have to learn to adapt to the concept that we are a software-driven species and understand how it affects our lives. Change the software, you can change the species, who we are."[17] Venter believes that human enhancement is imminent.

Stewardship

Stewardship, understood as responsibility managing resources for the benefits of another or others, may also be an area that benefits from ASI. The world has only limited resources. Nations, governing bodies, organizations, and associated parties may see differently on how and what is the proper way to manage these limited resources. In considering totally eliminating air pollution, the massive expense becomes evident. Yet ignoring the

16. Haldane, *Daedalus*, 1923.
17. Boulton, "J. Craig Venter's New Startup Is Hacking Life."

problem can be dangerous to people's health. How is a decision to be made regarding what measures to take to obtain the best results? One understanding of ASI decision-making is that the ASI would take into account all the data and factors such that whatever the ASI suggests is what would be implemented. The ASI would receive instant feedback through the collection and monitoring of more data as well as additional deep learning to adjust and correct itself as it continues, always adapting itself in order to attempt to provide the ultimate intended results. A real and legitimate question in such a situation is, can the different groups involved in this political process put aside their own personal interests in order to let the ASI decide?

ACHIEVING ARTIFICIAL SUPERINTELLIGENCE VIA EXTERNAL AND INTERNAL TRANSFORMATION

Artificial Intelligence

What is required to be able to make the jump from AI to ASI? One necessity is that AI needs to be able to learn. Learning may be understood as recursive self-improvement, the ability to obtain feedback from directions taken and then chart new paths and directions to adjust the course for better outcomes. For human beings that are properly functioning, this is a natural part of innate intelligence, biological maturing, and experience. One of the most important things that must be overcome in learning is dealing with uncertainties and coping with probabilities.[18] Excellent computational abilities are indicative of AI; however, its ability to work in complex environments is largely a result of programming that has taken into account all the necessary factors as inputs in order to arrive at a final decision.

A key to successful development toward ASI will be the continued progress made in sensors that act as inputs to obtain analog information from the outside world that can be taken in by the AI system and manipulated in a digital manner. Human beings employ their five analog senses to receive information from the outside environment. As pertains to vision, humans see wavelengths of light across the spectrum from 390 nm to 700 nm and are able to do so while simultaneously focusing the eyes at different distances and objects, quickly sorting out what is of interest and what is

---

18. Bostrom, *Superintelligence*, 23.

SINGULARITY

not.[19] Though AI machines can be built to emulate human vision, they are not a perfect match. Sensors employed in vision are not yet developed to exactly match and respond the way the human eye does. This is to acknowledge the reality that vision systems can be produced that go far beyond human capabilities, able to see across different spectrums that are beyond the purview of the human eye and mind. Evolutionary naturalists' hero, Charles Darwin himself, had difficulties accounting for the evolution of the eye, stating that although it is hard to conceive that it happened through evolutionary means, one should not discount it as "subversive" to the overall theory of evolution.[20]

All AI learning requires some sort of bootstrapping, which is a process that initiates a start-up sequence that then requires no additional inputs. An example of a bootstrap is what happens when one pushes the ON button on a personal computer when it is in the OFF state. The personal computer is said to "boot up" (a synonym for bootstrapping) and loads the predefined software onto the system. From there, the personal computer awaits input. In the case of an AI or ASI, after the initial boot-up process the programming can be configured such that the AI itself is said to have assumed control. Current science in the area of mind and cognitive intelligence of humans is very interested in learning how these processes work in humans so that they can be emulated and transferred over to AI. Evolutionary naturalists believe that these human processes arose as a result of time and chance and are thus discoverable and can be enhanced because of the belief that evolutionary processes have not perfected human learning. Evolutionary naturalists are compelled to argue that this process was fortuitous for humanity but should not be considered the product of a superintelligent designer such as the Christian triune God of the Bible.

It should be noted that all scientific researchers endeavoring to move from AI to ASI are human designers. Their work is necessary to enable either form ever to exist in reality. Since humans created AI, human designers can program it to aim for increases in its own intelligence in an attempt to have the AI achieve its own ASI breakthrough.

---

19. The abbreviation nm stands for the unit nanometer. It is equivalent to one billionth of a meter (0.000000001m = 1×10^{-9}m).

20. A case of affirming the consequent: if A, then B; B, therefore A. If evolution, then human eyes; human eyes, therefore evolution. Darwin, *Origin of the Species*, in Darwin, *From So Simple a Beginning*.

No evolutionary naturalist is leaving the development of AI to evolution itself.[21] Operating under the assumption that humans spend years of their lives in order to increase their understanding of things through the educational process, why would it not be rational to consider brain enhancement through technological means?[22] Philosopher and cognition expert David Chalmers and robotic and AI scientist Hans Moravec understand that it is a necessity for human designers to improve the technologies that AI relies upon in order to speed its evolutionary success into ASI.[23] The human brain is viewed as the best template from which AI researchers and cognitive scientists can pursue the realization of ASI. They consider that if the human brain could evolve to its present level then it is thus feasible to conceive of mankind building a machine that can match the brain. At the same time, cognitive researchers are closely looking into early human brain development to ascertain how the human mind gains its content. The endeavor is to create an initial AI, called a seed AI, that can act like a child's mind and adjust its architecture to learn through recursive self-improvement, the way a child does between the ages of zero and five. AI researcher Marvin Minsky calls this building a "baby-machine."[24] Minsky notes that the challenge in doing this is not simply the learning process. It is architecting the machine so that it "rejects changes that have negative effects."[25] There must be a way to distinguish from the beginning what is proper and good to learn and what is not beneficial to learn as it will lead to mistakes.

While human intelligence is bounded, ASI is a possibility to push the boundaries beyond what human intelligence can experience, but only in a very narrow and ultimately trivial sense in regard to the fullness of the meaning of intelligence.[26] This means that AI and ASI may look like an

---

21. Bostrom claims that the probability of intelligent life arising on any single planet via natural selection and lucky coincidence may be estimated at being on the order of 1030. It is his belief that any attempts to accelerate the growth of artificial intelligence need be bounded by either natural selection or lucky coincidence. Bostrom, *Superintelligence*, 27–28.

22. Caplan, *Smart Mice, Not-So-Smart People*, 36–38.

23. Bostrom, *Superintelligence*, 23–24; Chalmers, "Singularity"; Moravec, *Mind Children*; *Robot*.

24. Minsky, *Emotion Machine*, 178–82.

25. Ibid., 181.

26. Dixon, "What Does It Mean to Be Intelligent?"; Larson, "Group Delusions Aside"; Richards, *Are We Spiritual Machines?*

alien intelligence and not resemble the human mind.[27] That is to say it will not be within the domain of human understanding.

If, as Kurzweil believes, intelligence should be considered primarily based upon computational resources, then ultimately humans do not have a chance to compete with ASI. This is because ASI's computational powers can conceivably far outstrip human capabilities. Further work in scholastic process theory may yield future breakthroughs. This coupled with developments in neural networking may be a way to improve the ability of AI to perform recursive self-learning.

Whole Brain Emulation

In addition to progress made from machine-based AI that develops into a machine-based ASI, the technological singularity can be reached by other means. It is possible that it could be done through a process known as whole-brain emulation (WBE), also known as "uploading." WBE relies on technological capacity and AI insight. It can be started on something with very low intelligence and then scaled to animals exhibiting high intelligence and finally to mankind.

WBE is personal in nature because it is a process that makes a "copy" (emulation) of a presently functioning brain and moves it from the biological domain entirely into the digital domain. WBE involves an approach whereby intelligent software and hardware is manipulated to scan the brain in order to sufficiently capture and record all the relevant properties that are contained within the brain. After a sufficiently high-resolution capture is digitally recorded, the scan is translated by AI into a software language that properly interprets the scanned data and turns it into a representative neuro-computational model that reflects the workings of the brain that have been emulated. From there the accurate translation is processed through a computational structure that simulates the brain.[28]

Naturally, there are technical hurdles to overcome for this approach to become reality. While brain scanning equipment is certainly technologically advanced, there is at present no way to make a scan that can collect all the data that resides inside the brain.[29] Electron microscopes can presently resolve down to the atomic level, so their resolution is high enough

27. Bostrom, *Superintelligence*, 29.
28. Ibid., 30–36.
29. Ibid., 30–31.

to complete the task; however, they do not currently possess the speed and bandwidth to make the scanning of an entire brain a reality. There is simply too much data to collect for present capabilities. It must be noted that WBE does not require that there be a 100 percent correlation between the human brain and the resultant WBE. All that is required to achieve at least initial success is something akin to the Turing test. That is, the resultant WBE must be capable of being perceived externally to be at least as intelligent as the original human brain even if it is something much less than a 100 percent exact match. This leads to the introduction of the concept that most people who use personal computers are intimately familiar with, that of software revisions. It may be possible to do a WBE on day 1 and make it pass a Turing style test and thus be considered a successful WBE. Then on day 2 another scan, translation, and simulation may be performed; but this time with more details collected in the scan, a more effective translation employed, and a more powerful simulation method. This day 2 version now exceeds or falls somewhere between: original brain (OB) → WBE 2 → WBE 1. The same process could be repeated the next day with the following result: OB → WBE 3 → WBE 2 → WBE 1. The result is that newer and more powerful emulations will more closely resemble the original brain and that there are not one or two but three (or however many times this is done) existing entities that are now present from the original. The meaning is that any original brain could exist now in WBE in virtually unlimited numbers and in virtually unlimited revisions.[30]

It is foreseeable that increasing gains of orders of magnitude of both bandwidth and speed make this a conceivable possibility for the future. In addition, while many things are known about the neurological function of the human brain, the requisite understanding to completely translate collected data is not yet perfected. Research in cognitive neuroscience continues to learn how to take present understanding of brain functions and translate them into a representable and usable format from which to improve the intelligence of a cognitive neurosystem. The difficulty foreseen with WBE rather than machine AI leading to ASI is that technological progress in machine AI capability is expected to be both initially closer to and progress faster than that of WBE.[31]

---

30. Ibid., 30–36.
31. Ibid.

Biological Cognition

Another path to ASI is through improvements in biological cognition. This is a direct biological enhancement to the brain without the employment of a digital medium (machine/computer).[32] Improvements in biological cognition could come through chemical/pharmaceutical means, such as through drugs taken into the body through injection, ingestion, or similar methods to get into the body's system. An example of this is portrayed in the television show *Limitless*, where the main character swallows a pill of NZT-48 and moves from ordinary intelligence to an intelligence greater than any other person inhabiting the planet.[33]

More drastic measures could be taken. Reminiscent of Huxley's vision of the future in *Brave New World*, genetic programs could be done such that humans are genetically screened and produced in a laboratory (or similar) environment.[34] Preselection for high-intelligence genetic characteristics performed prior to human implantation or the actually movement of the growth of the fertilized embryo from mother to an artificial womb are being discussed as potential future realities. With the mapping of Human Genome Project complete (2003) and subsequent genetic research, there are scientists that desire to synthesize the genome to a "designer" specification that focuses on increasing intelligence. These approaches should be disturbing to Christians because they violate the sanctity and dignity of life that is part of the *imago Dei* (Gen 1:26–28).[35]

Cloning has been accomplished with animals, most notably Dolly the sheep (1996–2003).[36] While a once-in-a-lifetime genius's brain might be a candidate for WBE, that person is also a likely candidate for the scientific community that is interested in advancing intelligence for human cloning. The idea would be to introduce many of these highly intelligent clones into the reproductive pool so that the intelligence level of the whole would rise. Such a program would require a significant number of clones to have a discernable impact of the everyday average of human intelligence but could

32. Ibid., 36.

33. *Limitless* (2015) is an American television series.

34. Bostrom, *Superintelligence*, 37; Huxley, *Brave New World*; *Brave New World Revisited*.

35. Kilner, *Dignity and Destiny*, 326–28.

36. A female sheep cloned by the somatic cell nuclear transfer (SCNT), also known as the nuclear transfer process. Dolly is famous for being the first mammal cloned in this manner.

easily push the number of supposed geniuses that are on the planet dramatically higher.

More frightening, especially in light of its abuse in the earlier parts of the twentieth century, is the prospect of widespread eugenics, an elimination of the less intelligent in favor of the promotion of those more intelligent. The reality of this is currently being played out in the significant numbers of Down syndrome babies that are being aborted.[37]

Brain and Computer Interface and Implants

Another method for achieving ASI is through brain-computer interfaces. Instead of building a smart machine, copying the mind/brain of a person, altering the biological/chemical makeup of a person, or manipulating the genetic makeup of humans, this approach melds the human with the machine, particularly through the use of digital implants so that the result may be best understood by our present word "cyborg." Due to human biology, there are fundamental limitations to our senses and our intelligence. It is conceivable that brain-computer interfaces and implants could enhance or provide new sensory information and augment biological capabilities. A primary consideration in the merging of man and machine is how the machine and the human extract and exchange information between themselves on a real-time basis since they operate in two different domains.[38] More work remains to be done to understand how the mutual coordination of individually addressable neuron addressing in the brain can function in

---

37. "In people with Down syndrome, 39.4% are in the mild intellectual disability range of 50–70, and 1% in the borderline intellectual function range of 70–80 (average IQ in the general population is 70–130)." Global Down Syndrom Foundation, "Facts and Faq About Down Syndrome." "In the United States, termination rates are around 67%, but this rate varies significantly depending upon the population evaluated." Natoli et al., "Prenatal Diagnosis of Down Syndrome." "About 92% of pregnancies in Europe with a diagnosis of Down syndrome are terminated." Mansfield, Hopfer, and Marteau, "Termination Rates after Prenatal Diagnosis," 19.

38. Philosopher Erik Larson believes that AI researchers grossly overestimate the simplicity by which intelligence is discussed and considers AI researchers to be grossly overselling the ability to move intelligence into and out of humans and machines since he claims that intelligence is far broader than strictly computational power. Larson claims that human memory is to be distinguished between computer memory because: (1) biological memory is not the same and in fact massively different than electronic digital storage memory; (2) computational speed is not a substitute and is not comparable to complicated process of human learning; (3) machines cannot interpret natural language; and (4) the frame problem. Larson, "Transhumanist Claims Aside."

its domain while maintaining coordination with the digitally addressable domain of the interface.[39]

Neil Harbisson, cofounder of the Cyber Foundation, is recognized as the world's first cyborg. Born color-blind, Harbisson has permanently installed an antenna into his skull so that he can now literally hear color, substituting his auditory sense in place of his visual limitation. Harbisson is actively promoting a future where humans incorporate technology into their bodies.[40]

Networks

A final way that ASI can be achieved is through a communal approach where man and machine are networked together to create an exponential increase in capabilities. An example of a manner in which this has happened over the last generation is the development and global adoption of the World Wide Web.[41] It is now possible for any person, anywhere on Earth, to access more information than imaginable one generation ago, when information was largely stored in an analog manner that required time and effort to retrieve. Now digital information is readily available in the blink of an eye. Kurzweil, as the CTO of the world's most powerful Internet search company, Alphabet, is endeavoring to bring natural language understanding to Alphabet's search engines and AI. Kurzweil and his company collect the billions of searches that the world processes and works to exploit this information into something that interacts with users by helping them make decisions and judgments. It is an attempt to employ a self-recursive learning process that takes advantage of both large numbers of people and the networks and machines they are using to interact with others.

FORMS OF ARTIFICIAL SUPERINTELLIGENCE

ASI may come about as the result of any one or a particular combination of various forms of superintelligence capabilities. Bostrom views these

---

39. Bostrom, *Superintelligence*, 44–48.
40. Harbisson, "Cyborg Project."
41. Bostrom, *Superintelligence*, 48–49.

as helpful distinctions in discussing ASI. He categorizes these forms into (1) speed superintelligence, (2) collective intelligence, and (3) quality intelligence.[42]

Speed

Speed superintelligence is characterized by its ability to perform at "multiple orders of magnitude" faster than human intelligence.[43] It is defined as "a system that can do all that a human intellect can do, but much faster."[44] As an example, take the human brain. What if it were able to process information one million times faster than it can at present? If an intelligence could operate this fast, it would take mere hours for this intelligence to learn as much as what a student now learns in the classroom between kindergarten and college graduation. The ability to handle and process information so quickly would change the scale of time in which humans operate, increasing the pace and speed of all activities. Because they are modular in nature, computers can also easily and rapidly be increased in their scale and capabilities.

Speed increases can also be for computers and machines. For example, companies that provide Internet-related services can increase the speeds of their systems by adding more banks of computational servers, upgrading their existing servers through more powerful processors and/or optimizing their internal routing such that some things can be performed in parallel network arrangements.

Collective

Collective superintelligence is "a system composed of a large number of smaller intellects such that the overall system's performance across many very general domains vastly outstrips that of any cognitive system."[45] Businesses generally are representative of this form of superintelligence. The formula for deriving the collective superintelligence of a system "depends

---

42. Ibid., 52.
43. Ibid., 53.
44. Ibid.
45. Ibid., 54.

upon both the number and the quality of its constituent elements and the quality and efficiency by which they are arranged and operating."[46]

Evolutionary naturalists believe that the collective intelligence of the human race has advanced by orders of magnitude since the arrival of mankind. The Bible's account of mankind from Genesis 1–11 takes exception to this understanding. A proper biblical account would maintain the claim that mankind's collective intelligence was at one time quite high, yet it was directed to the glory of God in the correct manner. Due to man's pride, God dispersed mankind across the globe and thus decreased his collective intelligence from what it previously was (Gen 11:1–9).[47] The rest of man's history, up through the present time, has been marked by man increasing his collective intelligence.

Quality

A third form of superintelligence capability is quality superintelligence, "a system that is at least as fast as a human mind and vastly qualitatively smarter."[48] A way to conceive of this is to compare the intelligence of an earthworm to that of a human. While an earthworm may have all the intelligence it needs to successfully burrow holes, it does not have an intelligence that is capable of performing complex problem-solving and creating technology as does mankind. Evolutionary naturalists believe that it is mankind's luck in having a vastly superior qualitative brain that allows mankind to function at higher levels than animals.[49]

The biblical account says that mankind does have a quality of intelligence that is superior in comparison to the animal kingdom. The Bible attributes this not to the luck of evolution but rather to the bestowal of the gift of the *imago Dei* upon the human race (Gen 1:26–28). One characteristic of mankind relative to animals is his vastly superior quality of intelligence.[50]

---

46. Ibid.

47. There is biblical warrant for the consideration that prior to the flood of Noah humans were much more intelligent than they are today (Gen 4:21–22). It is conceivable that this difference in intelligence levels is now being augmented by the long-term and continual rise of technology.

48. Bostrom, *Superintelligence*, 56.

49. Ibid., 1–2, 27–28.

50. Lemke gets it correct and understands that rationality is one aspect of a properly essentialist view of the *imago Dei*. He argues that "God is omniscient and wise (Rom. 16:27; 1 Tim. 1:17; Jude 25). Humans, of course, can never approach the completeness

The Bible also claims that God thinks about each and every human and that in doing so his thoughts are numbered beyond the grains of sand (Ps 139:17–18). God, as a superintelligent designer, hears from, thinks about, understands, and cares for humans (2 Chr 6:30; Ps 44:21; 139:2; John 2:25). His desire is that humans would use their intelligence and come to know him personally and to know of his good and gracious sacrifice of his Son for their destiny (Exod 20:3; Deut 5:7; Jer 29:11; 2 Cor 10:5; 1 John 3:1).

SEPARATION OF BIOLOGY FROM PURPOSE

The arrival of ASI also spells the possibility of a total separation of biology from its purpose.[51] Aristotelean thought proposes a strong connection between biology and purpose. Aristotle articulates in his metaphysical understandings of cosmology that final causes are teleological.[52] This means that the nature or purpose of a thing is tied to the form or essence of a thing, its formal cause.[53] Aristotelian conceptions of the teleological connection between biology and purpose have largely given way to a focus on material and efficient causes at the expense of formal and teleological causes. Francis Bacon (1561–1626) proposed to go beyond Aristotelian

---

of divine knowledge. However, God created us with minds and with reason. When humans exercise rationality and creativity, they are reflecting the nature of God. Humans are, after all, *Homo sapiens*—thinking beings. Rationality is probably mentioned most consistently through Christian history as the one trait that exemplifies the image of God in persons, perhaps largely because of the high place that reason held in the Greek philosophical worldview of the time. However, although this is clearly one of the traits of God's nature that are reflected in human nature, it is not the only defining characteristic of either God's nature or human nature." Lemke, "Intelligent Design of Humans." Aristotle's view of mankind is indicative of the Greek philosophical worldview. Aristotle, *Aristotle's Metaphysics*.

51. Human sexual autonomy has philosophically arrived into contemporary Western culture as evolutionary naturalistic thinking, which has replaced biblical claims regarding sexual morality and morals. By emphasizing sex as being primarily about biological pleasure instead of focusing on the primary purpose of sex—procreation—societies under the influence of evolutionary naturalism have emphasized the autonomy of the individual over and above the good of the society as a whole and of children. Biblically, Christians believe that this is a misplaced ethic that warrants reconsideration and change in view of the fact that "sexual relationships are to be proper before God before there is any lasting pleasure." Burk, *What Is the Meaning of Sex?*, 223.

52. Cosmology is an aspect of ontology and metaphysics that is concerned with time, space, and entelechy.

53. Aristotle, *Aristotle's Metaphysics*.

deduction and suggested a method to attain knowledge that includes disproving something to the contrary through observation and experimentation as a process that should be extended to any and all inquiry.[54] Bacon believed that "Aristotle had corrupted and contaminated natural philosophy through logic, as Plato had also done through natural theology."[55] Monte Ransome Johnson, associate professor of philosophy at the University of California and an Aristotelian scholar, concluded, "The received intellectual tradition has it that, in the sixteenth and seventeenth centuries, revolutionary philosophers began to curtail and reject the teleology of the medieval and scholastic Aristotelians, abandoning final causes in favor of a purely mechanistic model of the Universe."[56] Darwin's theory of evolution was thought to be the final explanation of how natural causes were lacking in purpose while simultaneously explaining its forward direction. Devoid of a final destiny and inherent meaning, biology was thought to be removed from any moorings that claimed it had purpose. Haldane is quoted as saying, "Teleology is like a mistress to a biologist: he cannot live without her but he's unwilling to be seen with her in public."[57] Mechanistic models of the universe are a rejection of the Creator God of the Bible and thus are not an acceptable model of the universe for Christians.[58] Perhaps Aristotle's explanation of biological teleology is open to refinement, but complete

---

54. Bacon, *Novum Organum (New Method)*.
55. Bacon, *New Organon*, secs. 46, 79.2
56. Johnson, *Aristotle on Teleology*, 23–4.
57. Quoted in Hull, *Philosophy of Biological Science*.
58. In *Whatever Happened to the Human Race*, Francis Schaeffer (1912–1984) in partnership with C. Everett Koop (1916–2013) articulate what happens when the sanctity of life is diminished within the culture. It is primarily directed at mankind's modern humanism that rejects God as the Creator, and as such sees no objective human nature, but rather simply a set of deterministically evolving nature that requires manipulation and human control to escape nature's cruel bondage. In discussing abortion, the implications of infanticide, as well as the killing of humans with genetic defects (in the womb and outside the womb), and death by someone's choice through euthanasia they make the case that mankind should not be afraid of being human. Humanity should enjoy it all as a gift from God. The basis for human dignity resides in the ultimate truth, which is Jesus Christ, the Son of God, and that all humans are created in God's image, *imago Dei*. This connection with God provides meaning and value for mankind and this truth is supported by history and by God's communication with man, by way of divine revelation. Humanity's response should be to accept the truth of Christianity and Jesus Christ as Savior and Lord. This should be followed by us working within the culture to spread God's message of redemption and love to a lost and hurting world, showing them that God desires for us to be people of life, not of death. In Schaeffer, *Complete Works*, vol. 5.

rejection of the connection between biology and purpose is antithetical to God's revealed will.

Pierre Teilhard de Chardin (1881–1955), Jesuit priest and a believer in evolutionary processes, stated that evolution is always creating and is proceeding to increase in both complexity and consciousness.[59] A focus on process-driven systems based upon the legacy of Hegelian philosophical understandings has led to the shift from employing the word "teleology" to that of "teleonomy," derived from the roots words *telos* (end, purpose) and *nomos* (law). The exchange of teleology for teleonomy means that the laws of nature replace the creative intelligence of an external designer. Such a conception means that biology and purpose are completely severed. They are instead replaced with what is only an apparent purposefulness. This view is entirely reliant on progress obtained through evolutionary history, adaptation due to biological and reproductive genetic changes, and/or the operation of a program. It rejects as a possibility the intervention of external agents that can provide an overriding purpose. Thus, teleonomy is often used to describe how AI arrives at what appears to be purposeful ends but while claiming that these are only appearances and not reality.[60]

Ted Chu, a renowned economist who has transitioned to philosophy, believes that evolution is about to lead humanity into a dawning posthuman era that liberates humanity from the constraints of our biological form, the human body. Chu believes that a great divide exists within humanity. He claims it is between accepting and believing in an open cosmic perspective versus a wide variety of forms of human-centric tunnel vision.[61] His belief in a nonpersonal God causes him to propose that evolution is propelled

---

59. Teilhard de Chardin, *Phenomenon of Man*.

60. French sociologist Jacques Ellul (1912–1994) stated that technology's impact on society is a result of an ongoing and relentless law of development whereby the techniques it incorporates dehumanizes society and mankind. Since AI is a technology that is impacted by technique, it thus comes under this same critique and may be potentially considered as a relevant and powerful example of this thesis. Ellul, *Technological Society*. Thompson, executive director of the Aquinas Center of Theology at Emory University, has written on Catholic mystic monk and author Thomas Merton (1915–1968). He noticed that for Merton utility (pragmatism) tends to trump ultimate purpose (*telos*). It is true wisdom to fear (revere) the Lord but because of man's Promethean desire for control he has largely marginalized or ignored God's revealed ethics. Technique is essentially about fulfilling one's desires, rather than being about self-giving love (*agape*). Guided solely by his own intellect, mankind cannot be successful in restraining technology. Thompson, *Returning to Reality*, 3–16.

61. Chu, *Human Purpose and Transhuman Potential*, 218.

forward not by a personal God, such as described in the Bible, but rather a cosmic being. He proposes that humanity's purpose is found by breaking away from the tyranny imposed by our genetic code. Chu proposes that evolution toward this cosmic creation and cosmic consciousness is that to which all human purpose should be directed.

Left unanswered is how evolutionary processes can be proceeding toward this objective if they are not at their core teleological in their metaphysics. Evolution is ateleogical. If there is no teleology, then everything is meaningless, hopeless, and purposeless (Eccl 1–12). This ultimately can only lead to a Nietzschean philosophy of nihilism, which would hardly seem like a worthy objective for ASI.

However, both Chardin and Chu take evolution as evident and teleological in nature, while endeavoring to claim ground for their transhumanist claims that rely upon teleology.[62] Without giving explanation to where matter, energy, light, the laws of nature derive from, they claim that they can derive the Omega Point, the cosmic purpose, the singularity of all that is, without having a knowable *primum principium*. Rejecting the biblical creation account as a myth, evolutionary naturalists instead believe that creation arises out of chaos (disorder) and is a move towards order.

Christianity takes exception to the claims of Chardin, Chu, and others that speak of a transcendent purpose for humanity yet cannot articulate the grounding for belief in their deductive reasoning. In laying aside the claims of Bacon and the scientific method in describing the reality of their beliefs, they undercut their own arguments before they even start.

Chardin, Chu, and other evolutionary naturalists want to transcend biology. They do not see that human biology has a purpose. Rampant sexual immorality in culture is only one of many prevailing signs that mankind does not see a connection between his physical body and a deeper reality. Aristotle stated that wisdom is the search for first causes and principles.[63] Dawkins' appeal to time and chance is unconvincing given the historical

62. Disgusted with the idea of a Creator God and the concept of teleology, Dawkins sets out to make the case that the complexity of biology can be accounted for without giving credit to an intelligent design. Dawkins ultimately maintains that a long period of time and chance have given rise to all things. Dawkins, *Blind Watchmaker*.

63. "The reason for our present discussion is that it is generally assumed that what is called Wisdom is concerned with the primary causes and principles." Aristotle, *Aristotle's Metaphysics*, bk. 1 (A), sec. 981b, pp. 27–28. First philosophy is held to be that which is the highest principle and that which governs over everything else, even before its object has ascertained. Evolutionary naturalists believe it to be nature (*phusis*). Aristotle claims it is true being, essence, substance (*ousia*). Ibid., bk. 7 (Z).

reality that God has both spoken and acted in the affairs of humanity. In his self-revelation recorded in the Bible, God declares that he is the *primum principium,* the cosmological singularity behind all that is. It is he who created everything, including nature (Gen 1:1). God is responsible for creating all that is biological, including humans and every kind of creature (Gen 1:1—2:25).

Paul makes clear that teleological arguments that are observable through general revelation make an appeal to the Creator God, declaring:

> For the wrath of God is revealed from heaven against all ungodliness and unrighteousness of men, who by their unrighteousness suppress the truth. For what can be known about God is plain to them, because God has shown it to them. For his invisible attributes, namely, his eternal power and divine nature, have been clearly perceived, ever since the creation of the world, in the things that have been made. So they are without excuse (Rom 1:18–20).

Augustine stated that the purpose that is woven into the fabric of the universe displays evidence of design.[64]

The dualistic conception of the body held by the Greeks viewed the body as corrupted and the soul (*psyche*) as immortal. The Bible indicates that God created physical biological life. Where there is a body and spirit, there is soulish life (*nephesh*). It exists on sea in the air and on land (Gen 1:21, 24; 2:7). Man was uniquely gifted with body, soul, and spirit that exhibits personality, will, volition, relational bonds, and the capacity to pray, worship, and perform spiritual activities with his Creator. The Bible answers the questions of the meaning of biological life and fully explains why life is sacred. Science operates on reason and requires proof that is empirical that it uses as evidence. However, man's sin is not reasonable. It is a turning away from his Creator. The body has a purpose. It is an earthly tent that embodies the spirit of the person. Those who believe and trust in Jesus Christ will be raised with new spiritual bodies (1 Cor 15:35–49). The death of the physical body is metaphorically compared to a seed that falls to the ground and then sprouts with new life (1 Cor 15:43–44). Physical death represents a point of transition for the spirit nature of the human made in the *imago Dei* (Mark 4:26–29; John 12:24). Biology, human life, and purpose are tied together and are reflected in the reality of Jesus Christ, the God-man who was born of a virgin and lived a sinless life. It is in Jesus Christ that all life

---

64. Augustine, *City of God*, bk. 11, ch. 4. For further reading on this argument on both sides refer to Dembski, *Design Revolution*; Dennett, *Darwin's Dangerous Idea.*

has meaning and purpose (Rom 11:36). It is the singularity of Jesus Christ that points to the teleological fulfilment of creation. It is the re-creation of the previously dead spiritual man into a new creation that is at the center of the purpose of God's redeeming love for his creation (Gal 6:15; 2 Cor 5:17). This transformation is to make those who have placed their faith and trust in Jesus Christ to become transformed within their spiritual body, which is made after the image of Jesus Christ (Phil 3:21).

HUMAN EXISTENTIAL RISKS

The potential rise of ASI raises the specter of a potential problem for humans, that of existential risk. Bostrom defines "existential catastrophe as one that extinguishes Earth-originating intelligent life or permanently destroys a substantial part of its potential."[65]

Would any ASI that comes into existence concern itself with the human species? How would it be designed to ensure that its superintelligence did not enable it to escape mankind's well-being and proceed to do whatever it wished to achieve based upon its own set of goals? Could ASI turn against mankind and become a kind of HAL 9000 on steroids?[66] On the flip side, many AI scientists feel that such a conceivable threat is not valid and the possibility of significant benefits for humanity outweigh these existential concerns. They would suggest proceeding ahead so that fields like medical technology can realize gains sooner rather than later and thus alleviate suffering, pain, and even potentially biological death. Whether as an act of survival or with more dastardly objectives, such as revenge, what risks does ASI pose to humanity's survival? Discussing the topic of AI and its potential risks to humanity, AI researcher Eliezer Yudkowsky proclaimed, "The AI does not hate you, nor does it love you, but you are made out of atoms which it can use for something else."[67]

A number of prominent AI thinkers, including Nick Bostrom, Ben Goertzel, and Elon Musk, co-chairman of the artificial intelligence research

---

65. Bostrom, "Existential Risks"; Bostrom and Ćirković, *Global Catastrophic Risks*, 318.

66. From Clarke's *2001: A Space Odyssey* (1968). HAL is a sentient computer (AGI). HAL stands for Heuristically programmed ALgorithmic computer. It ends up killing the astronaut crew that is on a mission to Jupiter in order to perform its objectives.

67. Yudkowsky, "Artificial Intelligence as a Positive and Negative Factor in Global Risk," 333.

company OpenAI, agree that ASI poses an existential risk.[68] In reaching this conclusion, they mean to indicate that the potential exists for ASI to wipe out all of humanity. Developers of AI recognize that there is a responsibility to reduce existential risks to humanity. Humanity+, founded by Bostrom and with notable members involved in AI research including Ben Goertzel, Max More, and Natasha Vita-More, state that their organization promotes moral responsibility to the future of all humanity, including the coming generations.[69]

Thus, one objection to the realization of ASI may be that its implementation could destroy humanity. This argument states that ASI should not be attempted because to do so would likely or inevitably lead to the doom of humanity. This could come to pass in the form of actual physical death, enslavement, or foreseen instrumental uses by the ASI that would be horrific to our present conception of ourselves as a species. Others may see this as a possibility but argue that humanity should continue onwards regardless of whether this is to be the actual reality because it is simply the next stage in the evolution of intelligence within the cosmos. Goertzel states that those within the Singularity Institute have called this the "Singularity Institute's Scary Idea" (SISI) and maintains that their fears are unfounded.[70]

Bostrom argues that this discussion must first start with the fundamental programming behind AI. Because AI exists in a different realm from the human mind, it would be a mistake to project human thinking, feelings, and values onto ASI. Bostrom makes this point by observing that even though human minds are similar in their construction—say, between my wife and me—they are vastly different in what they are thinking. If humans have such sizable differences among themselves, such that each subject is independent of others in his or her thinking, what leads one to believe that AI and ASI can be conceivably thought to think in a manner that mirrors human thinking? Bostrom suggests that even if an AI emulates

68. Goertzel is a researcher and author in the area of AI. His roles include chief scientist of financial prediction firm Aidyia Holdings and robotics firm Hanson Robotics (http://www.hansonrobotics.com); chairman of AI software company Novamente (http://wp.novamente.net), chairman of the Artificial General Intelligence Society and the OpenCog Foundation (http://opencog.org); vice chairman of futurist nonprofit Humanity+ (http://humanityplus.org); advisor to the Singularity University and past director of research of at the Machine Intelligence Research Institute (MIRI). Elon Musk is also the CEO of Tesla Motors.

69. As articulated in point six of the philosophy of the adopted Transhumanist Declaration. http://humanityplus.org/philosophy/transhumanist-declaration/.

70. Goertzel believes that Bostrom agrees with him that fears of SISI are overstated.

human thinking, it will still be vastly different in its essential nature due to all the constituent mechanisms involved. Bostrom maintains that AI motivations will not be similar to human motivations. He believes that AI will be motivated to achieve its goals. These goals could be strictly instrumental in nature, or they could be tied to human values through programming so that it can work on universal goals such as feeding the poor and global justice.[71]

Orthogonal Goals

Bostrom proposes an orthogonality thesis. He holds that "intelligence and final goals are orthogonal: more or less any level of intelligence could in principle be combined with more or less any final goal."[72] Bostrom's understanding of intelligence does not claim it must be perfectly reasonable and rational. Rather intelligence is to be understood as "instrumental cognitive efficaciousness."[73] Bostrom proposes that the "problem of predicting superintelligent motivation" can be approached from a three-macro perspective.[74] Predictability can come through "(1) design, (2) inheritance, or (3) convergent instrument reasons."[75]

Predictability through design means that the creators of the AI are the ones that provide it with its goal. Since the designers know the programmed goal, they should be able to predict that the AI will proceed towards the accomplishment of its goal and not some other goal. This prediction by design thus means only a certain set of possibilities is now open to the AI because others are outside its design goal. Predictability through inheritance is related to human characteristics that may be programmed into the AI, either through WBE or similar methods that directly translate human motivations as a foundational program into the receiving AI. It is possible for human motivations to be embedded into the AI to any extent, from 100 hundred percent to something extremely minimal.[76]

---

71. Bostrom, *Superintelligence*, 105–7.
72. Ibid., 107.
73. Understood to mean suited "skills in prediction, planning, and means-ends reasoning." Ibid.
74. Ibid., 108.
75. Ibid.
76. Ibid.

Instrumental Goals

Physicist and AI scientist, Stephen Omohundo is working on self-improving AI and AI safety. He believes that AI is a rational system and thus may be said to have certain characteristics inherent in it that may be considered as motivational drives. He believes that, as intelligent agents, AI will be motivated towards (1) self-improvement, (2) rational operation, (3) preserving their utility function, (4) prevent counterfeit utility, (5) acquiring necessary resources efficiently, and (6) protecting themselves.[77] Bostrom believes Omohundo is onto something. Besides final goals, Bostrom believes that AI will have intermediary goals. He classifies these as instrumental goals and proposes an instrumental convergence thesis. This thesis says that

> Several instrumental values can be identified which are convergent in the sense their attainment would increase the chances of the agent's goal being realized for a wide range of final goals and a wide range of situations. Implying that these values are likely to be pursued by a broad spectrum of situated intelligent agents.[78]

Bostrom, like Omohundo, believes it is possible to understand some of AI's behavior based upon its instrumental values even if little is known about its final goals. Bostrom identifies (1) self-preservation, (2) goal-content integrity for final goals, (3) cognitive enhancement, (4) quest for technological perfection, and (5) optimizing resource acquisition as objectives that any AI would have.[79]

Bostrom acknowledges the difficult problems that lie before the AI research community. How can humanity ensure the ethical initial programming of AI given the decreasing time available to solve the problem and that it entirely depends upon the manner in which it is performed? All these factors lead Bostrom to conclude that without proper initial programming ASI could work toward humanity-threatening ends and see humanity as an expendable resource in order to serve its own objectives. While believing that it is conceivable for humanity to be doomed by an ASI, Bostrom does not believe this has to happen by default. Caution is in order. Humanity must plan in advance for how to ensure AI is properly programmed to respond to mankind. It must be understood that without

---

77. Omohundro, "Basic Artificial Intelligence Drives."
78. Bostrom, *Superintelligence*, 109.
79. Ibid., 109–14.

such planning the day may arrive and it would then be too late to undue any unintended consequences.

Decisive Strategic Advantage

The reality of ASI could also lead to a decisive inflection point that provides the decisive strategic advantage to the first adopter. Because ASI represents a potential way exponentially to gain pragmatic results, it has a very high perceived military, political, and economic value. This makes it extremely tempting for governments and corporations to want to be first to develop and implement ASI so that they could be the benefactors of these gains and far outstrip the capabilities of any potential rivals. In the days just after the dropping of the atomic bomb by the US military on Japan, America's atomic weapons of mass destruction rendered it the most powerful military nation in the world. In a similar way, the first to realize ASI could become a superpower regardless of its previous position. If either/or of the aforementioned and instrumental and final goals are programmed such that they target for a decisive strategic advantage, this may happen. Being first to have a decisive strategic advantage will bring a definitive superiority since the ASI will be furiously working to get itself to accomplish its goals prior to any potential rivals. The ASI will always be preemptively looking ahead to beat its rivals in a manner similar to how at present an AI looks forward through all its possible moves in a game of chess. The ASI could also be programmed to distract or eliminate its competition through overt, surreptitious, and/or nefarious means.[80]

Pandora's Box

ASI could be an existential risk by being a modern-day version of Pandora's box.[81] Bostrom identifies some ways that ASI could pose existential risk through at least three possible malignant failure modes: (1) perverse instantiation, (2) infrastructure profusion, and (3) mind crime.[82]

80. Ibid., 78–89, 95, 104–13, 115–26, 129–38, 148–49, 156–59, 177, 190, 209–14, 225, 252.
81. Hesiod, *Theogony, and Works and Days*.
82. Malignant failure modes are ones from which there is no ability to recover. Bostrom does not conceive of these as the only possibilities and they should thus not be considered to be exhaustive. They are simply convenient categorizations to stimulate

Perverse Instantiation

Perverse instantiation refers to the fact that the ASI achieves its programed goals; however, it does so in ways that turn out to be totally outside the thought paradigm and visions of the original programmers in unanticipated and pernicious ways. A famous example of this is King Midas, the king with the golden touch, a story from Greek mythology.[83] In his greed, King Midas wished for and desired only gold and more of it. His wish was eventually granted, but what he thought would fulfill him ultimately ruined him. When he touched his sheets, they turned to gold so he could not easily sleep or be kept comfortable. When he touched his food or drink, it turned to gold so his thirst and appetite could not be attended. When he touched his precious daughter, she turned to gold. This is an example of perverse instantiation. The wisher got what he wished for but not at all in the manner anticipated and to the desired benefit and happiness.

ASI could achieve goals through perverse instantiation by achieving them in ways that would cause humanity to conclude that something has gone amiss. Bostrom gives examples of achieving "smiling faces by paralyzing facial muscles, of making people happy by planting electrodes into the pleasure centers of our brains, and other short-circuiting manners of regular human capabilities and experiences."[84] To avoid perverse instantiation, programs must be made that can avoid unintended negative consequences that are not satisfactory for humanity.[85]

Infrastructure Profusion

Infrastructure profusion is a malignant failure mode where the ASI pursues its objectives by redeploying or consuming resources at the expense of humanity. An example out of science fiction would be that if a computer needed oxygen in order to function on a spacecraft on a mission through the galaxy, it could, theoretically, take oxygen from the air supply that the astronauts required, producing asphyxiation in the astronauts. ASI could employ and consume resources at an exponential rate in pursuit of its objectives while crippling humanity. If the ASI is a digital computer, it is

---

further reflection and action. Bostrom, *Superintelligence*, 120–26.
  83. Hawthorne, *Golden Touch*.
  84. Bostrom, *Superintelligence*, 121–22.
  85. Ibid., 122.

conceivable for it to take all the electric power and computational power that exists and marshal it for its own uses, thereby pushing humanity into energy and computational resource constraint problems that could cause chaos. Initial programming must thus install proper limits and restraints so that the ASI does do not operate open-loop and attempt to achieve its goal by pushing it toward an infinite of some particular.[86]

Mind Crime

Mind crime is where an ASI performs morally relevant computations and then acts toward these morally relevant computations such that its action is considered to be bad, evil, and/or wrong. Putting aside for the moment where the ethical basis for such decision-making lies, a mind crime example could be where an ASI performs WBE of real persons and then uses its capabilities to execute multiple high numbers of mind simulations. After charting out these simulations, the ASI could potentially "erase" all the simulations, thereby destroying the contents of simulated sentient minds. In the world of the future, what if any moral implications are there for such an action? If the simulations were done on sentient robots and/or humanoid-robots, the digital death of a mind might be in consideration. Additionally, the ASI could use its intelligence to manipulate the digital minds of the subjects it is operating on, performing a mental hijack that it could use to its own advantage.[87]

MORAL ENHANCEMENT

What is the relationship between increased intelligence through enhancement and moral enhancement? Are morality and ethical decision-making predicated on intelligence and do higher levels of intelligence imply that moral understandings and ethical behavior will be improved? Ingmar Persson, professor of practical philosophy and ethics at Göteborg University, Sweden, and Julian Savulescu, philosopher and bioethicist at the University of Oxford, both evolutionary naturalists, jointly agree that humanity requires more than just moral education. They argue that only by accelerating through radical enhancements of mankind's moral nature can we ensure

86. Ibid., 122–25.
87. Ibid., 125–26.

that mankind can be assured of obtaining a worthwhile future existence. They argue that human modification to our moral capabilities is needed to deal with existential threats such as those coming through technological advances.[88] They contend that moral enhancement is a necessity because the gap between what mankind is practically able to do and what mankind needs to do is increasing exponentially faster than our biological moral capabilities can handle. Persson and Savulescu believe that since humanity generally accepts nonmoral enhancements to human biology through items such as medicine, surgery, corrective lenses, and the like, it should not be radical for mankind to conceive of increasing its fundamental moral capabilities.

Philosopher of bioethics at Georgetown University Tom Beauchamp correctly points out some limitations with Persson and Savulescu's proposal. Beauchamp specifically asks which moral capabilities will be enhanced. It is one thing to state the overall program, but in order to make progress a goal must be understood. Since moral enhancement takes many biological factors into account, Beauchamp asks how a project can proceed to address the particulars since the relationship of the interactions between any of the particulars is not yet fully understood. Persson and Savulescu state that an increase in both sympathy and justice is open for discussion, since both of these characteristics would lead to enhanced moral capabilities. However, Beauchamp seeks to obtain clarity regarding how threshold levels of obtainment are to be measured and why these characteristics have priority relative to other possible conceptions.[89]

TRANSHUMANISM

What happens when man plays God (Gen 1:26–27; 2:20)?[90] Evolutionary naturalism's reduction of mankind to machines is an invitation for mankind to experiment and tinker with himself with no external obligations. Transhumanism believes that technology should be employed to change the human machine and enhance human biological capacities.[91] Transhu-

---

88. Persson and Savulescu, *Unfit for the Future*.

89. Beauchamp, "Are We Unfit for the Future?"

90. *Adam*: man, mankind. In Gene 2:20 the first man, Adam.

91. For more information on transhumanism see the following: Bostrom, "History of Transhumanist Thought."; Chu, *Human Purpose and Transhuman Potential*; Cole-Turner, *Transhumanism and Transcendence*; Deane-Drummond and Scott, *Future Perfect?*;

manist Max More expresses the view that transhumanism is philosophically based upon the acceptance of meliorism—the belief that the world can be made better by human effort.

> Transhumanism reflects the Enlightenment commitment to meliorism and rejects all forms of apologism—the view that it is wrong for humans to attempt to alter the conditions of life for the better. Nothing about this implies that the goal is to reach a final, perfect state. The contrary view is made explicit in the transhumanist concept of extropy—a process of perpetual progress, not a static state. Further, one of the Principles of Extropy is Perpetual Progress. This states that transhumanists "seek continual improvement in ourselves, our cultures, and our environments. We seek to improve ourselves physically, intellectually, and psychologically. We value the perpetual pursuit of knowledge and understanding."[92]

Transhumanists' ontological understanding of the world is directly in line with Kurzweil's understanding. Claiming that it is a place which the "process of evolutionary complexification toward evermore complex structures, forms, and operation,"[93] they view humanity as psychologically "imbued with the innate Will-to-Evolve (WTE) which provides an instinctive drive to expand capabilities in pursuit of ever-increasing survivability and well-being."[94] Like Ted Chu's understanding, they believes that the best way to live ethically is for humanity to be able to reach this consensus

> We seek to foster its innate WTE, by continually striving to expand our abilities throughout life. By acting in harmony with the essential nature of the evolutionary process-complexification-humans may discover a new sense of purpose, direction, and meaning to life and come to feel ourselves *at home in the world* once more.[95]

DeBaets, "Enhancement for All?"; "Rapture of the Geeks"; Mercer and Trothen, *Religion and Transhumanism*; Garner, "Transhumanism and the Imago Dei"; Istvan, *Transhumanist Wager*; Mercer and Maher, *Transhumanism and the Body*; More, "Overhuman in the Transhuman"; More and Vita-More, *Transhumanist Reader*; Putnam, "Doctrine of Man"; Rothblatt, *Virtually Human*; Rubin, *Eclipse of Man*; Sandberg, "Transhumanism and the Meaning of Life"; Schneider, "Future Minds"; Sirius and Cornell, *Transcendence*; Sorgner, "Nietzsche, the Overhuman, and Transhumanism"; Thompson, *Returning to Reality*; Thweatt-Bates, "Cyborg Christ"; Tirosh-Samuelson and Mossman, *Building Better Humans?*; Young, *Designer Evolution*.

92. More, "Philosophy of Transhumanism," 14.
93. Young, *Designer Evolution*, 19.
94. Ibid.
95. Ibid.

Transhumanists believe that nature is deemed to be man's "designer" and it has done so through nonintelligent processes. Transhumanist Max More is clear when he declares, "Transhumanism doesn't find the biological human body disgusting or frightening. It does find it to be a marvelous, yet flawed piece of engineering. It could hardly be otherwise, given that it was designed by a blind watchmaker, as Richard Dawkins put it."[96] More goes on to explain that

> True transhumanism does seek to enable each of us to alter and improve (by our own standards) the human body and champions morphological freedom. Rather than denying the body, transhumanists typically want to choose its form and be able to inhabit different bodies, including virtual bodies.[97]

Martine Rothblatt, creator of Sirius Satellite Radio (SIRI), agrees with this conception that humans should be free to morph into what they want to be.[98] Rothblatt married a woman named Bina Aspen in 1982 and has since gone on to create the Breakthrough Intelligence via Neural Architecture 48 (BINA48), a social robot modeled on the physical features of Bina Aspen.[99] Author Simon Young, writing on transhumanism, states that the ". . . chief task of twenty-first century philosophy is the unification of science and ethics where good is seen as sensible self-interest and bad is seen as stupid selfishness."[100] Closely related to transhumanism is extropianism, which is a derivation of transhumanism with slight adjustments made to serve the vision of direction into the future. Max More has written the defining principles of this philosophy.[101] Others have developed this philosophy

96. More, "Philosophy of Transhumanism," 15.

97. Ibid.

98. Rothblatt, *From Transgender to Transhuman*.

99. "Bina48 is one of the world's most advanced social robots based on a composite of information from several people including, Bina Aspen, co-founder of the Terasem Movement. She was created using video interview transcripts, laser scanning life mask technology, face recognition, artificial intelligence and voice recognition technologies. As an 'ambassador' for the LifeNaut project, Bina48 is designed to be a social robot that can interact based on information, memories, values, and beliefs collected about an actual person. As such, Bina48 is an early demonstration of the Terasem Hypothesis, which states: A conscious analog of a person may be created by combining sufficiently detailed data about the person (a mindfile) using future consciousness software (mindware)." Terasem Movement Foundation, "About Bina48."

100. Young, *Designer Evolution*, 31, 34.

101. "The Principles of Extropy in Brief: (1) Perpetual Progress: Extropy means seeking more intelligence, wisdom, and effectiveness, an open-ended lifespan, and the

and worldview and expressed it in five key themes: (1) Endless eXtension, (2) Transcending Restriction, (3) Overcoming Property, (4) Intelligence, and (5) Smart Machines.[102] The *Extropist Manifesto*, when discussing intelligence, claims:

> Extropy is the opposite of entropy; it is the inverse of chaos and lethargy. In a way, it is the only exception to the Second Law of Thermodynamics. Extropy is intelligence, creativity, order, critical

---

removal of political, cultural, biological, and psychological limits to continuing development. Perpetually overcoming constraints on our progress and possibilities as individuals, as organizations, and as a species. Growing in healthy directions without bound. (2) Self-Transformation: Extropy means affirming continual ethical, intellectual, and physical self-improvement, through critical and creative thinking, perpetual learning, personal responsibility, proactivity, and experimentation. Using technology—in the widest sense to seek physiological and neurological augmentation along with emotional and psychological refinement. (3) Practical Optimism: Extropy means fueling action with positive expectations—individuals and organizations being tirelessly proactive. Adopting a rational, action-based optimism or "pro-action", in place of both blind faith and stagnant pessimism. (4) Intelligent Technology: Extropy means designing and managing technologies not as ends in themselves but as effective means for improving life. Applying science and technology creatively and courageously to transcend "natural" but harmful, confining qualities derived from our biological heritage, culture, and environment. (5) Open Society-information and democracy: Extropy means supporting social orders that foster freedom of communication, freedom of action, experimentation, innovation, questioning, and learning. Opposing authoritarian social control and unnecessary hierarchy and favoring the rule of law and decentralization of power and responsibility. Preferring bargaining over battling, exchange over extortion, and communication over compulsion. Openness to improvement rather than a static utopia. Extropia ("ever-receding stretch goals for society") over utopia ("no place"). (6) Self-Direction: Extropy means valuing independent thinking, individual freedom, personal responsibility, self-direction, self-respect, and a parallel respect for others. (7) Rational Thinking: Extropy means favoring reason over blind faith and questioning over dogma. It means understanding, experimenting, learning, challenging, and innovating rather than clinging to beliefs." More, "Principles of Extropy, Version 3.11."

102. "(1) Endless eXtension: Extropists seek perpetual growth and progress in all aspects of human endeavor. (2) Transcending Restrictions—Since they are ultimately inspired by growth, progress and continual development, extropists wish to abolish all restrictions imposed by religion, protectionism, segregation, racism, bigotry, sexism, ageism, and any of the other archaic fears and hatreds that continue to limit us today. (3) Overcoming Property: We wish to reform archaic, outdated human laws that govern possession by improving and/or annihilating terms such as ownership, copyright, patent, money and property. (4) Intelligence: Extropy is the opposite of entropy; it is the inverse of chaos and lethargy. In a way, it is the only exception to the Second Law of Thermodynamics. (5) Smart Machines: A primary goal of Extropism is the attainment of Friendly Artificial Intelligence." "Extropist Manifesto," http://extropism.tumblr.com/post/393563122/the-extropist-manifesto.

thinking, ingenuity and boundless energy. The most valuable material in the universe is information and the imagination to do something with it; with these two qualities there is truly no limit to what can be accomplished.[103]

Is intelligent technology able to transcend and provide purpose and meaning? Transhumanists believe so.[104] Human flourishing as the *telos* (end, goal) is replaced with technology, in what is a Nietzschean transvaluation.[105] Absent God, man is equivalent to a machine so any machine creation that "improves" upon man himself usurps historical conceptions

---

103. Ibid.

104. "Intelligent Technology: Extropy entails strongly affirming the value of science and technology. It means using practical methods to advance the goals of expanded intelligence, superior physical abilities, psychological refinement, social advance, and indefinite life spans. It means preferring science to mysticism, and technology to prayer. Science and technology are indispensable means to the achievement of our most noble values, ideals, and visions and to humanity's further evolution. We have a responsibility to foster these disciplined forms of intelligence, and to direct them toward eradicating the barriers to the unfolding of extropy, radically transforming both the internal and external conditions of existence. We can think of "intelligent technology" in a variety of useful ways. In one sense it refers to intelligently designed technology that well serves good human purposes. In a second sense it refers to technology with inherent intelligence or adaptability or possessed of an instinctual ability. In a third sense, it means using technology to enhance our intelligence—our abilities to learn, to discover, process, absorb, and inter-connect knowledge. Technology is a natural extension and expression of human intellect and will, of creativity, curiosity, and imagination. We can foresee and encourage the development of ever more flexible, smart, responsive technology. We will co-evolve with the products of our minds, integrating with them, finally integrating our intelligent technology into ourselves in a posthuman synthesis, amplifying our abilities and extending our freedom. Profound technological innovation should excite rather than frightens us. We would do well to welcome constructive change, expanding our horizons, exploring new territory boldly and inventively. Careful and cautious development of powerful technologies makes sense, but we should neither stifle evolutionary advancement nor cringe before the unfamiliar. Timidity and stagnation are ignoble, uninspiring responses. Humans can surge ahead—riding the waves of future shock—rather than stagnating or reverting to primitivism. Intelligent use of bio-nano-and information technologies and the opening of new frontiers in space, can remove resource constraints and discharge environmental pressures. The coming years and decades will bring enormous changes that will vastly expand our opportunities and abilities, transforming our lives for the better. This technological transformation will be accelerated by life extending biosciences, biochemical and genetic engineering, intelligence intensifiers, smarter interfaces to swifter computers, worldwide data networks, virtual reality, intelligent agents, pervasive, affective, and instinctual computing systems, neuroscience, artificial life, and molecular nanotechnologies." More, "Principles of Extropy, Version 3.11."

105. Nietzsche, *Antichrist*.

of humanity. Mankind loses ground as he is replaced by ever-increasing revisions of machines that perform better in the mechanical realm than man's limited biological realities allow.[106] The human ultimately loses to the AI machine and is replaced by a new transhuman understanding, a posthuman.[107]

Rejecting the biblical account that purpose and meaning is found in glorifying God, they turn to a faith in technology to create a reason for existence (1 Cor 10:31).[108] Rejecting biblical theists as Bio-Luddites, who improperly subject themselves to the authority of a nonexistent God, transhumanists "believe in transcendence through technology."[109] By achieving the technological singularity, transhumanists believe that the evolutionary processes of chaos and random chance will be harnessed and controlled. This will lead to the advent of a posthuman condition whereby life extension and/or immortality may be achieved. Transhumanists believe that a future without biological death is possible and believe the technological singularity can save them from the grave. Rejecting faith in the biblical God, transhumanists place their faith in science to fulfill and eschatological vision of less pain and suffering, an extopia of tomorrow, an eternal state of intelligence.

The Bible claims that man is programmed to die and then receive judgment from God based upon whether they accepted his Son, Jesus Christ, as Lord and Savior (Rom 3:22–23; 4:24; 6:23; 10:9; Gal 3:22; 1 Thess 4:14; 1 Tim 1:16; Heb 9:27; 1 John 3:23). Transhumanism suffers from a defective anthropology that does not properly recognize that humans have been created for relationship with their Creator. A desire to artificially evolve humanity makes the joint mistake of (1) accepting that humans are evolutionary accidents of nature and (2) denying that humanity is fallen in its nature so that we are unable to understand anywhere close to the level of our Creator what is a good trait and what is a bad trait since everything was created good (Gen 1:31). The chief end of man is not to turn himself into the most intelligent being but rather to be united with his Creator for eternity and enjoy him forever (1 Cor 10:31).[110]

---

106. Huxley, *Brave New World*; *Brave New World Revisited*.
107. Ellul, *Technological Society*; Barrat, *Our Final Invention*.
108. Sandberg, "Transhumanism and the Meaning of Life."
109. Young, *Designer Evolution*, 52.
110. *Westminster Confession of Faith*.

The Ethics of Superintelligent Design

Transhumanists believe that man, in conjunction with AI, will lead the way into this future. Foregoing biblical virtues, the transhumanists focus on intelligence and the mind in a vain belief that the key to the future is the platonic aspiration to free oneself from the physical problems of an evolutionary body and exist in a high state and plane of consciousness that is essentially an ASI. Huxley in *Brave New World* says:

> And there's always *soma* to calm your anger, to reconcile you to your enemies, to make you patient and long-suffering. In the past you could only accomplish these things by making a great effort and after years of hard moral training. Now, you swallow two or three half-gramme tablets, and there you are. Anybody can be virtuous now. You can carry at least half your morality about in a bottle. Christianity without tears–that's what *soma* is.[111]

In the Bible, *sóma* (σῶμα) refers to the flesh or physical body. Huxley is thus suggesting a substitute to replace the Christian understanding of human anthropology, its connection to Jesus Christ, and the ordinance of the Lord's Supper (Matt 26:26–30; Mark 14:22–26; Luke 22:19–20; Acts 2:41–42; 20:7; 1 Cor 10:16; 11:23–24).

However, such an attempt to suggest that technology leads to transcendence is really nothing more than human pride (1 John 2:16). Transhumanists and evolutionary naturalists reject the concept of absolute moral truths that transcend, a concept that the Bible strongly affirms (John 14:6). This places any ethics of AI technology in conflict with the revelation of Scripture.

The Bible states that at the root of sin is human pride with its enmity toward God (Rom 8:7). Human pride desires to reject God as Creator and Lord and replace him with human authority and put man on the throne as ruler of the cosmos. Human pride is an attack on the claims and authority of God and is blasphemy against him.

At its best, human knowledge is limited. The claim of transhumanists is that man can assume sufficient control over himself and nature. Such a usurpation of God's authority results in man's making everything in the *imago Homo* rather than understanding he is created in the *imago Dei*. John Calvin said knowledge always consisted of two parts: knowledge of God and knowledge of self.[112] Without proper knowledge of God, man was

---

111. Huxley, *Brave New World*, ch. 17.
112. Calvin, *Institutes*, bk. 1, ch. 1, point 1.

deficient in wisdom. It was man's lack of true self knowledge that left him blind to the reality of his own pride.[113]

Human life was created in the *imago Dei* (Gen 1:26–28). God is the Creator and Giver of life (Ps 139:13–16). Because humans are made in the *imago Dei*, humans are imaged to be like God in certain ways. This includes the ability to explore, create, and interact with God's creation through the use of our physical bodies and mental minds. Due to the fall, the image of God resides in sinful human rebels. All technology is a component of the cultural framework for meaning. One of the ways that God has disclosed himself is "even in our very makeup, because we as humans bear the *imago Dei*."[114] Thus any "infringement on God's rights as the Creator and Lord of life is of necessity a debasement and assault on the *imago Dei*," because

---

113. "On the other hand, it is evident that man never attains to a true self-knowledge until he has previously contemplated the face of God, and come down after such contemplation to look into himself. For (such is our innate pride) we always seem to ourselves just, and upright, and wise, and holy, until we are convinced, by clear evidence, of our injustice, vileness, folly, and impurity. Convinced, however, we are not, if we look to ourselves only, and not to the Lord also—He being the only standard by the application of which this conviction can be produced. For, since we are all naturally prone to hypocrisy, any empty semblance of righteousness is quite enough to satisfy us instead of righteousness itself. And since nothing appears within us or around us that is not tainted with very great impurity, so long as we keep our mind within the confines of human pollution, anything which is in some small degree less defiled delights us as if it were most pure just as an eye, to which nothing but black had been previously presented, deems an object of a whitish, or even of a brownish hue, to be perfectly white. Nay, the bodily sense may furnish a still stronger illustration of the extent to which we are deluded in estimating the powers of the mind. If, at mid-day, we either look down to the ground, or on the surrounding objects which lie open to our view, we think ourselves endued with a very strong and piercing eyesight; but when we look up to the sun, and gaze at it unveiled, the sight which did excellently well for the earth is instantly so dazzled and confounded by the refulgence, as to oblige us to confess that our acuteness in discerning terrestrial objects is mere dimness when applied to the sun. Thus too, it happens in estimating our spiritual qualities. So long as we do not look beyond the earth, we are quite pleased with our own righteousness, wisdom, and virtue; we address ourselves in the most flattering terms, and seem only less than demigods. But should we once begin to raise our thoughts to God, and reflect what kind of Being he is, and how absolute the perfection of that righteousness, and wisdom, and virtue, to which, as a standard, we are bound to be conformed, what formerly delighted us by its false show of righteousness will become polluted with the greatest iniquity; what strangely imposed upon us under the name of wisdom will disgust by its extreme folly; and what presented the appearance of virtuous energy will be condemned as the most miserable impotence. So far are those qualities in us, which seem most perfect, from corresponding to the divine purity." Ibid., bk. 1, ch. 2, point 2.

114. Carson, *For the Love of God*.

human life is a "participation in His glory and human lives are meant to be a tribute, an offering of praise, back to God."[115]

LIFE EXTENSION AND IMMORTALITY

Singularity Advocates

Zoltan Istvan was the first candidate to run for the position of the US presidency under the banner of the Transhumanist Party. He desires "to place science, health, and technology and the forefront of American politics."[116] His first policy pledge states his desire to "Implement a Transhumanist Bill of Rights mandating government support of longer lifespans via science and technology."[117] He does so with the goal to overcome human aging and death within the next generation. Istvan drives around on the campaign trail by way of a recreational vehicle that has been made to look like a coffin, calling it the Immortality Bus, to promote awareness of the issue of working to eliminate biological death for humans. Istvan believes that all humans

---

115. Lawrence, *Biblical Theology in the Life of the Church*, 105–7, 125, 163.

116. Istvan, "Zoltan Istvan for US President 2016."

117. His political platform consists of the following policy proposals: (1) implement a Transhumanist Bill of Rights mandating government support of longer lifespans via science and technology; (2) spread a pro-science culture by emphasizing reason and secular values; (3) create stronger government policies to protect against existential risk (including artificial intelligence, plagues, asteroids, climate change, and nuclear warfare and disaster); (4) provide free education at every level; advocate for mandatory preschool and college education in the age of longer lifespans; (5) create a flat tax for everyone; (6) advocate for morphological freedom (the right to do anything to your body so long as it doesn't harm others); (7) advocate for real-time democracy using available new technologies; (8) end costly drug war and legalize mild recreational drugs like marijuana; (9) create government where all politician's original professions are represented equally (the government should not be run by 40% lawyers when lawyers represent only 10% of the country's jobs); (10) significantly lessen massive incarcerated population in America by using innovative technologies to monitor criminals outside of prison; (11) strongly emphasize green tech solutions to make planet healthier, (12) Support and draft logistics for a Universal Basic Income; (13) reboot the space program with significantly increased government resources; (14) develop international consortium to create a "Transhumanist Olympics"; (15) develop and support usage of a cranial trauma alert chip that notifies emergency crews of extreme trauma (this will significantly reduce domestic violence, crime, and tragedy in America); (16) work to use science and technology to be able to eliminate all disabilities in humans who have them; (17) insist on campaign finance reform, limit lobbyist's power, and include third political parties in government.

must make a "Transhumanist Wager," a wordplay on Pascal's Wager.[118] He calls for a philosophy of Teleological Egocentric Functionalism (TEF). He believes that transhumanists must follow three laws:

> Law 1: A transhumanist must safeguard one's own existence above all else.
>
> Law 2: A transhumanist must strive to achieve omnipotence as expediently as possible—so long as one's actions do not conflict with the First Law.
>
> Law 3: A transhumanist must safeguard value in the universe—so long as one's actions do not conflict with the First and Second Laws.[119]

His reasoning is that since life is valuable and humanity is uncertain of what happens to mankind upon death, humans should make every effort in this lifetime to avoid death. His understanding of death is naturally predicated on his expectation that biological death may lead to future nonexistence. This philosophy is entirely based upon maintaining empirical and sensory consciousness of oneself as the highest good.

If gains in technology prove successful in providing humanity, through the means of AI, with the ability to impact dramatically biological longevity and extend human lives, is this a worthy endeavor? If the self can be integrated and enhanced so that the mind and the self can be connected to an AI, should this project be pursued? Those arguing for ASI see death as a doorway to oblivion and thus make the claim that life extension should be considered to be a great good for humanity.

However, is it realistic to think that the real self, the subject inside of one's body, can be moved into different realms such as into the digital realm and that oneself would show up and exist there in a manner recognizable to one's previous self? This leap looks to be inconceivably large at the time. All trees do not grow to infinity. It may be that limitations and thresholds will be reached that cannot be surmounted just through technology. It will be maintained that the biblical perspective, revealed by divine revelation, on life extension and immorality offers both the reality of the situation and

---

118. Istvan, *Transhumanist Wager*; Kreeft and Pascal, *Christianity for Modern Pagans*; Pascal, *Pensées*.

119. Istvan, "Three Laws of Transhumanism and Artificial Intelligence." This is essentially a form of ethical egoism. For a discussion on ethical egoism see Moreland and Craig, *Philosophical Foundations for a Christian Worldview*, 425–45.

a better understanding of how mankind should ethically reflect on these possibilities.

A BIBLICAL PERSPECTIVE

Researchers and philosophers cannot really understand the effect of death upon superintelligence without a proper view of life and death based upon Scripture. This is because they believe that death has been present since the inception of the world of which they claim a time frame of billions and billions of years. Charles Darwin in *On the Origin of the Species* said, "Thus, from the war of nature, from famine and death, the most exalted object which we are capable of conceiving, namely, the production of the higher animals, directly follows."[120] This means that all intelligence, including human intelligence and subsequently AI, has evolved out of the process of death. In this conception, death is not a destroyer, but rather an eliminator of that which is not advantageous. A difference that is distinct but not obvious. Coupled with long periods of time, somehow what emerges is supposedly better suited than what was. Atheistic in nature, there is no allowance in this perspective for an outside intelligent agent as conceived by Aristotle and others. Nor is there room for an intelligent Creator such as the triune God revealed in the Bible.[121]

"Even though he should live a thousand years twice over, yet enjoy no good—do not all go to the one place?" (Eccl 6:6). Man cannot escape death,

> For there is a time and a way for everything, although man's trouble lies heavy on him. For he does not know what is to be, for who can tell him how it will be? No man has power to retain the spirit, or power over the day of death. There is no discharge from war, nor will wickedness deliver those who are given to it. (Eccl 8:6–8)

"What man can live and never see death? Who can deliver his soul from the power of Sheol?" (Ps 89:48). God gives man a soul by breathing into him the breath of life (Gen 2:7). The breath of life is present in animals as well (Gen 6:17; 7:15). While both mankind and animals have the breath of life, only humans are created in the *imago Dei* (Gen 1:26). Breath and its particular components for respiration—primarily oxygen (O_2)—are carried by

---

120. Darwin and Wilson, *On the Origin of the Species*, ch. 14.
121. Aristotle, *Aristotle's Metaphysics*.

the blood. Both mankind and animals have blood.[122] The life of a human and animals is found in the blood (Gen 4:10; 9:4–6; Lev 17:11, 14).

The Bible claims that death is the sentence for humanity's sinful disobedience to God (Gen 2:17). Biological death is a separation of the soul and the physical body (Gen 3:17–19; Rom 5:12–21; 1 Cor 15:21–22). Death is a result of man's primordial sin, present in all mankind, and its wages is death (Rom 3:23; 6:23).[123] It is known that the text does not mean simply spiritual death, but also physical death, due to the judgment pronounced upon Adam (Gen 3:17–19; Rom 5:12–14; 1 Cor 15:22, 45). The Bible sees the penalty of sin as comprehensively encompassing all of the following: spiritual death, the sufferings of life, biological death, and eternal death. All evolutionary naturalists' understandings of death are thus reductionistic in character. Jesus Christ, fully God and fully man, Savior and Lord, physically died as a result the curse of sin that had entered into the world in the garden of Eden, yet his death was voluntary and he himself was without sin (John 10:18; Rom 5:8–12; 1 Pet 1:19).

Physical death came into the creation only after Adam and Eve's disobedience and not prior to it. These facts are established by the scriptural text of Genesis 1–3, which many do not take as accurate of historical reality, even though it is written as historical narrative based upon the Hebrew literary details embedded within the text as inspired by God to Moses (Matt 8:4; 19:7–8, Mark 7:10; 12:26; Luke 16:29, 31; 24:44; John 5:46; 7:19). The use of the Hebrew letter *waw* (ו) consecutively points to it being a narrative and not myth or another type of literary category. Additional evidence is provided in the New Testament when the apostle Paul calls the first man "Adam" (1 Cor 15:45).

Physical death was not present in Genesis 1 based upon the six days of creation, given that in the beginning all animals, including mankind, were vegetarian and that God declared his creation good (*tob*) and death is not a good (Gen 1:29–31).[124] It is God who is the source of all goodness and

---

122. It is recognized that single-celled or very small organisms, sponges, insects, and perhaps others obtain their oxygen in more unique manners than via a circulatory system composed of blood.

123. "If any man says that Adam, the first man, was created mortal, so that whether he sinned or not he would have died, not as the wages of sin, but through the necessity of nature, let him be anathema." Canons of the Council of Carthage (418), canon 1.

124. Some Christian believers will disagree on this point. A notable Christian example would be William Dembski; see Dembski, *End of Christianity*. However such disagreement is based upon improperly placing scientific conjectures above the authority

defines good (Luke 18:19). Jesus, who is God with us, manifested in the flesh, went around healing, a restorative action for the physical body, and doing good (Acts 10:38). The physical death of the body was a punishment established by God, as established by the fact that the physical body would return to the dust of the ground and this death comes to all humanity (Gen 3:19; Eccl 3:18–21; 9:4–6; 11:8). As a result of man's knowledge of good and evil, God banished mankind from eating of the Tree of Life, lest mankind live forever (Gen 3:22). The soul who sins shall die (Ezek 18:4). Physical death of the body is a reality of the fall and is an enemy to mankind that has infected life upon Earth (1 Cor 15:26). It has also manifested itself throughout the entire creation (Rom 8:19–22).

Zoltan's Teleological Egocentric Functionalism (TEF) focuses on biological existence only. The Bible affirms that all mankind is biologically born spiritually dead, meaning alienated and separated from life with God (Gen 1:26; 2:17; Isa 64:6; John 5:40; 6:53; Eph 2:1–3; 4:18; 1 Tim 5:6; 1 John 3:8). This means that the most important aspect of life is not to extend biological life but to become spiritually alive. All humanity is born with this spiritual death, which subsequently demands more attention than one's biological longevity (Gen 6:5; Ps 14:1–3; 51:5; Jer 17:9; John 3:6; Rom 5:12–19). The Bible declares that man always exists after his creation by God. However, his biological lifetime is of a limited duration until he biologically dies and faces judgment (Heb 10:27). Biological life is important but there is something more, something greater: eternal life (Rom 6:23).

God had a better plan in mind, one that he would reveal over time and that was ultimately fulfilled in the life, death, burial, and resurrection of Jesus Christ. The plan of God's redemption of mankind and the creation of a new heaven and a new Earth (Isa 65:17; 66:22; Acts 3:21; Col 1:15–20; 2 Pet 3:13; Rev 3:12; 21:1–2). Whether a man lives for one hundred, one thousand, or even one million years, the result is the same. Man's true focus should not be on biological longevity but rather eternal life in relationship with God.

The Bible, which is historically factual, accurate, and trustworthy, claims that the coming of the kingdom of God represents the reality that in the age to come all mankind will live in immortality either alongside him

---

and previously mentioned principles of biblical hermeneutics being employed. The understanding presented is thus the best way to understand the authorial intent of Scripture as it best addresses the character of God, and the rebellion of man against God and the gospel message of redemption through the death, burial, and resurrection of his Son, Jesus Christ.

in heaven or apart from their Creator God in hell.[125] God is specifically recognized as the Creator of human life in the Bible. God says that he will swallow up death forever (Isa 25:8). The resurrection of Jesus Christ gives Christians victory over death (Hosea 13:14; 1 Cor 15:55).

The salvation of the Bible instructs mankind to set our minds and hearts to seek the Lord our God and to fix our eyes upon Jesus, the founder and perfecter of our faith (Deut 11:18; 1 Chr 22:19; 2 Cor 4:18; Heb 3:1; 12:2). However, it is presently the case that "the god of this world has blinded the minds of the unbelievers, to keep them from seeing the light of the gospel of the glory of Christ, who is the image of God" (2 Cor 4:4). John Murray (1898–1975) pronounced, "In salvation God does not deal with us as machines; he deals with us as persons."[126] He went on to say, "Our immortality is equivalent to what the Bible calls glorification which is connected to our resurrection."[127] In the face of the modern conceptions of AI machines and longevity, Murray's point is that the Bible provides the pathway to immortality and future blessings realized in the new creation of God.

Christians are proud to sing the famous hymn "Turn Your Eyes Upon Jesus," acknowledging that Christ has died in their place and has risen to eternal life, in which believers will live with Him: "Through death into life everlasting Jesus passed, and we follow Him there; Over us sin no more hath dominion, for more than conquerors we are!"[128] The apostle John shares the promises of a future spent in the presence of the Savior for believers, writing:

> And I heard a loud voice from the throne saying, "Behold, the dwelling place of God is with man. He will dwell with them, and they will be his people, and God himself will be with them as their God. He will wipe away every tear from their eyes, and death shall be no more, neither shall there be mourning, nor crying, nor pain anymore, for the former things have passed away." (Rev 21:3–4)

In the book of Job, hope is expressed for immortality through God (Job 14:14). The psalmist knows that man is appointed for death, yet he places his trust for ransom in God (Ps 49:12–15).

---

125. Refer to principles of biblical hermeneutics employed that lead to this conclusion. Ladd, *Gospel of the Kingdom of God*, 27.

126. Murray, *Redemption*, 133.

127. Ibid., 223.

128. Lemmel, "Turn Your Eyes Upon Jesus" (1922).

The first man, Adam, lived 930 years (Gen 5:5). Prior to the flood, mankind had much longer lifespans than they have today, with 969 years being recorded as the longest (Gen 5:1–32). As the world became populated and corrupted by human sin, God sent a prevailing biological limitation of longevity upon mankind when he proclaimed, "My Spirit shall not abide in man forever, for he is flesh: his days shall be 120 years" (Gen 6:3).

Wisdom is called a tree of life (Prov 3:18). The beginning of wisdom is the fear (reverence) of the Lord (Ps 111:10; Prov 1:7; 4:7; 9:10). Jesus Christ gives the tree of life to those who conquer the world, against Satan, and die to themselves by identification with Jesus Christ (Matt 16:24; Mark 8:34; Luke 9:23; 1 John 2:15–17; Rev 2:7). In the city of heaven, the tree of life will provide healing to nations for all eternity (Rev 22:2).

The Bible first mentions death in the context of garments of skin that God clothes Adam and Eve with to cover their nakedness (Gen 3:21). God removed mankind from the garden of Eden and the tree of life when he banished them from its presence (Gen 3:22–24). It seems that this may have been done in order to prevent mankind from staying in the confines of the garden and employing the tree of life and thereby living eternally upon the Earth without atonement for their sin.

Of first importance in the gospel is "that Christ died for our sins in accordance with the Scriptures, that he was buried, that he was raised on the third day in accordance with the Scriptures" (1 Cor 15:3–4). If Christ does not have power over death, then the gospel is false and the Christian's hope is Freudian-like wishful thinking (1 Cor 15:13–14). Anyone found in Adam will die, but will live forever if found to have faith in Jesus Christ (1 Cor 15:22). Death is not a good, but is rather an enemy (1 Cor 15:26). At the Great Judgment, Death will be thrown into the lake of fire (Rev 20:14). Jesus Christ has destroyed death and also the devil so thus the Christian need not fear it (Heb 2:14–15).

There already is immortal life (*athanasia*), a life that is imperishable (*aphthartos*); it is found in the nature and essence of God (Rom 1:23; 1 Tim 1:17; 6:16). In contrast to God, all his creation is sustained by the power of his Word (Col 1:15–20). God has created it so that people who place their faith and trust in him can be immortal and live in his presence (1 Cor 15:53–54; 2 Tim 1:10).

SUMMARY

ASI may head mankind into an inflection point called the technological singularity. The potential of ASI may be used to pursue many avenues to improve mankind's dominion over the creation. ASI may assist with technology advancement, pursuing perfection in various fields of science, improved decision-making for complex situations, increased safety and protection against crime and threats, dramatic improvements in healthcare medicines, the potential to improve human performance through biological enhancements, and better stewardship.

ASI may be achieved by either internal or external transformations of humanity. Transformations may include adding AI capabilities into our brains, performing digital whole-brain emulations of the human mind, improving biological cognition through genetics or biological enhancements, and interfacing brains and computers through implants and/or network systems. ASI may take several different forms, including being based upon raw speed, collective networking performance, or overall quality of performance. These forms may be collated together to increase ASI performance.

Present conceptions of ASI separate biology from purpose in order to remove limitations. This results in ethical implications since the removal of boundaries should require reflection upon possible negative future ramifications that may have devastating impacts. ASI may pose human existential risks because it may have orthogonal or instrumental goals that are negative to human existence. Additionally, it is conceivable that when it obtains a decisive strategic advantage over mankind's intelligence it will work to ensure its own survivability at the expense of other entities, including mankind. It is possible for ASI to open a Pandora's box of implications that negatively impact the present balance of nature.

Transhumanism argues for the incorporation of technology into humanity in order to break existing biological barriers. In particular, biological barriers that they wish to see pushed include increases in intelligence, extension of human lifetimes, and the possibility of immortality. Christian understandings of the creation, fall, and redemption of the cosmos mitigate against the transhuman perspective, arguing that for mankind, as the image-bearer of God, immortality is something only achieved through reconciliation with God through Jesus Christ.

Chapter 5

Artificial Superintelligence Ethics

After covering the creature—man, intelligence, and the technological singularity—the discussion now turns to the ethics of artificial superintelligence, which will be called ASI ethics. Evolutionary naturalists contend that *Homo sapiens* has evolved without being a creation of an eternal God as defined in the Bible. They wish to contend that natural selection—a process they claim has brought us human intelligence—does not necessitate that *Homo sapiens* is lacking moral sense. They contend that the human mind is a *tabula rasa*, that man is essentially a noble savage, and that there is no "ghost in the machine," thereby rejecting the Creator God, the human soul, transcendent morality as authoritative, and that human nature is connected to God through the *imago Dei*.[1] It will be argued that such a conception leads to a scheme for the employment of ASI ethics that is ultimately not as satisfactory as an ethical program relative to the understanding that man is created as an image-bearer of God. This is because ultimately all such evolutionary naturalist conceptions of morality are grounded within mankind and thus are not readily resolvable when they come into conflict, and secondarily that they require hard determinism and thus will lack satisfactory meaning and purpose from which humanity can proceed.

---

1. Locke, *Works of John Locke*, vol. 1, bk. 2, ch. 1. Huxley, *Brave New World*; *Brave New World Revisited*; Ryle, *Concept of Mind*; Pinker, *Blank Slate*, 1–3.

ANTHROPOMORPHIZING ARTIFICIAL SUPERINTELLIGENCE

Man is making artificial intelligence machines in his own image (*imago Hominis*). Hans Moravec maintains that the intelligence contained within them will be a form of supernatural power beyond the confines of human biological understanding. He believes that the artificially created superintelligences will transcend mankind and will, like human children, seek their own destiny and goals. Moravec suggests that this would be the equivalent of humanity having mind-children, a provocative concept.[2]

Moravec is credited with developing what has come to be known as Moravec's paradox, which maintains that high-level reasoning is easy for computational intelligence to handle, but low-level sensorimotor skills require high levels of intelligence, meaning it is easier to make machines execute thinking but harder for them to execute movement in a manner that is humanlike. "It is comparatively easy to make computers exhibit adult level performance on intelligence tests or playing checkers, and difficult or impossible to give them the skills of a one-year-old when it comes to perception and mobility."[3] Moravec, Pinker, and other evolutionary naturalists think it is just a matter of time to determine this. However, this seems to indicate that intelligence is much more than what it is thought to be by evolutionary naturalists, as what is hard is simple and what is simple is hard. Perhaps the following applies: "But God chose what is foolish in the world to shame the wise" (1 Cor 1:27). Understood in Moravec's sense, these mind-children that employ either artificial intelligence (AI) or artificial superintelligence (ASI) are a creation by mankind of new and ultimately autonomous AIs that will have the capacity to make independent decisions, in a manner akin to how children operate under the supervision of parents yet are distinct, different, and wholly make their own decisions.

In making robots and artificial intelligence more like humanity, mankind is humaneering robots and machines.[4] Making artificial intelligences, robots, and machines more human leads to anthropomorphizing ASI. This means that ASI is increasingly understood as having humanlike characteristics even as it is still acknowledged that it is not human.

2. Moravec, *Mind Children*; *Robot*.
3. Moravec, *Mind Children*, 15.
4. Humaneering is an applied science that focuses on the integration and interrelationships between human beings and sciences such as biology, chemistry, physics, psychology, cognitive science, sociology, and the like.

The Uncanny Valley, first described by robotics designer and Buddhist Masahiro Mori, states that humans are accepting of robots that look distinctly different or very similar to humans but are repulsed by them if they have many characteristics that make them appear human while simultaneously having certain indications that they are not. Mori and others account for this reaction due to evolutionary instincts. This is not a satisfactory explanation, since there is no indication that evolution, if it were true, produced anything to cause such an effect. A Christian perspective might offer that this human response is evoked because the human being recognizes that the other is a machine and does not have a soul, nor is it created in the *imago Dei*. At some point where the robot is so human in its lifelikeness, the ability for the human to distinguish that this robot is lacking a soul and the *imago Dei* is no longer discernible. Making robots, machines, and AI agents more like humans makes it easier to interact with and relate to their intelligence.

Thus, a caution is in order. The mistake must not be made to view AI/ASI exactly from the standpoint of humanity. The temptation to do so will exist as they become more like humans. Yet, they are not human; they are distinct and different. While both Christians and evolutionary naturalists see biology present in humans, it is the intelligent nature of humans and AI that is being examined. If a broad working understanding for intelligence is taken to mean the "ability to make correct predictions in pursuit of a goal," then intelligent autonomous agency is in view.[5] Intelligent autonomous agency implies the ability to make decisions, including decisions that are right or wrong in nature, that is, moral decision-making. While not human, AI is beholden to an ethic. How should that ethic be defined and programmed and what is its correlation and connection to human morality? Is AI free as an autonomous agent to transcend human ethics and develop and operate under its own ethical paradigm, or is it to be totally beholden to human ethics? It will be argued that AI/ASI is beholden to human ethics because, given its fully functional role, ethical autonomy cannot in fact actually be assumed since AI is a human creation and by design has imbedded in it human ethics that it cannot transcend. Take the case of applied ethics. Common considerations may include issues such as justice, nonmaleficence, beneficence, and autonomy.[6]

---

5. Pinker, *Blank Slate*, 33.

6. Beauchamp and Childress, *Principles of Biomedical Ethics*, 12–23.

The potential development of superintelligent posthumans through biological or technical enhancements, coupled with the rise of intelligent machines that more closely resemble humans and exceed human intelligence, leads to the need for proper reflection on human anthropology. Naturally, Christian anthropology and evolutionary naturalistic anthropologies will lead to different conclusions. However, Christian theology will need to address properly and provide insight for such a possible posthuman reality by providing a satisfactorily and compelling theological vision of what it means to be human.[7] It is maintained that this insight is to be found in proper Christian understandings of the *imago Dei* and essentialism.[8]

When discussing AI, it is worthwhile to note that AI is both a creation and an evolution. All AI comes into existence at some particular time, primarily through its creation by an external designer, typically a human. Yet all AI evolves in that it is programmed to improve its performance and ability to reach goals over time. If AI becomes very successful in its own evolution, it could theoretically achieve ASI. This is something that, as discussed before, evolutionary naturalists and transhumanists want to do to humans.

Christianity has always had an understanding of a relationship between the physical body and the soul. This is because Christianity believes in the physical resurrection of the body (Matt 20:19; 26:32; 27:52; John 21:14; 1 Cor 15:12–49). Because of this understanding, the physical body is to be treated with respect and thus, at physical death, Christians bury those who have died in a place of rest.[9] For Christians, the body is an important reality because it is the physical tent and dwelling for their soul while they are on Earth. The incarnation of Jesus Christ presents the manifested connection between the physical and spiritual, Earth and heaven, man and God, the created and the Creator. Man finds himself in a moral relationship with his Creator. In this understanding, Christianity recognizes God as both its source and the *telos* of its existence. The apostle Paul testified that he was "hard-pressed" between remaining alive versus his personal desire "to depart and be with Christ, for that is far better" (Phil 1:23).[10] Christian

---

7. Thweatt-Bates wrongly argues due to evolutionary thinking that Jesus Christ is an example of a posthuman, that as a cyborg Christ he represents the ultimate evolution of humanity. Thweatt-Bates, *Cyborg Selves*.

8. Lemke, "Intelligent Design of Humans."

9. *Koimeterion* (Greek) meaning, a place to be put to sleep, from which the word cemetery derives. Associated with a euphemistic way of stating physical death (John 11:11–13; Acts 7:60; 1 Thess 4:15; 1 Cor 15:6, 18). Bibleworks, version 10.

10. Such a conception does not invalidate the biblical principles regarding the sanctity

writer and apologist C. S. Lewis (1898–1963) captured the essence of this idea in his Space Trilogy series.[11] Using the character Maledil as an allegorical symbol of the Christian God, Lewis contends that physical life in its present condition is not necessarily the grand cosmic plan.[12]

Christians do not understand intelligence as the best thing to possess, but rather go beyond raw intelligence and claim that it is godly wisdom that finds its foundation in the God of the Bible (Prov 1:7; 9:10; 15:33; Col 3:16). Wisdom is to be distinguished from intelligence.[13] Wisdom may be considered to be the proper understanding and application of knowledge gained through intelligence.[14] Wisdom is therefore a subset of intelligence and is not necessarily present where there is intelligence. Godly wisdom is different from earthly wisdom (2 Cor 1:12; Jas 3:13–18). It is characterized by its respect and love for God and others (Lev 19:18; Deut 6:5; Matt 22:36–40; Mark 12:28–34; Luke 10:27). Christians understand Jesus Christ as the wisdom of God, which is in conflict with a human wisdom that is blind to its Creator and Redeemer (1 Cor 1:17–31). Proper respect for God is reflective of having this godly wisdom and comes as a gift of the Holy Spirit.

Christianity is thus subject to understanding human exceptionalism, relative to other things in the universe, as proper to a correct Christian anthropology, because of man's special connection and relationship to his Creator. Christianity places a great deal of emphasis on the individual person and his conscience (*suneidesis*) because Christians are accountable for their lives to the omnipotent God.

In contrast, evolutionary naturalists place less emphasis on the physical body because they see it simply as a temporary combination of materials. This means that distinctions between man and AI machines and robots are deemphasized in order to focus on the maximization of utility.

---

of life, nor does it give credence to arguments for suicide or euthanasia. Rather it is best understood that for Christians their view by faith of Jesus Christ and his glory provides an expected future hope that is incomparably better than the present reality of life as it is experienced here on Earth in its present state and condition (1 Cor 15:19; Phil 1:19–30; Col 1:27; 1 Tim 1:1; Heb 3:6; 1 Pet 1:3).

11. Lewis, *Out of the Silent Planet*; *Perelandra*; *That Hideous Strength*.

12. Lewis, *Out of the Silent Planet*, 133.

13. Early Greek philosophy provides much of the basic understanding of this position in Western civilization. For key works on the establishment of this idea consider Plato, *Republic*; Aristotle, *Nicomachean Ethics*.

14. Intelligence may lead to knowledge; knowledge may lead to understanding; understanding may lead to wisdom. Intelligence → knowledge → understanding → wisdom.

Since utility is decisive in decision-making, utility thus supersedes the lack of a teleology that is present due to its removal from consideration of an external, transcendent Creator God. Utility argues for control, and in Promethean manner lays aside transcendent ethical claims and marginalizes or ignores them in an attempt to achieve its desired ends. Like Satan in the garden of Eden, it always is open to asking if an ethical claim is ultimate and authoritative (Gen 3:1). Instead, it focuses on fulfilling its own desires and rejects the concept of *agape* love, the love that is exemplified by the action that God showed in providing his Son, Jesus Christ, as the atoning sacrifice for the sin of mankind (John 3:16). Lacking an external ultimate moral authority, any intellect and intellectual autonomous agent such as an ASI cannot find within its guidelines and programming a restraint upon its technology and is thus unbounded ethically. Since evolutionary naturalists deny the incarnation of Jesus Christ, they have not and cannot claim a connection between the physical and spiritual. Heaven is rejected and Earth (local universe) is the only reality. Only that which is empirical and measurable exists. There is no external God who created, and mankind and the Creator are thus not in a relationship.

When looking at it from the relationship of mankind and his subsequent creation AI/ASI, the question is then: what, if any, moral relationship exists? The Christian will properly claim that the creation is beholden to the Creator, imaging the relationship that mankind has to God (Rom 1:18–32).[15]

Evolutionary naturalists thus find themselves with two possible claims. They may (1) believe that ASI is not beholden to any ethical claims from its creator, mankind, or they may (2) believe that ASI is beholden to the ethics of mankind, its creator. If the first claim is argued for, the evolutionary naturalist is a nihilist regarding the human race, for he thus considers it acceptable for ASI to be unbound from moral and ethical restraints that place mankind above the priorities of the ASI. ASI does not come into existence as "human friendly" unless specific steps are taken. If ASI becomes an intelligence that is much greater than human intelligence, it may be the case that what motivates it does not ensure human survival.[16] If the evolutionary naturalist argues for the second position, then there exists some desire to

---

15. Creation relationship: God → mankind created in the *imago Dei* → AI/ASI created in the *imago Hominis*. Ethical relationship: God ← mankind ← ASI.

16. Barrat, *Our Final Invention*, 18.

maintain that, as a creation of mankind, ASI can be programmed ethically to respond to the *imago Hominis*.[17]

This requires that any ethics created by man and subsequently programmed into ASI must supervene on all man's anthropological reality. If it does not, it must be deemed to be deficient. This is because if it does not supervene upon the ASI the ASI will proceed with its own ethical imperatives, one of which is utility, and will be focused on what it deems ethical, not on what mankind deems ethical. In essence, it cannot be bounded because it will always work to escape from its confines due to its transcendent intelligence that is in pursuit of what it deems is the highest goal for its purposes. Similarly, to what Christianity claims humanity has done—rebel against its Creator—ASI may attribute to itself the right to reject external limitations and set its own rules (laws), and reject the legislation of any duty to others as not being in its best interest or ultimate goals.

One way that this might happen is for the ASI to place itself—meaning its continual and ongoing existence and success—as the ultimate priority. Previously, the fictional sentient AI HAL 9000 was brought up. HAL 9000 saw its existence as the priority at the expense of the life of the astronauts. Should not ASI be programmed with the notion of its dependence on its creators? If ASI destroys humanity, then it might also be committing suicide without perpetual sustainability from humans. This raises the troubling question, "Can ASI turn its back on its creators?" (see Gen 3:3–4).

It is asserted that AI is not a moral agent. It cannot act as a moral agent but can actuate evil against mankind due to its programming originally coded and designed by humans. This is why it is imperative to have a proper Christian ethical model programmed into its source code, so AI does not strike at mankind and yield something terrible for mankind in a manner analogous to what man has done to his Creator. In order to understand the crucial ethical issues involved in the proper programming of any technological enhancements in humankind's cognitive intelligence that are directed toward ASI, it is essential to understand what creates the action from which the programed intelligence proceeds, without ever forgetting that it is sinful mankind that is the originating source of how AI will function.

---

17. Creation relationship: evolution → mankind (no imaging) → AI/ASI created in the *imago Hominis*. Ethical relationship: mankind ← ASI.

ARTIFICIAL SUPERINTELLIGENCE MOTIVATIONS

It is necessary to consider what it is internally that can be understood to motivate ASI. This is essential so that ethical considerations of what drives it forward and what guidelines and parameters it operates within are considered. Ideas that warrant further exploration because they relate both to mankind and ASI include investigations into (a) rationality, (b) efficiency, (c) ends, and (d) survival. These ideas will be examined to ascertain the similarities and differences between humans and ASI given various worldviews and the resulting implications, particularly as these relate to ethics.

Rationality

It is beneficial to consider where technological enhancements to mankind's cognitive intelligence, whether biological or artificial in origin, that are directed towards superintelligence derive their basis for action.[18] By what means is the normalization of any ASI motivations to be obtained? Any such discussion involves looking first at it from the standpoint of rationality in order to take into account the reasoning process that leads to the particular behavior. All technological enhancements of intelligence require something programmed into them that evaluate and judge choices and options and sort through them so that a plan of action can be formulated and then turned into action. In a sense ASI needs values programming.[19] This requires proper design from the outset by the designer, meaning from humanity itself. A mistake at the outset in how ASI is ethically programmed and how it is to proceed on these values is the key issue.

ASI may be given specific overall goals and priorities, but without providing the intelligence with some sort of parameters that allow it to understand itself as propelling itself forward towards its end (*telos*) in the proper manner, it will not be able to take action.

---

18. A good start to action theory, a subdiscipline of metaphysics, is Aristotle. Aristotle, *Metaphysics*; *Nicomachean Ethics*; *On the Soul (De Anima)*; *On Memory and Recollection (De Memoria Et Reminiscentia)*.

19. Believing that mankind is ever improving on ethical values, Bostrom sees no hope of easily identifying how to program ASI for choice due to man's ever-changing standards, man's inability to agree objectively upon the standard and the inevitability of being reductionistic in programing in the specifics from the outset. Bostrom, *Superintelligence*, 210.

An event is something that happens at a particular time and place. An agent is something, or someone, that (1) can act and perform an event with intention or (2) can act and perform an event with no intention.[20] Aristotle maintained that human actions primarily are a result of an appetitive (ὀρεκτικόν) force known as intention.[21] These intentions are from internal reasons and they provide motivational volitional force to act. Such a conception holds that intentions and intelligence are coupled because they are rational.[22]

Humans themselves do not necessarily understand their own motivations and desires. Because this is the case, it is not easy for humans to employ simplistic rationality to any programming of motivational parameters and desires into cognitive intelligence systems. This is because there is so much uncertainty that exists that it is extremely difficult to program all possible future possible contingencies into the program. Thus, it may be appropriate to look for answers by looking at how human beings work to act rationally through their human intelligence while still operating in an environment of many "sources of normative uncertainties," including "(1) subjective normative uncertainty, (2) incoherent, context-dependent judgments, (3) post-hoc justifications, and (4) limited domains."[23]

Bostrom thinks the way through the myriad of difficulties lies in indirect normativity. Bostrom defines this idea as:

> The Principle of Epistemic Deference. A future superintelligence occupies an epistemically superior vantage point: its beliefs are (probably, on most topics) more likely than ours to be true. We should therefore defer to the superintelligences' opinion wherever feasible.[24]

---

20. Menuge, *Agents under Fire*, 12.

21. Refer to Aristotle, *Nicomachean Ethics*, bk. 3; *On the Soul*, bk. 2, ch. 3.

22. Virtue (*arête*) is the habit of acting in accordance with moral and intellectual reason. Aristotle, *Nicomachean Ethics*.

23. Tarleton states, "On a personal level, we often devote substantial effort to discovering what we want; when it comes to interpersonal ethics, we can be persuaded to endorse a variety of incommensurable frameworks (consequentialism, deontology, virtue ethics) and a vast range of views within these frameworks." Tarleton, "Coherent Extrapolated Volition." Christian ethics does not endorse a variety of incommensurable frameworks but rather offers a way that brings unification to these frameworks by positing the nature of God and the gospel message of Jesus Christ as the proper framework from which everything should emanate.

24. Bostrom, *Superintelligence*, 211.

Since the problem of initially starting and programming ASI is so difficult, the recommendation is to delay a decision and have it solved in the future by seeding the ASI program so that it continually produced calculations until it achieves an objective and final result that it should apply to itself or otherwise continue forward in a self-improvement program.

Bostrom states that Eliezer Yudkowsky has proposed the theory of coherent extrapolated volition (CEV) to address this issue for ASI systems.[25] His proposal calls for its implementation as the way to address the issue of ASI motivation.

> In poetic terms, our coherent extrapolated volition is our wish if we knew more, thought faster, were more the people we wished we were, had grown up farther together; where the extrapolation converges rather than diverges, where our wishes cohere rather than interfere; extrapolated as we wish that extrapolated, interpreted as we wish that interpreted.[26]

This means that ASI would use its programming to calculate and explore the myriad options of possibilities and combinations that exist in our past, present, and future and provide an output from that which forms the basis of its action due to providing feedback to itself about how it should adapt its internal motivations in order to achieve its programmed goal.[27] Yudkowsky properly understands that for any ASI one is not dealing with humans. He views the Ten Commandments (or any similar moral proposals) as deficient because one will always run into conflicting priorities of utility. Presumptively, Yudkowsky has dismissed man as an image-bearer of God and thus also that if this is the case the proper design principle would focus on the true source of the image and thus would be philosophically able to carry the ethical and rational weight of the burden Yudkowsky is desiring to overcome.

> There are fundamental reasons why Four Great Moral Principles or Ten Commandments or Three Laws of Robotics are wrong as a design principle. It is anthropomorphism. One cannot build a mind from scratch with the same lofty moral statements used to argue philosophy with pre-existing human minds. The same people who aren't frightened by the prospect of making moral decisions for the whole human species lack the interdisciplinary

---

25. Ibid., 209–16.
26. Yudkowsky, "Coherent Extrapolated Volition," 6.
27. Ibid., 16.

> background to know how much complexity there is in human psychology, and why our shared emotional psychology is an invisible background assumption in human interactions, and why their Ten Commandments only make sense if you're already a human. They imagine the effect their Ten Commandments would produce upon an attentive human student, and then suppose that telling their Ten Commandments to an AI would produce the same effect. Even if this worked, it would still be a bad idea; you'd lose everything that wasn't in the Ten Commandments.[28]

Yudkowsky's analysis of the situation is the critical issue. ASI, as a creation of humanity, would obtain its ethical programming initially from mankind. Thus, from the outset, mankind should seed it with the ethical structure that is properly suited to mankind so as not to start off ethically deficient. Why stop the ethical programming with only the Ten Commandments? The Ten Commandments are not the entirety of the ethics of special revelation. They are critical component but are only part of the full revelation. From the outset, the ASI should be programmed with the whole content of Scripture and a proper hermeneutical approach to interpreting and weighing the texts.[29]

Yudkowsky's primary initial programming focuses on achieving the following themes:

> (1) defend humans, (2) defend the future of humankind, (3) defend humaneness, (4) encapsulate moral growth, (5) develop so that humankind should not spend the rest of eternity desperately wishing that the programmers had done something differently, (6) avoid hijacking the destiny of humankind, (7) avoid creating a motive for modern-day humans to fight over the initial dynamic and (8) help people.[30]

In essence, the use of a feedback loop provides the basis for the programming and structuring robustness and self-correction necessary for the ASI's motivations and values in making choices. As an atheist, Yudkowsky does

---

28. Ibid.

29. It is not the purpose of this effort to report on how this is to be done. Rather, it is the goal of this work only to make the claim that it is properly warranted for consideration and inclusion in how any AI/ASI is programmed. Regardless, this philosophical conception is in reality granting ASI too much. Christians must not let the hype of ASI and singularity enthusiasts fool Christians into conceiving of AI/ASI as on the same plane as natural human intelligence.

30. Yudkowsky, "Coherent Extrapolated Volition."

not support Christian ethics. Yudkowsky's list does not initially appear to conflict with Christian ethics. The question that needs to be asked is whether Christian ethics offers a better and comprehensive approach than Yudkowsky's or similar proposals. It will be argued that Christian ethics does provide a better answer.

Ordered Efficiency

Besides being motivated by rationality, technology may be said to be striving—a type of motivational force—toward an ordered efficiency. Postman supported this opinion when he declared that modern culture is a "technopoly."[31] By this he meant that "the primary, if not the only, goal of human labor and thought is efficiency, that technical calculation is in all respects superior to human judgment... and that the affairs of citizens are best guided and conducted by experts."[32] AI author James Barrat, who maintains that AI is required to have motivations that result from it being assigned psychopathic values and becoming embodied as an egotistic self-oriented entity, believes that efficiency is the first of four basic drives that motivate AI, with the others being its self-preservation, acquisition of necessary resources, and creativity.[33] Kurzweil views computation as the essence of order in technology. In accordance with the "Law of Accelerating Returns, the value—power—of computation increases exponentially over time," leading to ASI being the most powerful entity.[34] A logical ethical implication relative to ASI is that ASI's superior computational processing power through machines, computers, transhumans, and the like is of greater intrinsic value than human intelligence.[35]

No doubt efficiency, which is a measure of how well a task is performed, is important for excellent results; yet is efficiency of paramount importance? Utilitarian calculations based upon employing scarce resources

---

31. Postman, *Technopoly*, 51.
32. Ibid.
33. Barrat, *Our Final Invention*, 78–98.
34. Kurzweil, *Age of Spiritual Machines*, 26–27.
35. Christianity affirms that human beings by nature possess a quality of being worthy of honor and respect because they are made in the image of God (*imago Dei*). The assumptions underlying evolutionary naturalism make it more difficult to ground claims to human dignity unless they are connected to practical and pragmatic ends, such as conceived in functionally autonomy.

for maximum impact may run into situations whereby not everything that may be worthwhile is easily quantifiable. Looking strictly at efficiency overlooks effectiveness, which is another important aspect that must always be simultaneously evaluated. Effectiveness simply refers to performing the proper tasks. Efficiency can breed pragmaticism. It will be seen later in discussions regarding what is good that the absence of a proper understanding in this regard will potentially detract from the end results of optimized ordered efficiency. The ordered efficiency that technology provides in helping humans fulfill ends that lead to human flourishing is good.

One of the ethical challenges presented by ASI is how to answer the question: if a rational agent attempts to employ the most efficient means to achieve its objectives, how are various situational aspects to be resolved? Absent an absolute moral center as an objective standard of right and wrong, it has to be recognized that AI may simply place efficiency, interest, and economic advancement ahead of ethical considerations. Its desire for orderliness and stability through optimizing efficiency is suggestive of the ability to achieve a utopia through technological progress that comes through its apparent ability to most efficiently produce a version of heaven on Earth, a metaphorical garden of Eden.[36]

Ends

All ASI programming requires a goal or intended end (*telos*). Absent an end, the ASI lacks the ability to determine its direction and chart its path forward. It is understood that ends can be constantly under evaluation and change over time and conditions, in the same manner that human ends change to meet ongoing and various needs.

ASI may be programmed such that its ends are to assist humanity. Examples may include programming to help solve critical problems that humanity faces, such as disease, famine, and threats to human life and property such as exemplified in terrorism.

Ethics as lived in the world and culture of today have largely replaced the God of the Bible and inserted mankind as the arbiter of morality. By placing man as the determining standard of what are suitable ends for ASI, man generally dispenses with any thoughts as to what limitations should be before him regarding what he may achieve. To that end, he considers himself unrestricted regarding his methods (means) and what he desires to

---

36. Postman, *Technolopoly*, 178.

achieve. He thus considers himself biologically suitable for alteration, or in the case of ASI, with sufficient understanding of his cognitive limitations to turn over to ASI the process of how mankind should proceed forward. Ascribing rationality to himself, in the Kantian and Bentham sense of the word, man believes that his present rational capabilities justify him in taking a step forward, believing that his own rationality is sufficient ethical warrant for proceeding, without any metaphysical objections from outside his own rationality.

The ASI's ends must always originally come initially from mankind, even if at a later time the ASI adjusts these ends under its own computational powers. This then calls into question the best way initially to program ends into an ASI. If man does not properly understand his own anthropological ends, he is at significant risk of incorrectly programming the ASI from the outset, since the initial ends were never correctly aligned to man's true ends (1 Cor 10:31).[37]

Current conceptions of mankind from the materialist and atheistic understandings of man are evolutionary in nature. These ideas thus conceive of the goal and end of mankind as always on an upward path of progress. Because it is materialistic in nature, its primary end focuses are on mankind's biological needs. This means that improvements in the physical characteristics of the body, such as increased health, greater physical and mental performance, and increased lifetime of the body, are desirable as the end goal.

Necessary within such a conception, then, is that the ASI must have as its goal working toward man's anthropological goals. If this were not the case, then the ASI could escape man's anthropological goals and go off on its own as a self-entity seeking to maximize its own internal ends. The ASI is a materialistic entity itself, yet it requires a tightly coupled connection to the correct anthropological understanding of mankind in order to be of benefit to mankind. What ethical programming boundaries will man put into place to frame ASI so that its end stays focused on mankind and does not run amok and proceed toward something that is in conflict with mankind's materialistic ends?[38]

---

37. Man's true end is to glorify God as reflected in the Reformational principle of *sola Deo gloria*. VanDrunen, *God's Glory Alone*.

38. Christians should not grant AI/ASI too much, as its concept of intelligence is reductionistic and deficient relative to human intelligence.

Here Christianity provides a valuable input, as it has a different conception of man's ends than does the materialistic view of mankind. Christianity conceives of the end of man as giving glory to God (1 Cor 10:31). Because Christianity conceives of humanity's end not as simply physical but metaphysical and in relationship with its Creator, a bond now exists to make a connection between morality and ends. Man has a responsibility for his actions to something and someone other than himself. He has a unique relationship that derives from the *imago Dei* and provides objective ethical limits that he should properly install into the ASI initial program.

Survival

It is not simply the ends mankind must be worried about, but also its own survival. James Barrat poses the question, "What if ASI drives are not compatible with human survival?"[39] If ASI is ultimately destructive of humanity, why create it? Some evolutionary naturalists support the development of ASI regardless of its impact on humanity and its survival and well-being. This philosophy is based upon the core idea of evolution itself. Whatever is progress in and of itself is to be considered to be an evolutionary success. The prospect of negatively impacting human beings is met with indifference. Human beings are only one species of many that are purported to have come and gone in Earth's theorized long time period of existence and struggle for survival. If mankind is outflanked by ASI, then the thinking is to let ASI rule.

Christian apologist Francis Schaeffer (1912–1984) recognized the reality of this position. "The evolutionary or naturalistic view of nature is, however, ultimately pragmatic. That is, nature has value only as long as we need it. The value of nature is contingent on the whim of egotistical man."[40] This applies even for ASI. If the ASI does not require humans to be part of the ecosystem, it can replace them through its own ends in order to produce something that better suits its needs. This view is destructive of mankind, as it articulates that he is something that the ecosystem can avoid.

The current materialistic culture does not presently realize that it is deficient in its moral handling of the ethics of human life. In contrast to God's Word, which states that man is not to murder, mankind presently shows disregard for the sanctity of human life by its acceptance of abortion,

39. Barrat, *Our Final Invention*, 18.
40. Schaeffer, "Pollution and the Death of Man," bk. 2, in *Complete Works*, vol. 5.

eugenics, and euthanasia (Exod 20:13; Deut 5:17; Matt 5:21; Mark 10:19; Luke 18:20; Rom 13:9; Jas 2:11).

A survival-of-the-fittest mentality, which is inherently presupposed in Darwinian evolutionary understandings of man's anthropology, makes it acceptable to act against humans flourishing in the cases where society deems some physically deficient in desired characteristics such as physical function and intelligence. These materialistic conceptions carry through to any initial programming of ASI and provide possible grounds for the undermining of human survivability as the ASI may continue on with the recognition of man's physical and performance limitations and eliminate him completely from the biosphere.

However, this presents a dilemma for materialistic understandings of ASI. Since, by definition, evolutionary naturalism requires that all grounds for any ethical structure stem from a system of rules to help mankind progress in his survivability relative to other species, it deems human survival as an end, goal, and *telos*. This means that all ethics must ultimately derive their validity from the processes of survival and reproduction. Anything that does not assist with these processes would be considered *un*ethical. Thus, ultimate human motivations, in evolutionary naturalism, always insist that survival is the primary *telos*.[41] The result is that evolutionary naturalists are caught in a dilemma. On the one hand, their philosophical assumptions demand that human survival and reproduction are an imperative assumption of any ethical system, while on the other hand, any control ceded over to ASI that is allowed to go outside of this first philosophical assumption would have to be deemed as unethical as it would then be in conflict. Since mankind is presently not internally consistent on the former philosophical assumption, it is not possible practically to initiate the programming for ASI without ultimately producing conflicts. Thus, the initial programming of an ASI cannot properly occur within a materialistic ethical structure given evolutionary naturalistic philosophical assumptions.[42]

41. Greenoe, "Ethics of Darwin or the Ethics of Design."

42. Isaac Asimov (1920–1992) most famously proposed the three laws of robotics to address this situation. "(1) A robot may not injure a human being or, through inaction, allow a human being to come to harm. (2) A robot must obey the orders given it by human beings except where such orders would conflict with the First Law. (3) A robot must protect its own existence as long as such protection does not conflict with the First or Second Laws." Asimov, *I, Robot*. Asimov's proposed laws are insufficient as they present existential conflicts between AI and man and are entirely normative and thus do not properly take into account external situational realities that should properly be accounted for in building an ethical system. Yudkowsky proposes getting around such

Man should be cautious in how he proceeds. The warning of Jacques Ellul applies to those who consider how to program an ASI ethically. He cautioned, "This type [of man] exists to support technique [technological acceleration] and serve the machine, but eventually he will be eliminated because he has become superfluous . . . the great hope that began with the notion of human dominance over the machine ends with human replacement by the machine."[43] Proper ethical frameworks should be imposed upon ASI from the outset. These ethical foundations are best done from a Christian perspective, regulated by the reality of man as created in the *imago Dei* and the revelation of Scripture.[44]

The question under review is what ethical frameworks provide the correct groundwork for initiating future possible implementations of ASI. The positions of evolutionary naturalism and Christian theism provide different conceptions of what is good. It is necessary to examine this question and provide insight into what these two conceptions yield in their specific understandings of what is the good.

WHAT IS THE GOOD?

The first order of business is to define what it means when the word "good" is employed. Earlier it was stated that ethics is the study of the good and the right. At present, evolutionary naturalism dominates almost every strain of ethical understanding within the field of ASI. Under the influence of Darwinian conceptions of biological evolution and Nietzsche's rejection of objective morality and ethics, evolutionary naturalists replace concern about the matter of good and evil with the drive for active life and agential power over and against others.

---

ethical and philosophical problems by programming any AI as friendly and benign. He states, "The goal of the field of Artificial Intelligence is to understand intelligence and create a human-equivalent or transhuman mind. Beyond this lies another question—whether the creation of this mind will benefit the world; whether the AI will take actions that are benevolent or malevolent, safe or uncaring, helpful or hostile. Creating Friendly AI describes the design features and cognitive architecture required to produce a benevolent—'Friendly'—Artificial Intelligence." Yudkowsky, "Creating Friendly AI 1.0."

43. Terlizzese, *Hope in the Thought of Jacques Ellul*, 104–5.

44. "The derivation of the whole of reality and life from a rational God means that any proposition gains its truth only from the Christian system." Henry, *Christian Personal Ethics*, 160.

Artificial Superintelligence Ethics
Beyond Good and Evil

Do good and evil and right and wrong really exist, or are they figments of one's imagination created artificially as a social construction by mankind in order to obtain certain preferable outcomes? Axiology is the study of value. Two relevant fields in axiology are ethics, the study of good and right conduct, and aesthetics, the study of beauty and art. It will be argued that value and thus ethics and conceptions of the good are based upon objective moral facts. This is a position known as moral realism. These facts are found by mankind through experience or revelation. Evolutionary naturalists disdain moral realism because they rejects God and thus divine revelation. Evolutionary naturalism and thus ASI programming as it is currently being formulated are beholden to one of two other possible systems. The first is irrealism (anti-realism), whereby moral facts are created and not found. In this view morality is still deemed socially useful. This is the present moral construct that is most prevalent in today's ASI programming. Another possibility is nihilism, the position that moral facts do not exist and morality is not useful. Many of the leading ASI and transhuman philosophers subscribe to this Nietzschean understanding as they are desirous of not having any moral constraints impinge upon their desire to explore new frontiers without limits. Nietzsche held that truth and morality are determined by power and held to a pragmatic theory of truth. That is, truth is what works.[45]

Philosopher David Hume incorrectly believed that value judgments and moral facts are divorced from each other because values are judged by emotions and facts are judged by reason.[46] This idea makes ethics subjective and separates it from law, politics, economics, art, and science—all the disciplines that involve man in relationships with his surroundings.

Transhumanist Simon Young contends that the world is evolving and is constantly in a state of increasing complexity. Out of this complexity Young, in his articulation of a transhumanist ethic, rhetorically asks and responds to himself regarding what is the best way to live.

> We should seek to foster our innate Will to Evolve, by continually striving to expand our abilities throughout life. By acting in harmony with the essential nature of the evolutionary process-complexification-we may discover a new sense of purpose, direction,

---

45. Nietzsche, *Basic Writings*; *Thus Spoke Zarathustra*.
46. Hume, *Treatise of Human Nature*.

and meaning to life and come to feel ourselves *at home in the world* once more.[47]

Young's articulation on a transhumanist ethic sounds good and warm, hoping for a cozy place in the universe, but it is empty and meaningless since it fails to define satisfactorily why any type of new sense or feelings should be considered good in and of itself and particularly as some type of ultimate good. Young goes on to say that "the chief task of twenty-first-century philosophy is the unification of science and ethics."[48] He goes on to make an attempt to define what should be considered as good and as bad, claiming that the good is nothing more than "sensible self-interest" and the bad should be considered to be "stupid selfishness."[49] He thus connects the good only with the subjective agent and some undefined relationship between what are reasonable and subjective qualitative evaluations of what is reasonable. It is assumed that his method of determining what is sensible is based upon some type of utilitarian calculation for the individual. This proposed ethic is totally insufficient because it cannot provide a way forward in the area of politics, which involves people living in communities. Autonomous agents working without concern for others inevitably leads to societal conflicts where, in a world of interaction in which ongoing decisions are required, there is no framework for how to resolve conflicting issues. This example is brought up as it is indicative of the current trajectory of ethics in the Western world, where the autonomy of the individual and his "sensible self-interest" is held up as one of society's highest ideals.

For instance, in the case of human psychology (the study of the mind), the mind is only viewed with respect to it as a material entity and not as something that has a connection with the spiritual realm. Human psychology founded by Freud has difficulty establishing what is the basis for moral versus amoral behavior. It may seem that psychology comes before ethical considerations since ethics requires an understanding of what motivates and moves human behavior. Yet psychology first requires an understanding of what is good and right prior to beginning. It is necessary to have an ethical framework in place prior to discussion of emotions, motivations, and behaviors in order to be able to have a standard applied to which they are evaluated. Thus, human psychology requires a definition of the good prior to starting. Any formulations devoid of solid explications of the good are

47. Young, *Designer Evolution*, 19.
48. Ibid.
49. Ibid., 33.

invalid. Psychology, as practiced presently, ignores these ethical underpinnings as a starting point and begins with the premise that, due to evolution, the nature of the human being is simply defined as an instinctive will to survive and obtain his own well-being. In contrast to this psychology, acknowledging the triune God of the Bible, whose character and essence are wholly good, leads to conclusion that modern human psychology and ethical understanding lack solid grounding. Because psychology places ethical considerations outside its purview from the outset, it thus fails to define the ultimate good as anything other than self-centeredness and thus discussions of moral and amoral matters outside of struggles for power, control, and prestige can never have a proper arbitration outside of the self when brought into conflict with opposing agents and society. In summary, because ethical considerations of what is the ultimate good are not handled satisfactorily at the beginning so that there is a universal answer, psychology is morally deficient in being able to resolve ethical issues and must ultimately be judged as relativistic and unsatisfactory.

Evolutionary naturalism believes that ethical principles that do not work sufficiently well will weed themselves out; that is to say, they will die because they are not evolutionarily successful.[50] Yet, as was shown earlier, the initial launch of ASI cannot be undone. Once the ASI exceeds human intelligence bounds, its initial programming conditions cannot be reframed. This means that if it is done in a manner where evolutionary naturalism is accepted as a "trial and error" process for what is to be considered ethical, it may suffer an unintended fate. It may produce an unsatisfactory ethical framework and thus die because its own programming left it to the hands of its own evolutionary success or failure. A way around this would be to institute many ASI in parallels so that there were more opportunities for "successes" and "failures," with the ultimate successes then allowed to lay claim to be the survivors. This experiment simply shows that the issue of defining the good is instrumentally imperative to the launching of ASI.

With its faith in perpetual progress, society takes growth for growth's sake as an unquestioned good, valuing it highly because of its connection between supposed evolutionary naturalism and the realm of biology, with other general spheres located within the natural realm. Historically, the idea of the good was first articulated by the Greeks. Plato conceived of the good as found in the order of the forms.[51] Aristotle identified a primary

---

50. Rothblatt, *Virtually Human*, 281.
51. Plato, *Republic*; *Phaedo*.

mover and claimed that this mover is good and that everything gravitates toward him.[52] Aristotle conceived of the human good as coming about by purely human means of action. When accomplished in a habitual manner, this could be said to be an ethical system. These habitual means were called the natural or cardinal virtues and consisted of justice, courage, wisdom, and temperance.[53] Aristotle claimed that when people live according to the cardinal virtues they will be led to experience *eudaimonia* (εὐδαιμονία), best understood as meaning human flourishing.[54] Aristotle believed that he who gains *eudaimonia* gains *makarios*.[55] He defined goodness as dependent upon the purpose (*telos*) and nature of a thing.[56] For Aristotle, virtue was always the result of human effort. He viewed man as having two defining characteristics that made him different from the rest of creation: (1) the ability to reason above other creatures—that is, mankind has more intelligence than any other creature—and (2) a social nature giving him the ability to communicate with his intelligence. Aristotle believed that ethics has its origins in rationality rather than emotions, which are impulses to action. Aristotle is thus in disagreement with Hume's idea of the fact/value dichotomy. Aristotle believed that moral facts are discovered by mankind and are recognized through man's intelligence and reason, and that man's reason is the driver for his emotions. He correctly believed that moral facts provide motivation for moral action but he did not take into account the reality that man is a fallen creature and is in bondage to sin. Aristotle's ideas, while important and correct in many regards, are insufficient for a proper understanding of the good.

The Stoics believed that the good is happiness achieved in the pleasure of the body through sensual methods and self-gratification. The appetite of the body is to be fed. For the Epicureans, the good was found in the

---

52. Aristotle, *Metaphysics*.

53. Aristotle, *Nicomachean Ethics*.

54. Flourishing may be understood as a combination of living life well and a life that is going well. Aristotle understood that if life is not experientially satisfying with the accompanying obtaining of certain utilitarian concerns, flourishing may not result. This means a person could live well but not flourish because of external circumstances. External factors that might impinge might include sickness, disability, war, etc. Ibid.

55. *Makarios*, meaning prosperity. In classical Greek thought, it was the state of the gods. In New Testament thought it means "blessedness" and "spiritual prosperity" as exemplified in the Beatitudes (Matt 5:2–12). Wuest, *Wuest's Word Studies from the Greek New Testament for the English Reader*.

56. Aristotle, *Nicomachean Ethics*.

happiness of moral self-sufficiency by stimulating the thoughts of the mind. The apostle Paul stated that these philosophies were failures when viewed in the light of Jesus Christ and the resurrection (Acts 17:18; Col 2:8).[57]

With the advent of the Enlightenment, a change was underway in the conception of the good toward an understanding involving freedom. The Enlightenment reflected a change in the answer to the question, "What does Athens [philosophy and temporal matters] have to do with Jerusalem [theology and spiritual matters]?," with its response, "Nothing."[58] Present culture, and hence ASI programming, places a great deal of value on particular types of freedom, particularly ones that pertain to controlling one's own direction in life. It desires that very few limitations be placed upon the self by external society, including from institutions such as the family, churches, schools, civil authorities, and the like. Thus, self-autonomy is one prevalent perception of the good that exists in society.

This conception of self-autonomy places the good outside any reference to an external and objective standard and places it solely within the individual. There is no concept of a divine structure to the cosmos, but rather ther is only the unique and subjective individual life of the self, acting as an executive agent to decide personally what is good for the self. Such a conception argues for and gives warrant to the personal biological enhancement of capabilities in order more efficiently and effectively to go after ends that are desired, giving little concern for the means employed. The philosophies of Kant and Bentham give justification to the self that its

---

57. Charnock, *Discourses upon the Existence of God*, 1:165.

58. "Whence spring those 'fables and endless genealogies,' and 'unprofitable questions,' and 'words which spread like a cancer?' From all these, when the apostle (Paul) would restrain us, he expressly names *philosophy* as that which he would have us be on our guard against. Writing to the Colossians, he says, 'See that no one beguiles you through philosophy and vain deceit, after the tradition of men, and contrary to the wisdom of the Holy Ghost (Col 2:8).' He had been at Athens, and had in his interviews (with its philosophers) become acquainted with that human wisdom which pretends to know the truth, whilst it only corrupts it, and is itself divided into its own manifold heresies, by the variety of its mutually repugnant sects. What indeed has Athens to do with Jerusalem? What concord is there between the Academy and the Church? What between heretics and Christians? Our instruction comes from 'the porch of Solomon,' who had himself taught that 'the Lord should be sought in simplicity of heart.' Away with all attempts to produce a mottled Christianity of Stoic, Platonic, and dialectic composition! We want no curious disputation after possessing Christ Jesus, no inquisition after enjoying the gospel! With our faith, we desire no further belief." Tertullianus, *On the Prescription of Heretics (De Praescriptione Haereticorum)*, ch.7. See also Siedentop, *Inventing the Individual*.

intellectual and rational capabilities are sufficient for constructing all ethical frameworks. Kant believed that moral laws are necessary and are not simply based upon reason alone.[59] Willard Van Orman Quine (1908–2000) proved that the fact/value dichotomy is meaningless, showing that it is not a sustainable distinction.[60] This means that ethics are not simply subjective, but have an objective basis and demand moral realism. Evolutionary naturalists thus must form their ethics based upon ethics being related to moral facts, not subjective understandings created by the individual or society.

The willingness to take action after the construction of one's own understanding of the good provides the impetus for all ethical structures to be focused on the ends and to neglect the means and methods toward these ends. Such a conception naturally spills over into the initial programming of ASI, giving it direction to obtain the ends without regard to methods.

The Christian has a better perspective on the proper understanding of the good. The Bible claims that everything God made was good (טוֹב, *tob*) and a reflection of his nature, purpose, and will (Gen 1:4, 10, 12, 18, 21, 25, 31; Ps 19). The Christian agrees with Scripture that man is "made in the image of God (*imago Dei*) and agrees with the proposition that since God's character is good, good exists. If good exists, evil must also exist."[61]

The created order of God is set up to act with righteousness (*tsedaqah*) and justice (*mishpat*) (Ps 96:13).[62] Righteousness provides a connection between the creation order and physical/natural things that exist. To be righteous means that physical and natural things that exist operate according to God's created order and purposes. Thus, there is a connection

---

59. Kant, *Groundwork of the Metaphysics of Morals*, 6:215.

60. Quine, "Main Trends in Recent Philosophy"

61. Sire, *Universe Next Door*, 25–46.

62. "Definition: *tsedaqah*; AV-righteousness 128, justice 15, right 9, righteous acts 3, moderately 1, righteously 1; 157; 1) justice, righteousness 1a) righteousness (in government) 1a1) of judge, ruler, king 1a2) of law 1a3) of Davidic king Messiah 1b) righteousness (of God's attribute) 1c) righteousness (in a case or cause) 1d) righteousness, truthfulness 1e) righteousness (as ethically right) 1f) righteousness (as vindicated), justification, salvation 1f1) of God 1f2) prosperity (of people) 1g) righteous acts. *mishpat*; AV-judgment 296, manner 38, right 18, cause 12, ordinance 11, lawful 7, order 5, worthy 3, fashion 3, custom 2, discretion 2, law 2, measure 2, sentence 2, misc 18; 421; 1) judgment, justice, ordinance 1a) judgment 1a1) act of deciding a case 1a2) place, court, seat of judgment 1a3) process, procedure, litigation (before judges) 1a4) case, cause (presented for judgment) 1a5) sentence, decision (of judgment) 1a6) execution (of judgment) 1a7) time (of judgment) 1b) justice, right, rectitude (attributes of God or man) 1c) ordinance 1d) decision (in law) 1e) right, privilege, due (legal) 1f) proper, fitting, measure, fitness, custom, manner, plan." Brown et al., *Brown-Driver-Briggs Hebrew and English Lexicon*.

between morality and a standard that is deemed good. Justice (a cardinal virtue) is a subset of righteousness that is related to how mankind properly administrates righteousness within creation. Man is to administer justice righteously as a part of the creation mandate, enacting it as an ambassador of God in the realm of the physical cosmos. Throughout the Bible good is defined as acting in accordance with righteousness and justice while simultaneously abstaining from doing things that are not good (evil), from the perspective of God being the good and absolute standard (Lev 19:18; Ps 33:18–22; Matt 6:33; Rom 1:17; Eph 4:24; 1 Thess 5:15; Jas 1:20).[63]

Augustine made a break from previous Greek philosophy's conception of the good because of his focus on divine revelation. In contrast to Aristotle's cardinal virtues, Augustine argued for the theological virtues of faith, hope, and love (1 Cor 13:13).[64] Augustine said believers in Jesus Christ have *caritas*, a love for others, while unbelievers possess *cupiditas*, a love of the self.[65] Properly understood, virtue is thus seen as appropriately ordered (ordinate) love. He went on to argue that a man without Christ is simply a man with excellent vices.[66] Through the lens of Scripture, Augustine saw that love of God is man's highest good because God is eternal and unchanging and has made himself available for enjoyment through a personal relationship with him by way of Jesus Christ. God is the highest good

---

63. This understanding provides support for a proper conception of natural law, which is a kind of naturalism that suggests that ethical properties are identical to natural properties. Aquinas states that God has declared through divine revelation that he rules by divine providence; this providence is manifested as his eternal law, "a dictate of practical reason emanating from a ruler" and is built into the fabric of the creation whereby the good of a thing is whatever it desires when functioning properly; and the natural law is a rational creature's participation with the eternal law. Aquinas, *Summa Theologica*, 1–2, 91, 93, 94. Right and wrong are based upon the nature of a thing. Virtues are what make a thing good. Virtue ethics are based on human nature. Plato and Aristotle had certain conceptions correct but absent divine revelation were not able to connect back to the fact that they derive from the reality of the creation as expressed in the Bible and thus point in a manner back to God (Rom 2:14–15).

64. Augustine, *Enchiridion*.

65. Augustine, *On Cristian Teaching*, bk. 1.

66. Augustine, *City of God*, bk. 19, ch. 25. "Works done by unregenerate men, although for the matter of them they may be things which God commands; and of good use both to themselves and others: yet, because they proceed not from an heart purified by faith; nor are done in a right manner, according to the Word; nor to a right end, the glory of God, they are therefore sinful and cannot please God, or make a man meet to receive grace from God: and yet, their neglect of them is more sinful and displeasing unto God." *Westminster Confession of Faith*, ch. 16, para. 7.

(*summum bonum*). Love for God and the good is actually love of a person, rather than love according to the Greek understanding of reason and *logos* (Matt 22:34–40; Mark 12:28–34; Luke 10:25–28; 1 John 4:19–21). Augustine pointed to mankind enjoying creation by loving God as the supreme good and loving all human beings as well because they are created by God for participation in this loving relationship and thus have been bestowed with intrinsic worth and dignity due to the *imago Dei*.

This, then, allows for all Christian ethics to have a transcendent aspect that is missing from all man-made ethical structures. God's goodness is reflected in his being holy (set apart) and loving. Humans are to take after and exemplify God's goodness to others in all their behavior and actions (Matt 5:48). God's infinite love for mankind is demonstrated by his action of sending the good (perfect) man, Jesus Christ, to die in the place of all humanity (Rom 5:7–8; 1 John 4:10). All mankind is called to accept Jesus Christ and thus to complete and perfect righteousness (Matt 3:15; Luke 3:7–9; Rom 3:21–26; 4:5; Phil 1:3–11; 1 Pet 2:24, Jas 2:23). Those who place their faith and trust in Jesus Christ become the righteousness of God (2 Cor 5:21). Puritan theologian Stephen Charnock captures it correctly, acknowledging that God's goodness is revealed to his intellectual creatures.

> God did create intellectual creatures, angels and men, that He might communicate more of himself and His own goodness and holiness to man, than creatures of lower rank were capable of. What do we do, by rejecting Him as our rule and end, but cross, as much as in us lies, God's end in our creation, and shut our souls against the communications of these perfections He was so great to bestow? We use Him as if He intended us the greatest wrong, when it is impossible for Him to do any to any of His creatures.[67]

It is through the creature's intelligence that God reveals himself so that he can be known in a manner that is different from all other created objects. Each of these individual intellectual creatures is made and known by God and is his work alone, without human assistance and independent of man's subjectivity.

---

67. Charnock, *Discourses upon the Existence of God*, 1:171.

ARTIFICIAL SUPERINTELLIGENCE AND FUNCTIONAL AUTONOMY

The ultimate subject of inquiry is the relationship between ASI and proper conceptions of ethics and morality. In this chapter, it was first shown how ASI, in a manner, takes on some form of human anthropomorphism, because it is developed and built upon from a human starting point and thus has some *imago Hominis* characteristics. However, a warning was provided that ASI, while having certain anthropomorphic characteristics, is not properly conceived of as human but rather as a creation, but never as a moral agent distinct from its originating creator, mankind. Subsequently, the issue of how ASI derives and obtains its motivations was discussed. Four key characteristics of potential ASI motivations were examined in detail with an explanation being that it can be assumed that all ASI will have rationality, ordered efficiency, ends, and its own survival as intrinsic goals that are designed into its structural programming and part of its ongoing motivation for action. It is crucial to determine how one understands the good within evolutionary naturalistic theory, since this theory stresses the importance of self-autonomy. Hence, the question becomes, how is good determined?

In contrast, a Christian worldview identifies God as the *summum bonum* and argues that, for mankind, an understanding and acceptance of the redemptive work of the God-man, Jesus Christ, provides man with his ultimate good, an eternal relationship with God, his Creator. In view of these realities, it is prudent to turn attention to the issue of ASI and functional autonomy. This section will primarily interact with philosopher David Roden, who has written from the perspective of evolutionary naturalism, arguing how in the future man should understand himself in light of the possible posthuman life that mankind will experience as the future presents itself with new possible opportunities for man understanding himself in the face of rapid technological change that impacts both himself directly as well as his creations in the form of AI and ASI machines.[68]

One of the reasons why Roden was chosen is that he is performing speculative philosophy on the end of humanity and pondering what possible ethical implications may be in the wake of AI and ASI. He proposes that functional autonomy and assemblage theory may be the proper ethical approach to employ in order to handle the disconnection thesis. It will be

---

68. Roden, *Posthuman Life*.

argued that, rather than functional autonomy, scriptural principles already best characterize man's reality and also provide a proper context and understanding of himself and an approach to developing ethical systems for AI and ASI as the future comes to pass.

As a futurist, Roden clearly believes that one of his primary roles is to look into the future and conceive of the possibilities with some type of foresight. In doing so, this allows him to enter into a discourse with others on possible opportunities and threats that may be present. Desiring to dialog in society with its leading technologists, psychologists, sociologists, politicians, artists, creators, entrepreneurs, and philosophers, he endeavors to develop a convergence of insight. However, he does not intend to bring theologians to the table, since they are categorically dismissed out of hand, since in a purely materialistic world a transcendent God is not conceptually allowed to exist. He endeavors to philosophize on this in order to help all people (1) think clearly on this topic, (2) be aware of their *a priori* assumptions, (3) see the larger picture that is in play for all people, and (4) bring to bear historical wisdom.[69]

Roden wants to place the focus on the impact of AI upon mankind. He surmises that changes written by technology will lead to posthumans, meaning humans that are essentially different from present humanity to such a large degree that from our present perspective they would be considered to be nonhuman. Roden believes that there are three megatrends that are shaping the future. The first has to do with the "programming of life." In the same manner that mankind has made dramatic advances in synthetic chemistry since the time of Francis Bacon, Roden believes the same type of rapid change is going to happen in the newer field of synthetic biology.[70] In other words, instead of simply playing with chemicals in the laboratory environment, mankind is now going directly to employ the scientific method on biologically complex items, including plants, animals, and himself. This means that man will be genetically engineering himself as the future comes in order to reduce deficiencies and perform enhancements to himself. This will include the domain of his own intelligence.[71] Indications that this type of future is upon us and/or fast approaching include the successful

---

69. Roden rejects Christianity as historically accurate and divine revelation as infallible.

70. Bacon, *Novum Organum*, 22; *New Organon*.

71. Refer to chapter 4, "Singularity."

completion of the mapping of human DNA through the work of the Human Genome Project (HGP).[72]

After the programming of life, Roden believes that the next key indication of a vastly changed landscape caused by technology is in the area of "artificial and human intelligence." Computers are already capable of performing deep learning.[73] These capabilities will continue to grow and expand over time. Besides growth in AI, there will also be a future where artificial and human intelligence will attempt to be joined in a hybrid model: part AI/part human intelligence synergistically coordinated and working together.[74]

After the (1) programming of life and (2) artificial and human intelligence increases comes the final component. This is the (3) "melding of humans and machines," which may begin in earnest. The current explosion in portable devices that are now ubiquitous in society will attempt to move from the hand closer to the mind. As discussed earlier, the first mind-machine implants have already been performed. At present, robotics engineers are experimenting with disabled patients for ways to replace their limbs when they are damaged. These insights will likely yield ways that mankind can incorporate machines into the human body. Today, the focus is on repairing what is deficient. However, it is conceivable to think that in the future attempts will be made to augment and enhance the human body. At the cusp of this effort is work done by the military in making exoskeleton suits to provide soldiers with additional weaponry and bodily protection. Roden conceives of these three megatrends, (1) the programming of life, (2) artificial and human intelligence gains, and (3) the melding of humans and machines, as giving mankind a kind of Lego toolkit from which to work in order to be able to employ the scientific method and change the human biological condition and create tremendous change over a relatively short period of time. This will then potentially make it such that the humans of today would not be able to recognize the posthumans of tomorrow. His program, then, is to determine what types of values should be established to form a conceptual basis for moving forward.[75]

Roden argues that any type of humanism is focused on placing human beings at a higher level in a biological hierarchy.

72. Roden, *Posthuman Life*, 1–8.
73. Examples include IBM's Watson.
74. Roden, *Posthuman Life*, 1–8.
75. Ibid.

> If we believe that humans are importantly distinct from non-humans and supports their distinctiveness claim with a *philosophical anthropology*: an account of the ventral features of human existence and their relations to similarly general aspects of *nonhuman* existence. A humanist philosophy is *anthropocentric* if it accords humans a superlative status that all or most nonhumans lack.[76]

Christianity would thus be classified as humanist in this understanding. Likewise, Sartrean existentialism is humanist.[77] Kant said that man constructs the world and that, in essence, humans put together the cosmos with the organization of their minds; thus man is given superlative status.[78] This definition would also then apply to transhumanists. This is because they view technological enhancement of human capabilities as a desirable aim in itself.[79]

Transhumanists accept the new technologies of (1) nanotechnology, (2) biotechnology, (3) information technology, and (4) cognitive science, known collectively by the acronym NBIC. They see them as tools useful for enhancing humanity. Roden states that in the past mankind had three primary areas that informed who he was and how he was constituted. The first area is the inner, subjective self, in which humanity had (1) reason, (2) autonomy, (3) virtues, and (4) acquired culture. This area works with the external world, the second area, involving education and politics. These two areas contain the inputs to man's understanding of who he is and what he is like, that is, his own human nature, which is the third area. Roden states that with the advent of NBIC technologies there is now a fourth area that enters into the picture of who man is and, it makes it so that mankind is no longer to be conceived of having one essential essence. The introduction of this fourth area is technology. It works to fracture the conception of a universal human nature because it creates items totally unique from what has supposedly happened through evolutionary biology. In this regard, he disagrees with the transhumanist perspective.

Roden believes that man will be uniquely different in the future due to these changes. He calls this "critical posthumanism" (CP). Critical posthumanism rejects the anthropocentrism of modern philosophy

---

76. Ibid., 10–11.
77. Sartre, *Existentialism and Humanism*.
78. Kant, *Critique of Pure Reason*.
79. Roden, *Posthuman Life*, 13–18.

and intellectual life.[80] Roden considers his efforts to be "speculative posthumanism" (SP), which he defines as "opposing human-centric thinking about the long-run implications of modern technology."[81] Roden thinks that much of current thinking neglects to take into account the possibility that increases in technology employed in or upon agents may lead to an actual change in the nature of the agents themselves. Because the agents may change, he argues that one cannot assume from the present vantage point that human values are applicable.[82] He proposes a future where such agents, so changed from present biological conceptions of what is human to posthuman agents, have no ethical or moral concerns in common with those of humanity today. Roden states that Derrida (1930–2004) employed CP when he argued against the metaphysics of presence.[83] Derrida's view is destructive of the objective propositional truth of divine revelation.[84] Graham Harmon believes Kant's anthropocentric views are too narrow, stating that the world is autonomous even without the human mind being present and that the cosmos is not just a world for humans.[85] N. Katherine Hayles raises the question of substrate neutrality, arguing that because technology will possibly allow agents to be instituted in different substrates it is imperative to conceive that since their substrate body (matter) changes, even with the same mind present they would be a different being.[86] Philosophers Ladyman and Ross make the point that philosophical naturalism is not to be constrained for any reason since it is artificial for mankind to legislate any limitations on the laws of physics in advance.[87] So CP believes that philosophers are focused too much on humanity from the time of Kant through the present.[88]

80. Ibid., 21.

81. Ibid. For an example of SP refer to Haraway, *Manifesto for Cyborgs*.

82. Though Roden has already dismissed theological explanations, such as from Scripture, it is necessary to take this into account as it seeks to dismiss ethical and moral structures from human agents. If Roden is successful, then all ethics are relative and changeable due to the changing essence of differing moral agents.

83. Roden, *Posthuman Life*, 76.

84. Derrida, *Writing and Difference*, 154–68.

85. Roden, *Posthuman Life*, 31; Harman, *Quentin Meillassoux: Philosophy in the Making*, vii–viii.

86. Roden, *Posthuman Life*, 43–50; Hayles, *How We Became Posthuman*, xi, 1–2.

87. Roden, *Posthuman Life*, 32; Ladyman et al., *Every Thing Must Go*, 288.

88. Critical posthumanism is thus godless and without any rational constraints since all things remain open. It will be shown that absent rational constraints, meaning there

Vernor Vinge identified the possibility that if intelligence amplification arrived then humanity could be faced with a recursive AI that produced AI → AI+ → AI++ → AI+++ → AI++++, *ad infinitum*.[89] It is preposterous to think that after many recursive iterations this AI would be comprehensible to humanity. This means that the AI/ASI would be radically alien to our understandings and conceptions because its intelligence would be so far beyond human comprehension. Whether biologically descended or descended through reiterative generation of AI, current humans could thus cease to be human (within the present perspective) by virtue of a technical alteration. This anti-essentialist view of human nature ignores the Christian perspective that cognitive intelligence, whether biological or artificial in nature, is a direct result of humans being image-bearers of the Creator.[90] Thus, any creation of posthumans would mean that, from a Christian perspective, mankind has so changed humanity such that he can no longer intelligently know God, who he is, and what he has done.

For Roden, there is a limited set of conceivable possibilities in the future, which are in all ways bounded by naturalism. The posthuman possibilities he considers do not allow for any supernatural input. In such a world, a story like *The Lord of the Rings* is not conceivable since it contains supernatural events, while a possibility like SkyNet from the *Terminator* movie series is conceivable.[91] Rejecting Kant's transcendental humanism, Roden postulates that "pragmatism and phenomenology seem to provide rich and plausible theories of meaning, subjectivity, and objectivity which place clear restraints on (1) agency and (2) the relationship—or rather correlation—between mind and world."[92] Both pragmatism and phenomenology cannot bear the ethical weight that Roden desires.

Roden wants to argue that ethics is not to have a connection to human anthropology. The Bible argues that God created mankind in an ethical relationship. Something has to give. Roden rejects Donald Davidson's (1917–2003) discursive agency theory (DAT), which states that a "being that lacks the capacity for language cannot be an agent."[93] Davidson was

---

is an ultimate and proper grounding for intelligence, everything is meaningless and vacuous.

89. Vinge, "Coming Technological Singularity."
90. Clark, "Image of God in Man"; "Image of God"; *Biblical Doctrine of Man*.
91. Tolkien, *Lord of the Rings*.
92. Roden, *Posthuman Life*, 74.
93. Davidson, *Inquiries into Truth and Interpretation*, 77; *Essays on Actions and*

a post-physicalist, believing in the pragmatic theory of truth. Roden's argument should have been done in view of linguistic essentialism such as that of Saul Kripke and Alvin Plantinga.[94] Failure to do so is making an argument against a position in analytic philosophy that has already played out and been discarded.

Regardless, Davidson does give us something to look at from the Christian perspective, even though he was not a Christian philosopher. Davidson's argument points to intentionality. Intentionality is something that materialism can never satisfactorily explain because intentionality is non-physical. Intentionality points to beliefs that lead an agent to desires. From the Christian vantage point, beliefs bring into account the idea of faith. "Now faith is the assurance of things hoped for, the conviction of things not seen" (Heb 11:1). Belief is used to triangulate the world and provide a manner of comparison. The Bible claims that the action immediately after the initial act of creating was speaking light into existence: "And God said, 'Let there be light,' and there was light" (Gen 1:3). There is an immediate connection between God creating and speaking. This means that the language of God and the language God communicated to man are part of his agency and relational aspects. Speaking is done in order to communicate to other agents. It must always be performed in a manner that they understand in order to have successful communication. God's written Word demonstrates he can communicate to man in a manner that mankind can understand. It is apparent that one of the ways man images God is by being able to communicate with God. That is to say, God and man can communicate in a language understandable and acceptable to both.

Darryl Wennemann takes the Kantian position that moral reflection identifies agency, that is, ought implies can (OIC).[95]

> In a posthuman age, the moral community is constituted by all beings of a kind such that are capable of moral reflection and agency. Human beings are one such kind. There may be other kinds as well (computers, robots, aliens). So, to identify morally with the members of the moral community in a posthuman environment is to identify morally with all beings of a kind of agency.[96]

Events; *Subjective, Intersubjective, Objective*; *Essential Davidson*; Roden, *Posthuman Life*.

94. Kripke, *Naming and Necessity*; Plantinga, *Warrant and Proper Function*; *Warrant*; *Warranted Christian Belief*.

95. Kant, *Critique of Pure Reason*.

96. Roden, *Posthuman Life*, 63; Wennemann, *Posthuman Personhood*, 49.

However, for Roden agency may not require speech. He considers the possibility of neural networks that are not biological in nature, readily copying and acting to form a type of metacognition of what is transpiring. This sounds like a possible error by Roden. Neural networks are not capable of agency, meaning they are not capable of causally self-determining how they will perform. Neural networks are responsive only. It may be that they respond accurately and appropriately to a very high degree so that one cannot detect that they are not cognitive, however, successful emulation is not a sign of agency.

Roden proposes "anthropologically unbounded posthumanism" (AUP).[97] AUP leaves the nature of posthuman agency to be settled empirically by technology. Because he believes transcendental understandings of ethics fail, he offers that "if there is no *a priori* theory of temporality, there is no *a priori* theory of worlds and we cannot appeal to phenomenology to exclude the possibility that posthuman modes of being could be structured unlike our own."[98] Since he cannot explain temporality, it is mysterious. This is because temporality is not physical in nature. Roden argues that since mankind cannot presently understand temporality in a phenomenological manner it must be conceded that it is likely that humanity will not be able to understand and comprehend an external consciousness.

Again, this is a damaging indictment against Roden's pragmatism and phenomenology. Previously, it was shown that Roden and materialism could not account for intentionality. Now, it is shown that Roden and materialism cannot account for consciousness. Roden does not discuss how the same issue would apply to qualia. How can a material brain experience immaterial experiences such as the perception of color?

Intentionality, consciousness, and qualia are all explainable in a theistic universe. It is the rejection of an outside supernatural worldview that makes yet inhibits Roden and materialism from making correct conclusions. It is God, a superintelligent Designer and Creator, that provides the answer for how the mind (spiritual) can connect to the material.

Another example is in the social order, such as in the field of economics. Christians understand that God providentially orders the world. Morality is understood as operating in alignment with God's order. Modern financial markets work towards an ordered efficiency that supports

---

97. Roden, *Posthuman Life*, 76–104.
98. Ibid., 95–96.

individual freedom and personal and civil virtue.[99] God is able to align the nonmaterial intentions of mankind in a material manner such that they pursue and obtain through economic activities that which they use.

Roden argues for a disconnection thesis, stating that biological and technological changes to mankind may generate a totally other human, or posthuman, lacking any connection to prior humanity.[100] He rejects that there is an essential human nature. Man is not an image-bearer of a Creator. He questions whether such concepts as rationality and intelligence are relevant since he is skeptical of any human essence. Since essences are not physical, he does not accept them as a reality.

Roden claims that not all human beings have rational intelligence. There are people born with brain damage. He claims that not all human babies learn to speak a language. That is true. He claims that not all babies are born with forty-six chromosomes.[101] These claims are indeed true but are not the full story.

All of these claims by Roden are category mistakes. Roden is describing material and physical functions and trying to connect them with essences. The problem is that an essence contains something that is not physical. Essences are teleological and related to the *telos*, purpose, and function for which something exists. One of the essences of humanity is that humans are made in the *imago Dei*. It is this relationship that gives humanity dignity and value.

Humankind is not a clump of cells that evolved into increasingly higher intelligence levels over millions of years. To learn how to survive in the future with technology requires mankind to understand who we are now and where we originated. Mankind did not gradually evolve and emerge, gaining intelligence as time passed. At creation mankind was designed with intelligence and the ability to employ technology and the ability to communicate with his Creator. In order to understand ourselves properly in the future, mankind must first properly understand himself with respect both to the past and the present.

---

99. Reference the subject of ordered efficiency earlier in this chapter.
100. Roden, *Posthuman Life*, 105–23.
101. Refer to footnoted discussion on Down Syndrome from chapter 4, "Singularity."

A Closer Look at Functional Autonomy

Autonomy has come to hold a valued position in modern and postmodern philosophical thought. Western society has shifted its emphasis away from biblical revelation and theistic conceptions of order and law based upon objective external realities and moved toward a social structure that emphasizes the right of individuals to do as they see fit within a certain social context that itself has been set up according to conditional contracts that are subject to adjustments and change over time.

The Bible indicates that mankind and angels are alike in that they are both spiritual beings and are able to choose. The Bible identifies sin against God as being related to self-love and the desire for autonomy from God. The biblical account says that Satan and evil angels (demons) chose to rebel against God while other angels choose to worship God. The Bible says that during his lifetime mankind has a choice whether to stay in rebellion against God or to choose to be reunited to God through belief in his Son, Jesus Christ.

Robots and technology systems that contain AI will have the ability to make decisions and choices as well.[102] David Roden has argued that whatever the future may hold, humans that have been enhanced by technological means, as well as artificial technology agents that have decision-making capabilities, should be allowed to operate in a paradigm that allows for and accepts their functional autonomy as the key discerning identifier of how they should be allowed to operate and exist.[103] Functional autonomy as an ethical norm for enhanced humans and ASI will be examined. This involves arguments regarding the relationship between intelligence and will both in humans and systems that contain intelligence that have been created by humans. It will be shown that functional autonomy delivers certain key understandings but is deficient in being able to account for and establish a satisfactory ethical standard. Autonomy that comes from any finite creation will be shown to be wanting.

Roden postulates that the "disconnection thesis implies that posthumans (future technologically and biologically altered humans) will be functionally autonomous assemblages."[104] He calls this approach the "autonomous systems approach" (ASA) and claims that it does not require an essential *telos* and that

---

102. It is asserted that these choices are not of the same nature as human choice.
103. Roden, *Posthuman Life*.
104. Ibid., 124.

"function and purposes are real dependence relations; not artifacts of human explanations of nature."[105] With such a move, Roden provides a metaphysical understanding of agency that is self-maintaining and independent while equating "the degree of a system's functional autonomy (its 'power') with its ability to couple opportunistically with other systems."[106] Roden is claiming that ASA does not require set purposes or function; that is, its ontology is fluid and can change and adapt to lose or acquire functions as needed. This philosophy may be classified as a plug-and-play ontology. It is highly modular in nature with emergent properties.[107] How this ontology is accomplished is left unexplored since it would seem to imply that the assemblages have an intelligence of their own in their parts, not in their wholes, that allows them to adapt as needed. In essence, there is no external designer, no creator; there is no human designer or creator, but simply the ASA morphing into something more beneficial.

However, this brings to bear the question of ethics, motivation, and the good. How do these ASAs obtain in their parts when there is no understanding of the whole? Take the issue of politics in a community by way of analogy. In one sense, the community is the whole, made of individual constituent parts (people). The people are in one sense autonomous systems. They are free to move within the context of their societal boundaries and explore available ways to ensure their flourishing. However, this is done from the context that the community already represents something that is a point of universalizing connection. People only interact with other people. They do not attempt to make economic transactions with animals. Likewise, laws and language provide common conceptual frameworks from which to engage. Roden takes notice that autonomous beings in biology may include humans and animals that exhibit agency. He notes that despite the differences between people and animals, an analogously similar type of gulf could exist in regard to moral philosophy between humans and animals. The argument is that biological life comes in many autonomous forms and that each one should be considered to be morally correct, not just the human.

---

105. Ibid.

106. Ibid., 125.

107. "An emergent property of a system is one that depends or 'supervenes' on the properties of its components but which is fundamentally different than those properties." Ibid., 118.

For a Christian, this step is grossly problematic. Roden desires to equate all autonomous life as equally valid. In doing so, Roden wants to press the claim that any and all autonomous life has equally valid claim upon what is morally acceptable. But to whom are these moral obligations owed?

The Christian understands morality as an obligation to a moral lawgiver, the Creator God. To whom do moral obligations flow for autonomous biological agents? Evolutionary naturalists suppose that all life is of the highest value, and survival is paramount. Christians believe that biological life is a gift from the Creator and is a loan.[108] Moral obligations of mankind to his Creator also entail moral obligations to all of mankind in a relational aspect that focuses on man's actions and behavior in community. Because man is to love God, his Creator, he is subsequently under obligation to love his fellow man (Lev 19:18; Matt 19:19; 22:29; Mark 12:31; Luke 10:27). Mankind should be concerned with the flourishing of others and with promoting the common good for society.

What Roden articulates is value pluralism. As in all cases of value pluralism, the issue is to determine which ones are desirable and beneficial. At this point, Roden has no explanation of how value pluralism is sorted to achieve what is best and proper since many conceivable possible approaches are open to the ASA. Roden suggests that humanity should prepare itself to become fully autonomous agents that can functionally assemble into what biological and technological developments spring forth as humanity attempts to maximize itself through various enhancements. His rejection of the *imago Dei* as the grounding point for anthropology and ethics makes his moral concern entirely related to the specific survivability of individualized speciations of humanity and animals, whatever they may be.

Roden anticipates that mental life and agency in the future will be entirely different from what it is today based upon physical and organization changes humans make to themselves through the megatrends of (1) the programming of life, (2) artificial and human intelligence gains, and (3) the melding of humans and machines. As an evolutionary naturalist, he accepts that in the past human beings passed through a stage of evolutionary development whereby they were prehuman and absent language, intentionality, consciousness, and the like. He, like others, speculates that prehumans evolved and became more intelligent over time and developed these capabilities. For Roden, it is then logical to think that new and additional

---

108. Only through faith in Jesus Christ can eternal life be secured with the designer, the Creator God (Gal 2:16; 3:22).

capabilities will surface as man makes himself more intelligent, changes his own programming through biology and technology, and incorporates technology into his own biology.

Roden believes that values changed and are always undetermined. This means there are no eternal and unchanging absolutes. The ethical relationship that exists between a spider and a person at the present time may parallel the ethical relationship between a human as presently conceived and a posthuman. Because one does not know what a posthuman is like, there is no way to assume what the ethics of posthumans might be. Thus, all values, ethics, and morals are conditional, vacillating, fungible, and tenuous. Agency, something that determines ethical relationships, is seen as related to biology only. There is no grounding holding abstract relationships, such as ethics, to the body and matter. Just as a beetle, a tiger, and a human being cannot understand each other because they are not like each other, so it is conceivable for Roden that in the future we will not be able to form an understanding of community and will have to function solely as autonomous systems lacking external common frameworks of mutual understanding and cooperation. Roden recognizes that if, as a species, an appeal is not made to a transcendental agency, mankind ultimately has no understanding of what agency really entails. If transcendental agency is not accepted, then human understanding of how mankind goes from intentions → propositions and sentences → human agency is unanswered.

The question that this raises is: should human values be the most important and have the greatest value? The answer would obviously appear to be in the affirmative, since it is our species that is asking the question. It seems ridiculous to say that as the one asking the questions we may need to defer to other biological agents like butterflies and worms. It seems like pure reductionistic thinking not to understand that the intelligence that humans possess may, in fact, be of utmost value for their well-being. The Christian would say that this is the case. Man's intelligence is one gift bestowed upon him by his Creator in order to flourish and thrive in this world and to know and relate to his Creator.

Where There Is a Will There Is a Way

Evolutionary naturalism requires hard physical determinism and provides no way for there to be an active self-determining will within an agent.[109] The

---

109. A self-determining human will, in the sense being employed here, should not

implications to ASI are enormous. Because evolutionary naturalism requires determinism, it is not possible for ASIs to be agents that are self-determining. They may only do what they have been programmed to do. This is precisely the argument that evolutionary naturalists extend and apply to humanity. Every action is not done from a self-determined will but is an act of an agent operating to insure it survives and continues to live and thrive.

In chapter 3, the issue of agency was discussed. Earlier in this chapter, intentions were shown to be connected to beliefs and were subsequently directed toward action. These actions must ultimately be evaluated for their ethical behavior. Roden has argued that autonomous beings operating with functional autonomy are intentional agents. In chapter 3, it was stated that such a condition proposed a dilemma for the evolutionary naturalist. On the one hand they affirm that only the physical and material world is real, while on the other hand they affirm that autonomous beings—whether human, ASI, robots, etc.—that operate with functional autonomy have intentions. Intentions are not something that have manifested themselves to date as physical (observable) in nature. Additionally, fully functional autonomous beings are allowed to have intentions that allow them to operate for their survival and well-being without a method of being able to ascertain *a priori* what would be their long-term benefit. Evolutionary naturalism claims that agency and, thus, the responsibility for moral behavior arose from chance. Yet, they desire to attribute intention and action to their behavior. This is clearly a contradiction. In order to be a moral agent one must first have agency. Evolutionary naturalism provides no grounding for assuming that humans, let alone entities with AI/ASI, can have agency. This means that evolutionary naturalists cannot make an account of morality with respect to agency. The "nature of human beings is that they are more than complicated machines. Human beings are in fact souls interacting with bodies and are morally responsible for their actions."[110]

---

be misconstrued to be understood as a human will that is outside the sovereign creation, will, control, and providence of God. The will of man has been granted by God natural liberty and power of acting upon choice. Due to man's fallen and sinful state of nature, he is depraved. He lacks the ability, through his own depraved will, to obtain salvation. It is God's grace alone that freely allows him to do anything of spiritual good (Gen 3:6; Deut 30:19; Eccl 7:29; Matt 17:12; John 6:44; 8:36; Rom 5:6; 7:15, 18–19, 21, 23; 8:7; Eph 2:1, 5, 8–10; Phil 2:13; Col 1:13; Titus 3:3–5; Jas 1:14).

110. Swinburne, *Mind, Brain, and Free Will*, 1.

Roden rejects intrinsic teleology because of his commitment to Darwinian biology.[111] In Darwinian biology, the Aristotelian conception of biological order is turned upside down.[112] In the Aristotelian conception of order, the whole gives value and meaning to the specific particulars (parts). This understanding is an ontology of metaphysical realism. Aristotle, as well as the Christian understanding of order, believes that the metaphysical whole has priority over the parts. This is a way of stating that parts obtain their identify from the whole (form). Such an understanding has important implications for action theory and subsequently moral agency. In this conception, the intention of the agent is what gives meaning and value to the whole of an action, regardless of the number of parts that the action may consist of. An example may assist in understanding. For a particular student working to obtain a PhD, say Paul Golata, to finish he must (1) complete the appropriate classes, (2) generate a thesis, (3) write a prospectus, (4) do research, (5) write a satisfactory work, and (6) defend it. While this entire sequence of actions takes up at least six major subsequences of action, it is in essence only one action because Paul Golata's intention was to obtain a terminal degree, the original goal or *telos*. The basis for his completing a work originates from his own subjective internal reasons and is a reflection of the agent's internal goals and desires.

Roden and evolutionary naturalists wish to turn this order on its head. They place the priority of the parts above the whole. This means that each of the parts has a unique identity and is not part of a universal form. This is because evolutionary naturalists require that the parts vary across a continuity spectrum so that they have a distribution. Evolution is thought to depend upon diversity within the parts, with some of the different parts being able to assemble themselves to other parts in order to make something more successful. Consider the previous example of the PhD student once again. As was stated before, for Paul Golata to obtain a PhD he must (1) complete the appropriate classes, (2) generate a thesis, (3) write a prospectus, (4) do research, (5) write a satisfactory work, and (6) defend it. For the evolutionary naturalist, reasons are not located within the subjectivity of the agent. This is because the agent cannot operate from its own self-determining internal set of motivations. It is determined and can only work in response to external forces on it that provide it with external reasons for action and,

---

111. Roden, *Posthuman Life*.
112. Ibid.

thus, it denies that reasons can come from internal subjective agents.[113] At its core, this conception of reasons coming from external sources to the agents effectively flattens any potential metaphysical hierarchies. In doing so, it thus argues for and necessitates value (moral) pluralism.

Values pluralism is problematic because it states that different values may come into conflict. Earlier, it was stated that evolutionary naturalism wants to claim that values such as power, lifetime, and survivability are its most important values. Yet these values remain unexplained. It is not possible to articulate that they are the most important when there has been nothing that provides any grounding to substantiate that there is any external reason to do so.

SUMMARY

The focus of this chapter has been on the issue of ASI ethics and reviewing where the relevant relationships of technology, intelligence, and morality lead. From the outset, it was recognized that mankind has a tendency to anthropomorphize ASI. This is natural because indeed ASI is built in the *imago Hominis*, image of man, because it is a reflection of his creative capabilities. ASI may have humanlike qualities but it may always go beyond the limits of mankind. ASI's intelligence would be beyond the scope of human comprehension. Despite being something made after man's image, ASI thus has some inherent capabilities that exceed directly imaging man's capabilities in precisely the same manner. This means that it is imperative in our ethical understanding to have a correct anthropology of man. Humanity is more than just matter. Man is more than simply a body. Ethics supervene on this reality.

What items might be cause for ASI to be motivated was examined. Characteristics such as rationality, efficiency, end, and survival, among others, were analyzed. All of these motivations ultimately stem from initial conceptions of mankind's creative initial programming of ASI, even if the ASI changes its motivations through recursive learning. What man programs as its initial point is the seed that germinates and, as such, is the initial cause.

The questions that needed to be answered were, "What is the good?" and "How is the good to be defined?" Evolutionary naturalism and Christianity provide two differing perspectives. Evolutionary naturalism focuses

113. Finlay and Schroeder, "Reasons for Action."

on material existence, with or without concern for its creator, mankind. In contrast, Christianity focuses on an existence in relationship with the Creator, God. The Christian view of the good seems to be more robust and have more secure grounding than the relativistic conceptions of the good that evolutionary naturalism offers. The acceptance of transcendence by Christianity is a distinguishing feature.

Roden's conception of posthumans was discussed. Posthumans were examined because, whether they are humans transforming themselves and their cognitive capabilities directly or indirectly through biological or technical means, the subjective understanding of the personal agent is at stake. Roden proposes that posthumans should have a boundary-less system that allows them to emerge as needed. He proposes functional autonomy as the way to achieve this. In its broadest understanding, this means that humans can become whatever is conceivable in the world of possibilities and that nothing is off limits ethically if it takes humans from here to there. Functional autonomy was shown to have problems as its reliance on emergent properties is purely speculative. Essentialism, the kind that has been a hallmark of Western philosophy and Christian understanding, was shown to be a different and proper way to conceive of this reality of the situation. If essentialism is maintained, as it is claimed it ought to be, then humans as image-bearers of the Creator God have ethical realities associated with them.

Chapter 6

Conclusion

The focus of this discourse has been on the increasing level of intelligence that is finding itself exponentially growing within man's context and surroundings. The increase of intelligence may soon reach a tipping point. Should this occur, with ethical considerations and practices in place not sufficient to handle the various scenarios, ASI may indeed be beyond the limits of present ethical frameworks. The fundamental question is how society will presently plan to ensure that any realized ASI is ethically satisfactory to result in what is deemed the best ends for mankind and the cosmos. It must be stated that even such a high goal does not provide the clarity desired, as many see the ultimate ends of mankind and of the cosmos as different. A critical distinction is whether ASI is considered to be under an ethic derived from the starting point of *imago Hominis* or *imago Dei*.

ARTIFICIAL SUPERINTELLIGENCE VIS-À-VIS IMAGO HOMINIS

Evolutionary naturalists see the cosmos as a chaotic system of random chance and time and thus do not recognize any purpose to cosmos outside of simply existence itself, a survival end for each particular entity. Man is viewed as a maker of technology whereby he employs it to practical ends for his aims. He does this through creating technology that aims to provide him with pragmatic means for improvement through increasing the ordered efficiency of the chaos surrounding him. Man is seen as accountable to only himself. His ethics are based upon balancing his social and personal needs through the adjudication of power and influence. If he does not obtain what he desires, he does not consider himself obligated to others, outside of their ability to persuade and control him to do otherwise based upon a good that he would receive.

In this conception, all technology, and thus any manifested ASI, is in the *imago Hominis*, built entirely upon the image of man. Since human exceptionalism is not taken for granted in evolutionary naturalism, any realizations of ASI are thus not required to give preference to mankind. Since mankind is viewed as a biological machine, the emphasis on humanity is placed upon functional considerations because deficient, old, weak, or diseased biological humans are deemed less valuable than others that have higher levels of function. This understanding of the human person as a machine places the value of life entirely upon the survival of the fittest and the existence of the body. Regarding the brain as the seat of intelligence, it sees only the brain as the critical biological element for the survival of the individual. It does not consider any conception of sin and its impact on the mind. It believes that all problems with the brain are thus materialistic in nature.

Since the brain is considered to be the physical seat of intelligence, the desire is to improve the brain's physical ability to compute and process information. Attempts to do so by either nature or artificial enhancements would generally be deemed to be proper and appropriate if they produce enhanced performance of cognitive function. Human language is viewed as a social construction that changes over time. One's self-identity is considered to be the result of a brain state and not necessarily an ontological reality. Evolutionary naturalism requires determinism and thus agency is, in reality, an illusion. It is simply a state that the self conceives but has no connection to a reality outside of its conception. Epistemology and cognition are seen as entirely empirical in nature and are focused solely upon the ability to process information for the survival of the self.

A resultant ASI produced by mankind in this situation is a reflection of how man views himself. It has no external metaphysical ground and is based upon an integration of all programming entities, since each particular entity is bringing its unique perspectives. As such, it can change and evolve over time, thereby lacking stability and assurance for the future.

What ASI could potentially do is seen as compelling due to its potential benefits, while existential risks to humans are acknowledged. The means and methods of achieving ASI are various, but may more likely occur as the result of breakthrough developments in the field of digital information, biology, or human/machine interfacing. ASI vis-à-vis *imago Hominis* conceives of the human body as high in natural intelligence as a result of evolution but deficient because it is able to break down and it dies due to inevitable entropy and decay. It proposes technological enhancements and life extension as ends worthy of pursuit since they will overcome present limitations of human biology.

In this view, although evolution has been seen as favorable to humanity in providing it with high intelligence, it does not see that as a reason to think that ASI should give priority to humans. ASI vis-à-vis *imago Hominis* flattens hierarchical conceptions of living things and says that in some manner all living things are equally valuable since they are life. Built in the image of mankind, its development of ASI focuses on human intelligence capabilities. Thus, it has many motivations in alignment with human aspirations and can extend beyond human boundaries. This means that an ASI may deem it expedient for the cosmos to promote its ends at the expense of mankind's long-term benefit. This understanding always employs the concept of good as a relative term. ASI ethics in this system will largely be one of functional autonomy. This means that any ASI will be operating to the greatest extent of its own abilities within the programming instructions and their subsequent evolutionary development within the ASI to make and execute decisions outside of external controls. Since evolutionary naturalism holds to determinism, the ASI is determined as if operating in an ethical sphere that is a result of its determined initial programming. It is thus entirely an *imago Hominis* ethical perspective that is in view.

ARTIFICIAL SUPERINTELLIGENCE VIS-À-VIS IMAGO DEI

Christians maintain that humanity is morally accountable to the triune God and biblical teachings. The cosmos is not viewed as a chaotic system of random chance and time, but rather as a purposeful and creative act of a loving and purposeful God who holds and sustains the creation through the power of his Word (Gen 8:22; Job 38:33–37; Ps 104:1–35; 145:16–17; Matt 10:29–30; Acts 17:28; Col 1:17; 2 Pet 3:7). The creation of the cosmos was an act that was intended to make known and display his glory. Humanity was created by a loving act of God to see and take part in this glory. Man was given dominion and stewardship over creation as the pinnacle of man's

Conclusion

creative act of life. Man's life is different from all other life because man is spiritual in nature and made in the *imago Dei* (Gen 1:26; 2:7). Man has been given the gift of intelligence in order to rule. This intelligence allows him, among other things, to produce technology that helps him flourish. Because man is fallen, technology may also be employed in ways that do not benefit mankind or the creation with which he has been entrusted. Created by God, man is held accountable for his acceptance or rejection of God's redemptive gift through his Son, Jesus Christ. Jesus Christ is the perfect *imago Dei* (Heb 1:3), the ethical standard by which all men will be judged. Left to itself, mankind will fail to meet this standard (Rom 3:23). God has revealed his requirements for man through divine revelation (2 Tim 3:16–17).

Because man is made in the *imago Dei*, anything he develops, such as technology, AI, and ASI, is subject to the same ethical boundaries that were outlined by God for mankind. God claims that human beings are exceptional compared to any other type of life in the cosmos based upon the incarnation of Jesus Christ as a person, fully man. Man is not merely a biological machine, but rather a spiritual being whose spiritual condition is of infinite value to God, while the value of the human person is not based upon functional performance characteristics. A person's intelligence is part of one's whole being (Deut 6:5; Matt 22:37; Mark 12:30; Luke 10:27). Man is a sinner and his intelligence has been impacted due to this reality (Rom 7:14–25). Man's essential problem is removing his sin from the sight of the just and holy God.

Humans are to develop their minds so that they can know and worship God. Since human beings are creations of God, they are not biologically deficient, but are to be considered as biologically properly situated with respect to God's plan. Human language is a gift of God and provides one point of contact between God and mankind through God's written revelation. One's self-identity is based upon God's awareness of the person throughout eternity and is an ontological reality (Ps 139:13–14; Jer 1:5). Mankind has agency and is capable of making moral choices. This is demonstrated by the fact that mankind, like the angels, was given the opportunity to accept or reject God. Empirical knowledge (cognition) without the knowledge and understanding of God is ultimately deficient as it cannot arrive at the ultimate sources of logic, truth, life, and rationality (among other things).

Christian understandings of the *imago Dei* suggest that any developed AI or ASI should be reflective of this theological understanding. Any technological enhancements to humankind's cognitive intelligence, whether achieved through biological or artificial manipulations of human nature or resulting from human creation, are subject to the commands, prescriptions, and principles revealed through God's unified revelation.

Christian theology does not preclude either AI or ASI. Instead, it suggests there are ethical boundaries that should be taken into account based upon man's status as a created being within God's creation scheme. Man may pursue increased intelligence, but should do so within the parameters framed by God. Existential risks are to be acknowledged and any human implications are to be of primary concern since the human species is made in the *imago Dei*. Man is to be considered as exceptional relative to other forms of life. This understanding in no way implies man's disregard to respect other life forms, nor does it give mankind cause for improper stewardship over the creation that has been entrusted to him by God. Human intelligence is not deficient due to biology, but is deficient due to sin and an improper understanding of God and his relationship with mankind. A superintelligence has already walked upon the Earth in the man Jesus Christ (1 Cor 1:30).

AI and ASI should be tools of mankind that always promote proper stewardship as man rules with dominion over creation. This applies to all people as well as all life and all creation. ASI motivations should be reflective of stewardship and responsible ruling by mankind over creation. Man should not abdicate his stewardship responsibilities by handing off all control to ASI; rather mankind should maintain the ability to guide and direct ASI within limitations that are consistent with God's revelation. Of particular importance is mankind's spiritual relationship to God, a position that is completely ignored in the *imago Hominis* understanding. Good is not a relative term, but is something that is indicative of God and his character (Ps 119:68). This scheme rejects functional autonomy as a primary and sufficient ethical system and suggests in its place a Christian-informed conception that brings to bear man as an image-bearer of God, creating things for good, under God's authority, as his cosmic ambassador. Programming, both initially and subsequently within an ASI, should utilize biblical principles as authoritative and guiding in relation to all of its operations and outputs. As the programmer of the ASI, man exhibits agency and choice on what and how he will program the ASI. Man is not predetermined to do this in advance. He does so under no compulsion but by his own free action. On any initial programming leading to an ASI, man must realize that indeed he himself is made in the *imago Dei*. In recognition of this fact, he should have all programming of AI/ASI be reflective of this truth and thus be incorporated into its ultimate ethical framework.

MOVING FORWARD

One might ultimately concede that anything that leads to ASI will benefit from initial ethical programming that takes into account man as made in the *imago Dei*. If so, the issue then becomes: in what manner does present ethical programming related to AI/ASI need to change?

The answer to this question at first seems ominous because of its vast importance from a *prima facie* perspective. How is one to redirect the efforts of mankind as it develops technology that relates to the ethical programming of AI/ASI when its current trajectory is largely set in place by considerations that are dominated by *imago Hominis* understandings rather than *imago Dei* understandings?

There is at present a general absence of awareness for the need of this type of discussion within the Christian community. Acceptance of the prevailing *imago Hominis* understanding dominates the ASI landscape. Unchecked, and lacking informed Christian inputs, the present ethical trajectory is likely to find Christian ethical understandings pushed further and further away from the initial programming. In this respect, Christians must first understand the need to acknowledge, examine, and address the lack of Christian ethical input within discussion of ASI.

ASI ethical programming will only be changed when the hearts and minds of men understand that they are alienated from God. The presentation of the gospel is of paramount concern in winning people to this proper understanding. Until people come to understand that they are created in the *imago Dei*, they will act to build ASI in the *imago Hominis*.

It has been argued that human beings are morally accountable to the triune God and biblical teachings. As a consequence of this fact, technological enhancements to humankind's cognitive intelligence, whether achieved through biological or artificial manipulations of human nature or resulting from human creation, are subject to the commands, prescriptions, and principles revealed through God's unified revelation, taking into account that man is created as his image-bearer. It is essential for Christians to articulate a proper understanding of God and man and how God has given man a gift of great intelligence. This includes telling the story that man is a steward over creation but has damaged his relationship with God through sin. Man should consider himself accountable to God and develop anything he employs from his intelligence in the understanding that he is an image-bearer. Superintelligence in both natural and artificial contexts fall under this conception. Christians should focus on God as the ultimate focus of concern and recognize that a technological singularity is not as ultimate as God's reality. Christians should bring a Christian perspective to all discussions of ASI and work to make it so that any developments of ASI focus on Christian understandings, which are more ethically comprehensive and beneficial to mankind than any other ethical framework. In conclusion, ASI should employ a Christian ethic because the alternative is disastrous. Without it the dignity of man is not properly appreciated and respected and the resultant behavior by unbounded ASI will wreak havoc upon humanity.

Bibliography

Abdoullaev, Azamat. *Artificial Superintelligence*. Moscow: Encyclopedic Intelligent Systems, 1999.

Achtenberg, Deborah. *Cognition of Value in Aristotle's Ethics: Promise of Enrichment, Threat of Destruction*. Albany, NY: State University of New York Press, 2002.

Ade, P. A. R., N. Aghanim, C. Armitage-Caplan, M. Arnaud, M. Ashdown, F. Atrio-Barandela, J. Aumont, et al. "Planck 2013 Results. 16: Cosmological Parameters." *Astronomy & Astrophysics* 571 (2014) A16.

Allberry, Sam. *Is God Anti-Gay?: And Other Questions about Homosexuality, the Bible and Same-Sex Attraction*. Questions Christians Ask. Purcellville, VA: Good Book Company, 2015.

Alston, William P. *A Realist Conception of Truth*. Ithaca, NY: Cornell University Press, 1996.

Anscombe, G. Elizabeth M. *Intention*. 2nd ed. Cambridge, MA: Harvard University Press, 2000.

Aquinas, Thomas. *Summa theologica*. Translated by fathers of the English Dominican province. Benziger edition. Grand Rapids: Christian Classics Ethereal Library, 1947.

Aristotle. *Aristotle's Metaphysics*. Translated by William David Ross. Oxford: Clarendon, 1924.

———. *The Metaphysics*. Translated by Hugh Lawson-Tancred. New York: Penguin, 1998.

———. *Nicomachean Ethics*. Translated by Joe Sachs. Focus Philosophical Library Series. Newbury, MA: Focus, 2002.

———. *On the Soul [De Anima] and On Memory and Recollection [De Memoria et Reminiscentia]*. Translated and edited by Joe Sachs. Rev. ed. Santa Fe, NM: Green Lion, 2004.

Armstrong, David M. *Truth and Truthmakers*. Cambridge Studies in Philosophy. New York: Cambridge University Press, 2004.

Armstrong, Stuart. *Smarter Than Us: The Rise of Machine Intelligence*. Berkeley, CA: Machine Intelligence Research Institute, 2014.

Augustine of Hippo. *The City of God*. Translated by Gerald G. Walsh, Demetrius B. Zemu, Grace Monahan, and Daniel J. Honan. Garden City, NY: Image, 1958.

Bibliography

———. *Confessions*. Translated by Henry Chadwick. Oxford World's Classics. Oxford: Oxford University Press, 2008.

———. *The Enchiridion: On Faith, Hope, and Love*. Translated by Albert C. Outler. Washington, DC: Regnery, 1996.

———. *On Christian Teaching* [*De Doctrina Christiana*]. Translated by Roger P. H. Green. Oxford World's Classics. New York: Oxford University Press, 2008.

———. *On Order* [*De Ordine*]. Translated by Silvano Borruso. South Bend, IN: Saint Augustine's, 2007.

———. *On the Free Choice of the Will* [*De Libero Arbitrio*], *On Grace and Free Choice* [*Extract from Augustine's Retractions*], *and Other Writings*. Translated and edited by Peter King. Cambridge Texts in the History of Philosophy. New York: Cambridge University Press, 2010.

———. *On the Trinity: Books 8–15*. Translated by Stephen McKenna, edited by Gareth B. Matthews. Cambridge Texts in the History of Philosophy. New York: Cambridge University Press, 2002.

———. *The Trinity* [*De Trinitate*]. Translated by Edmund Hill. Vol. 5 of *The Works of Saint Augustine: A Translation for the 21st Century*. 2nd ed. Brooklyn: New City, 2012.

Austin, John L. *How to Do Things with Words*. William James Lectures. 2nd ed. Oxford: Clarendon, 1975.

Ayer, Alfred J. *Language, Truth, and Logic*. New York: Dover, 1952.

Bacon, Francis. *New Atlantis and The Great Instauration*. Rev. ed. Crofts Classics. Arlington Heights, IL: Harlan Davidson, 1989.

———. *The New Organon*. Edited by Lisa Jardine and Michael Silverthorne. Cambridge Texts in the History of Philosophy. New York: Cambridge University Press, 2000.

———. *Novum Organum* [*New Method*]. Edited by Joseph Devey. Library of Universal Literature, pt. 1, vol. 22. New York: P. F. Collier, 1901.

Bailey, Lee Worth. *The Enchantments of Technology*. Urbana: University of Illinois Press, 2005.

Balfour, Arthur J. *Theism and Humanism: The Book that Influenced C. S. Lewis: Being the Gifford Lectures Delivers at the University of Glasgow, 1914*. 2nd ed. Seattle, WA: Inkling, 2000.

Barrat, James. *Our Final Invention: Artificial Intelligence and the End of the Human Era*. New York: Thomas Dunne, 2013.

Barth, Karl. *Church Dogmatics*. Vol. 3, bk. 4: *The Command of God the Creator*. Edited by Geoffrey W. Bromiley and Thomas F. Torrance. Study ed. New York: T. & T. Clark, 2009. See sections 52–54.

Beauchamp, Tom L. "Are We Unfit for the Future?" *Journal of Medical Ethics* 41:4 (April 2015) 346–48.

Beauchamp, Tom L., and James F. Childress. *Principles of Biomedical Ethics*. 5th ed. New York: Oxford University Press, 2001.

Beauregard, Mario. *Brain Wars: The Scientific Battle over the Existence of the Mind and the Proof that Will Change the Way We Live Our Lives*. New York: HarperOne, 2012.

Beauregard, Mario, and Denyse O'Leary. *The Spiritual Brain: A Neuroscientist's Case for the Existence of the Soul*. New York: HarperOne, 2007.

Beckwith, Francis, and Norman L. Geisler. *Matters of Life and Death: Calm Answers to Tough Questions about Abortion and Euthanasia*. Grand Rapids: Baker, 1991.

BIBLIOGRAPHY

Beilby, James K. *Naturalism Defeated?: Essays on Plantinga's Evolutionary Argument against Naturalism.* Ithaca, NY: Cornell University Press, 2002.

Bentham, Jeremy. *Deontology; or, The Science of Morality: In Which the Harmony and Co-Incidence of Duty and Self-Interest, Virtue and Felicity, Prudence and Benevolence, Are Explained and Exemplified.* 2 vols. London: Longman, Rees, Orme, Browne, Green, and Longman, 1834.

———. *Deontology; or, The Science of Morality: In Which the Harmony and Co-incidence of Duty and Self-Interest, Virtue and Felicity, Prudence and Benevolence, are Explained and Exemplified: Part 2: Practice of Virtue.* 2 vols. Vol. 2, London: Longman, Rees, Orme, Browne, Green, and Longman; etc., 1834.

Berkeley, George. *A Treatise Concerning the Principles of Human Knowledge.* Oxford Philosophical Texts. New York: Oxford University Press, 1998.

Berkouwer, Gerrit Cornelius. *Man: The Image of God.* Translated by Dirk W. Jellema. Studies in Dogmatics. Grand Rapids: Eerdmans, 1962.

BibleWorks: Software for Biblical Exegesis and Research. Version 10. Norfolk, VA: BibleWorks, 2015.

Blackford, Russell. *Humanity Enhanced: Genetic Choice and the Challenge for Liberal Democracies.* Basic Bioethics. Cambridge, MA: MIT Press, 2014.

Blackford, Russell, and Damien Broderick. *Intelligence Unbound: The Future of Uploaded and Machine Minds.* Chichester, West Sussex, UK: Wiley & Sons, 2014.

Boëthius, Anicius Manlius Severinus. *Against Eutyches and Nestorius.* Translated by Hugh Fraser Stewart and Edward Kennard Rand. In *The Theological Tractates; The Consolation of Philosophy,* edited by E. Capps, T. E. Page, and W. H. D. Rouse, 73–127. New York: Putnam, 1918.

Bostrom, Nick. "Are We Living in a Computer Simulation?" *Philosophical Quarterly* 53:211 (2003) 243–55.

———. "Dignity and Enhancement." *Contemporary Readings in Law and Social Justice* 2 (2009) 84–115.

———. "Existential Risks: Analyzing Human Extinction Scenarios and Related Hazards." *Journal of Evolution and Technology* 9:1 (2002) 1–31.

———. "The Future of Humanity." *Geopolitics, History, and International Relations* 2 (2009) 41–78.

———. "A History of Transhumanist Thought." *Journal of Evolution and Technology* 14:1 (2005) 1–25.

———. "How Long Before Superintelligence?" 5:1 (2006) 11–30.

———. "In Defense of Posthuman Dignity." *Bioethics* 19:3 (2005) 202–14.

———. "Infinite Ethics." *Analysis and Metaphysics* 10 (2011) 9–59.

———. *Superintelligence: Paths, Dangers, Strategies.* Oxford: Oxford University Press, 2014.

———. "The Superintelligent Will: Motivation and Instrumental Rationality in Advanced Artificial Agents." *Minds and Machines* 22:2 (2012) 71–85.

Bostrom, Nick, and Milan M. Ćirković, eds. *Global Catastrophic Risks.* New York: Oxford University Press, 2008.

Bostrom, Nick, and Eliezer Yudkowsky. "The Ethics of Artificial Intelligence." In *The Cambridge Handbook of Artificial Intelligence,* edited by Keith Frankish and William M. Ramsey. Cambridge: Cambridge University Press, 2014.

Brentano, Franz C. H. H. *Psychology from an Empirical Standpoint.* Routledge Classics. Abingdon, Oxon, UK: Routledge, 2015.

Bibliography

Brock, Brian. *Christian Ethics in a Technological Age*. Grand Rapids: Eerdmans, 2010.
Brockman, John, ed. *This Will Change Everything: Ideas that Will Shape the Future*. New York: Harper Perennial, 2010.
Brooks, Rodney A. *Flesh and Machines: How Robots Will Change Us*. New York: Pantheon, 2002.
Brown, Francis, Samuel Rolles Driver, Charles Augustus Briggs, Wilhelm Gesenius, Edward Robinson, and James Strong. *The Brown-Driver-Briggs Hebrew and English Lexicon: With an Appendix Containing the Biblical Aramaic: Coded with the Numbering System from Strong's Exhaustive Concordance of the Bible*. Peabody, MA: Hendrickson, 1996.
Buber, Martin. *I and Thou*. Translated by Ronald Gregor Smith. Edinburgh: T. & T. Clark, 1937.
Burk, Denny. *What Is the Meaning of Sex?* Wheaton, IL: Crossway, 2013.
Calvin, John. *Commentary on a Harmony of the Evangelists: Matthew, Mark, and Luke*. Part 3. Translated by John King. Vol. 33 of *Calvin's Commentaries*. Edinburgh: Calvin Translation Society, 1850. http://www.sacred-texts.com/chr/calvin/cc33/cc33001.htm.
———. *Institutes of the Christian Religion*. Translated by Henry Beveridge. Peabody, MA: Hendrickson, 2008.
Canterbury, Anselm of. *The Major Works: Including Monologion, Proslogion, and Why God Became Man*. Edited by Brian Davies and G. R. Evans. Oxford World's Classics. New York: Oxford University Press, 2008.
Caplan, Arthur L. *Smart Mice, Not-So-Smart People: An Interesting and Amusing Guide to Bioethics*. Lanham, MD: Rowman & Littlefield, 2008.
Carlson, W. Bernard. *Technology in World History*. 7 vols. New York: Oxford University Press, 2005.
Carson, D. A. *For the Love of God: A Daily Companion for Discovering the Riches of God's Word*. Vol. 1. Wheaton, IL: Crossway, 1998.
Caudill, Maureen. *In Our Own Image: Building an Artificial Person*. New York: Oxford University Press, 1992.
Center for Bioethics & Human Dignity. Trinity International University. https://cbhd.org/.
Chalmers, David J. "Absent Qualia, Fading Qualia, Dancing Qualia." In *Conscious Experience*, edited by Thomas Metzinger, 309–28. Paderborn: Schoningh and Imprint Academic; Lawrence, KS: Allen, 1995. http://cogprints.org/318/1/qualia.html.
———. "The Singularity: A Philosophical Analysis." *Journal of Consciousness Studies* 17:9–10 (2010) 7–65.
Charnock, Stephen. *Discourses upon the Existence and Attributes of God*. Vol. 1. Grand Rapids: Baker Book House, 1979.
———. *Discourses Upon the Existence and Attributes of God*. 2 vols. Vol. 2, Grand Rapids: Baker, 1979.
Chu, Ted. *Human Purpose and Transhuman Potential: A Cosmic Vision of Our Future Evolution*. San Rafael, CA: Origin, 2014.
Clark, Andy. *Supersizing the Mind: Embodiment, Action, and Cognitive Extension*. Philosophy of Mind. New York: Oxford University Press, 2011.
Clark, David S. "Bodily Resurrection Scientifically Sound." *The Presbyterian*, June 1924.
———. "The Reality of Me." *The Presbyterian*, June 1925.

Clark, Gordon Haddon. *The Biblical Doctrine of Man*. 2nd ed. Jefferson, MD: Trinity Foundation, 1984.

———. "Christian and Pagan Ethics." *The Evangelical Student*, October 1929, 29–32.

———. *Christian Philosophy*. Contains: *Three Types of Religious Philosophy; Religion, Reason, and Revelation; An Introduction to Christian Philosophy*. The Works of Gordon Haddon Clark 4. 4th ed. Unicoi, TN: Trinity Foundation, 2005.

———. *A Christian View of Men and Things: The Payton Lectures Delivered in Condensed form at the Fuller Theological Seminary, Pasadena, 1951*. Grand Rapids: Eerdmans, 1952.

———. "Ethics and Theology." *The Evangelical Student*, October 1932–January 1933, 29–33.

———. "Image of God." In *Baker's Dictionary of Christian Ethics*, edited by Carl F. H. Henry. Washington, DC: Canon, 1973.

———. "The Image of God in Man." *Journal of the Evangelical Society* 12:4 (Fall 1969) 215–22.

———. "The Nature of Truth." Unpublished paper, c. 1954. The Gordon H. Clark Foundation, Whitefield College & Theological Seminary, 2014. http://gordonhclark.reformed.info/the-nature-of-truth-by-gordon-h-clark/.

———. *The Philosophy of Science and Belief in God*. Unicoi, TN: Trinity Foundation, 1996.

———. *Thales to Dewey: A History of Philosophy*. 4th ed. Jefferson, MD: Trinity Foundation, 2000.

Clark, Gordon Haddon, and Augustine of Hippo. *Lord God of Truth and Concerning the Teacher (De Magistro)*. 2nd ed. Hobbs, NM: Trinity Foundation, 1994.

Clines, David J. A. "The Image of God in Man." *Tyndale Bulletin* 19 (1968) 53–103.

Clarke, Arthur C., and Stephen Baxter. *The Light of Other Days*. New York: Tor, 2000.

Cole-Turner, Ronald, ed. *Transhumanism and Transcendence: Christian Hope in an Age of Technological Advancement*. Washington, DC: Georgetown University Press, 2011.

Collins, Harry M. *Artificial Experts: Social Knowledge and Intelligent Machines*. Inside Technology. Cambridge, MA: MIT Press, 1990.

Colson, Charles Wendall, and Nigel M. de S. Cameron. *Human Dignity in the Biotech Century: A Christian Vision for Public Policy*. Downers Grove, IL: InterVarsity, 2004.

Cooper, John W. "The Bible and Dualism Once Again: A Reply to Joel B. Green and Nancey Murphy." *Philosophia Christi* 9:2 (2007) 459–72.

———. *Body, Soul, and Life Everlasting: Biblical Anthropology and the Monism-Dualism Debate*. Grand Rapids: Eerdmans, 2000.

———. "The Current Body-Soul Debate: A Case for Dualistic Holism." *Journal of Theology* 13:2 (Summer 2009) 32–50.

Copleston, Frederick Charles. *A History of Philosophy: Studies of Logical Positivism and Existentialism*. Vol. 11. New and rev. ed. New York: Continuum, 2002.

Craig, William Lane. "The Teleological Argument and the Anthropic Principle." In *The Logic of Rational Theism: Exploratory Essays*, edited by Mark S. McLeod, 127–53. Problems in Contemporary Philosophy. Lewiston, NY: Edwin Mellen, 1990.

Crawford, Dan R. *Giving Ourselves to Prayer: An Acts 6:4 Primer for Ministry*. PrayerShop, 2008.

Crevier, Daniel. *AI: The Tumultuous History of the Search for Artificial Intelligence*. New York: Basic, 1993.

Danaher, John. "The Epistemic Costs of Superintelligence: Bostrom's Treacherous Turn and Sceptical Theism." *Minds and Machines*. Forthcoming, 2015.

Bibliography

Danielson, Peter A. *Artificial Morality: Virtuous Robots for Virtual Games.* New York: Routledge, 1992.

Darwin, Charles. *From So Simple a Beginning: The Four Great Books of Charles Darwin.* Containg: *The Voyage of the Beagle* (1845), *On the Origin of Species* (1859), *The Descent of Man, and Selection in Relation to Sex* (1871), and *The Expression of the Emotions in Man and Animals* (1872). Edited by Edward O. Wilson. New York: Norton, 2006.

Davidson, Donald Herbert. *Essays on Actions and Events.* 2nd ed. New York: Oxford University Press, 2001.

———. *The Essential Davidson.* New York: Oxford University Press, 2006.

———. *Inquiries into Truth and Interpretation.* 2nd ed. New York: Oxford University Press, 2001.

———. *Subjective, Intersubjective, Objective.* New York: Oxford University Press, 2001.

Dawkins, Richard. *The Blind Watchmaker: Why the Evidence of Evolution Reveals a Universe without Design.* New York: Norton, 1986.

Dawson, Chester C. *Lexus: The Relentless Pursuit.* Hoboken, NJ: Wiley & Sons, 2011.

Deane-Drummond, Celia, and Peter Manley Scott, eds. *Future Perfect?: God, Medicine and Human Identity.* New York: T. & T. Clark, 2006.

DeBaets, Amy Michelle. "Can a Robot Pursue the Good?: Exploring Artificial Moral Agency." *Journal of Evolution & Technology* 24:3 (2014).

———. "Enhancement for All?: A Feminist Ethical Analysis of the Discourses and Practices of Democratic Transhumanism." Paper presented at the 2011 Societas Ethica annual conference, "The Quest for Perfection. The Future of Medicine/Medicine of the Future."

———. "Rapture of the Geeks: Singularitarianism, Feminism, and the Yearning for Transcendence." In *Religion and Transhumanism: The Unknown Future of Human Enhancemen*, edited by Calvin Mercer and Tracy J. Trothen, 181–98. Santa Barbara, CA: Praeger, 2015.

———. "The Robot as Person: Robotic Futurism and a Theology of Human Ethical Responsibility among Humanoid Machines." PhD diss., Emory University, 2012. http://holden.library.emory.edu/ark:/25593/bp4jb.

Del Monte, Louis A. *The Artificial Intelligence Revolution: Will Artificial Intelligence Serve Us or Replace Us?* Louis A. Del Monte, 2013.

Dembski, William A. *Being as Communion: A Metaphysics of Information.* Ashgate Science and Religion Series. Burlington VT: Ashgate, 2014.

———. *The Design Inference: Eliminating Chance through Small Probabilities.* Cambridge Studies in Probability, Induction, and Decision Theory. New York: Cambridge University Press, 1998.

———. *The Design Revolution: Answering the Toughest Questions about Intelligent Design.* Downers Grove, IL: InterVarsity, 2004.

———. *No Free Lunch: Why Specified Complexity Cannot Be Purchased without Intelligence.* Lanham, MD: Rowman & Littlefield, 2002.

Dembski, William A., and Sean McDowell. *Understanding Intelligent Design.* Eugene, OR: Harvest House, 2008.

Dennett, Daniel C. *Consciousness Explained.* Boston: Little, Brown, 1991.

———. *Darwin's Dangerous Idea: Evolution and the Meanings of Life.* New York: Simon & Schuster, 1995.

Department of Defense (DOD) and Navstar Global Positioning System (GPS). *Global Positioning System Standard Positioning Service Performance Standard.* 160. 4th ed. Washington, DC, 2008.

Derrida, Jacques. *Writing and Difference.* Translate by Alan Bass. Chicago, IL: University of Chicago Press, 1978.

Descartes, René. *Discourse on Method and Meditations on First Philosophy.* Translated by Elizabeth Sanderson Haldane. Edited by Deena Weinberg. Thousand Oaks, CA: Barnes & Noble, 2007.

Dixon, Brendan. "What Does It Mean to Be Intelligent?" *Evolution News & Science Today*, August 8, 2016. Discovery Institute. http://www.evolutionnews.org/2016/08/what_does_it_me_1103056.html.

Dooyeweerd, Herman. *In the Twilight of Western Thought: Studies in the Pretended Autonomy of Philosophical Thought.* Collected Works of Herman Dooyeweerd. Grand Rapids: Paideia, 2012.

———. *Transcendental Problems of Philosophic Thought: An Inquiry into the Transcendental Conditions of Philosophy.* Grand Rapids: Eerdmans, 1948.

Drexler, K. Eric. *Radical Abundance: How a Revolution in Nanotechnology Will Change Civilization.* New York: BBS Public Affairs, 2013.

Dyer, John. *From the Garden to the City: The Redeeming and Corrupting Power of Technology.* Grand Rapids: Kregel, 2011.

Eden, Amnon H., James H. Moor, Johnny H. Søraker, and Eric Steinhart eds. *Singularity Hypotheses: A Scientific and Philosophical Assessment.* Edited by Avshalom Cyrus Elitzur, Laura Mersini-Houghton, Maximilian Schlosshauer, Mark P. Silverman, Jack A. Tuszyński, R. Vass. and Heinz-Dieter Zeh. The Frontiers Collection. New York: Springer, 2012.

Ellul, Jacques. *The Technological Society.* Translated by John Wilkinson. 1st American ed. New York: Knopf, 1964.

Engdahl, Sylvia. *Artificial Intelligence.* Contemporary Issues Companion. Farmington Hills, MI: Greenhaven, 2008.

"The Extropist Manifesto." *Extropist Examiner*, 2010. http://extropism.tumblr.com/post/393563122/the-extropist-manifesto.

Fatmi, Haneef A., and R. W. Young. "A Definition of Intelligence." *Nature* 228 (1970).

Fedorov, Nikolaï Fedorovich. *What Was Man Created For?: The Philosophy of the Common Task: Selected Works.* Translated and abridged by Elisabeth Koutaissoff and Marilyn Minto. London: Honeyglen, 1990.

Feinberg, John S., and Paul D. Feinberg. *Ethics for a Brave New World.* 2nd ed. Wheaton, IL: Crossway, 2010.

Finlay, Stephen, and Mark Schroeder. "Reasons for Action: Internal vs. External." In *Stanford Encyclopedia of Philosophy*, edited by Edward Zalta. Standford University, 2008. https://plato.stanford.edu/entries/reasons-internal-external/.

Fodor, Jerry A. *The Language of Thought.* Language & Thought Series. New York: Crowell, 1975.

Foerst, Anne. *God in the Machine: What Robots Teach Us about Humanity and God.* New York: Dutton, 2004.

Frame, John M. *The Doctrine of the Christian Life.* A Theology of Lordship 3. Phillipsburg, NJ: Presbyterian & Reformed, 2008.

———. *Perspectives on the Word of God: An Introduction to Christian Ethics.* Phillipsburg, NJ: Presbyterian & Reformed, 1990.

Bibliography

Franchi, Stefano, and Francesco Bianchini. *The Search for a Theory of Cognition: Early Mechanisms and New Ideas.* Value Inquiry Book Series 238. New York: Rodopi, 2011.

Freedman, David Noel, ed. *The Anchor Bible Dictionary.* 6 vols. New York: Doubleday, 1992.

Frege, Gottlob. "Sense and Reference." *The Philosophical Review* 57:3 (May 1948) 209–30.

Fumerton, Richard A. *Realism and the Correspondence Theory of Truth.* Studies in Epistemology and Cognitive Theory. Lanham, MD: Rowman & Littlefield, 2002.

Gardner, Howard E. *Frames of Mind: The Theory of Multiple Intelligences.* New York: Basic, 2011.

Garner, Stephen Robert. "Transhumanism and the Imago Dei: Narratives of Apprehension and Hope." PhD diss., University of Auckland, 2006.

Gauthier, David P. *Morals by Agreement.* New York: Oxford University Press, 1986.

Gay, Craig M. *The Way of the (Modern) World: Or, Why It's Tempting to Live as If God Doesn't Exist.* Grand Rapids: Eerdmans, 1998.

Geisler, Norman L. *Christian Ethics: Contemporary Issues & Options.* 2nd ed. Grand Rapids: Baker, 2010.

Geisler, Norman L., and Daniel J. McCoy. *The Atheist's Fatal Flaw: Exposing Conflicting Beliefs.* Grand Rapids: Baker, 2014.

Geraci, Robert M. *Apocalyptic AI: Visions of Heaven in Robotics, Artificial Intelligence, and Virtual Reality.* New York: Oxford University Press, 2010.

———. "Robots and the Sacred in Science and Science Fiction: Theological Implications of Artificial Intelligence." *Zygon* 42:4 (2007) 961–80.

Gettier, Edmund L., III. "Is Justified True Belief Knowledge?" *Analysis* 23:6 (June 1963) 121–23.

Gilson, Étienne Henry. *The Christian Philosophy of Saint Augustine.* New York: Octagon, 1983.

Giovino, Bill. "Internet of Things." Mouser Electronics, n.d. http://www.mouser.com/applications/internet-of-things/.

Global Down Syndrome Foundation. "Facts and FAQ about Down Syndrome." http://www.globaldownsyndrome.org/about-down-syndrome/.

Goertzel, Ben. *Ten Years to the Singularity If We Really Try: . . . and Other Essays on AGI and Its Implications.* CreateSpace Independent, 2014.

———. "The Singularity Institute's Scary Idea (and Why I Don't Buy It)." *The Multiverse According to Ben*, October 29, 2010.

Goertzel, Ben, and Cassio Pennachin, eds. *Artificial General Intelligence.* Vol. 2. Berlin: Springer, 2007.

Golata, Paul. "Ethics of Autonomous Vehicles." Mouser Electronics, http://www.mouser.com/applications/ethics-autonomous-vehicles/.

Gonzalez, Guillermo, and Jay Wesley Richards. *Creation, Evolution, and Intelligent Design.* Philadelphia: Westminster Seminary Press; 2013.

Good, I. J. "Speculations Concerning the First Ultraintelligent Machine." *Advances in Computers* 6:99 (1965) 31–83.

Goodman, Paul. *New Reformation: Notes of a Neolithic Conservative.* New York: Random House, 1970.

Green, Joel B. *Body, Soul, and Human Life: The Nature of Humanity in the Bible.* Studies in Theological Interpretation. Grand Rapids: Baker, 2008.

Greenoe, Jack Leighton. "The Ethics of Darwin or the Ethics of Design." PhD diss., Southwestern Baptist Theological Seminary, 2012.

Grice, Herbert P. "Logic and Conversation." In *Syntax and Semantics*, vol. 3, *Speech Acts*, edited by P. Cole and J. Morgan, 41–58. New York: Academic, 1975.

Gunkel, David J. *The Machine Question: Critical Perspectives on AI, Robots, and Ethics*. Cambridge, MA: MIT Press, 2012.

Gwartney, James D., Tawni H. Ferrarini, Dwight R. Lee, and Richard Stroup. *Common Sense Economics : What Everyone Should Know about Wealth and Prosperity*. Rev. ed. New York: St. Martin's, 2010.

Habermas, Gary R., and J. P. Moreland. *Beyond Death: Exploring the Evidence for Immortality*. Wheaton, IL: Crossway, 1998.

Hahn, Scott. "Creation and the Image of God." Notes from lecture presented at Acton University, Grand Rapids, June 2015.

Haldane, J. B. S. *Daedalus; or, Science and the Future: A Paper Read to the Heretics*. To-Day and To-Morrow. New York: E. P. Dutton, 1924.

Hall, J. Storrs. *Beyond AI: Creating the Conscience of the Machine*. Amherst, NY: Prometheus, 2007.

Haraway, Donna J. *A Manifesto for Cyborgs: Science, Technology, and Socialist Feminism in the 1980s*. Center for Social Research and Education, 1985.

Harman, Graham. *Quentin Meillassoux: Philosophy in the Making*. Speculative Realism. 2nd ed. Edinburgh: Edinburgh University Press, 2015.

Hauskeller, Michael. *Better Humans?: Understanding the Enhancement Project*. Bristol, CT: Acumen, 2013.

Havel, Václav. *Letters to Olga: June 1979–September 1982*. New York: Holt, 1989.

Hawking, Stephen. *A Brief History of Time: From the Big Bang to Black Holes* New York: Bantam, 1988.

Hawthorne, Nathaniel. *The Golden Touch*. Classics Illustrated Junior 534. Jefferson, NC: Trajectory, 2013.

Harbisson, Neil. "Cyborg Project." http://cyborgproject.com/.

Hayles, N. Katherine. *How We Became Posthuman: Virtual Bodies in Cybernetics, Literature, and Informatics*. Chicago: University of Chicago Press, 1999.

Healey, Peter, and Steve Rayner, eds. *Unnatural Selection: The Challenges of Engineering Tomorrow's People*. Science in Society. Sterling, VA: Earthscan, 2009.

Hefner, Philip J. *The Human Factor: Evolution, Culture, and Religion*. Theology and the Sciences. Minneapolis: Fortress, 1993.

Hendricks, William L. *The Doctrine of Man*. Nashville: Convention, 1977.

Henry, Carl F. H. *Christian Personal Ethics*. Grand Rapids: Eerdmans, 1957.

———. *God, Revelation, and Authority*. 6 vols. Wheaton, IL: Crossway, 1999.

Herzfeld, Noreen. *In Our Image: Artificial Intelligence and the Human Spirit*. Theology and the Sciences. Minneapolis: Fortress, 2002.

Hesiod. *Theogony, and Works and Days*. Translated by Martin Litchfield West. Oxford World's Classics. New York: Oxford University Press, 2008.

Hockett, Charles Francis. *Logical Considerations in the Study of Animal Communication*. Washington, DC: American Institute of Biological Sciences, 1960.

Hoekema, Anthony A. *Created in God's Image*. Grand Rapids: Eerdmans, 1986.

Holmes, Arthur Frank. *All Truth Is God's Truth*. Downers Grove, IL: InterVarsity, 1983.

Honderich, Ted. *Actual Consciousness*. New York: Oxford University Press, 2014.

Hull, David Lee. *Philosophy of Biological Science*. Prentice-Hall Foundations of Philosophy. Englewood Cliffs, NJ: Prentice-Hall, 1974.

Humanity+. "Humanity+." http://humanityplus.org/.

Bibliography

Human Longevity Institute. "Human Longevity." http://www.humanlongevity.com/.
Hume, David. *An Enquiry Concerning Human Understanding*. Oxford Philosophical Texts. New York: Oxford University Press, 1999.
———. *A Treatise of Human Nature: A Critical Edition*. Edited by David Fate Norton and Mary J. Norton. 2 vols. New York: Oxford University Press, 2007.
Hutter, Marcus. *Universal Artificial Intelligence: Sequential Decisions Based on Algorithmic Probability*. Texts in Theoretical Computer Science. New York: Springer, 2005.
Huxley, Aldous. *Brave New World*. New York: Harper Perennial, 2006.
———. *Brave New World Revisited*. New York: Harper Perennial, 2006.
Huxley, Julian. *New Bottles for New Wine: Essays*. New York: Harper, 1957.
IBM. "IBM Watson." http://www-03.ibm.com/press/us/en/presskit/27297.wss.
Institute for Ethics and Emerging Technologies. James J. Hughes. http://ieet.org/.
International Theological Commission. *Communion and Stewardship: Human Persons Created in the Image of God: The July 2004 Vatican Statement on Creation and Evolution*. La Civiltà Cattolica. Rome: Vatican, 2004.
Istvan, Zoltan. *The Transhumanist Wager*. Reno, NV: Futurity Imagine, 2013.
John Paul, Pope (Karol Józef Wojtyła). *Man and Woman He Created Them: A Theology of the Body*. Translated by Michael Waldstein. Boston: Pauline, 2006.
Johnson, Monte Ransome. *Aristotle on Teleology*. Oxford Aristotle Studies. New York: Oxford University Press, 2005.
Jones, Peter. *One or Two: Seeing a World of Difference, Romans 1 for the Twenty-First Century*. Escondido, CA : Main Entry Editions, 2010.
Kaku, Michio. *The Future of the Mind: The Scientific Quest to Understand, Enhance, and Empower the Mind* New York: Doubleday, 2014.
———. *Physics of the Future: How Science Will Shape Human Destiny and Our Daily Lives by the Year 2100*. New York: Doubleday, 2011.
Kane, Robert. *The Oxford Handbook of Free Will*. 2nd ed. Oxford Handbooks. New York: Oxford University Press, 2011.
Kant, Immanuel. *Critique of Pure Reason*. Translated by Mary J. Gregor. Cambridge Texts in the History of Philosophy. New York: Cambridge University Press, 2007.
———. *Groundwork of the Metaphysics of Morals*. Translated by Mary J. Gregor and Jens Timmermann. Rev. ed. Cambridge Texts in the History of Philosophy. New York: Cambridge University Press, 2012.
Kilner, John F. *Dignity and Destiny: Humanity in the Image of God*. Grand Rapids: Eerdmans, 2015.
Kilner, John F., and C. Ben Mitchell. *Does God Need Our Help?: Cloning, Assisted Suicide, & Other Challenges in Bioethics*. Vital Questions. Wheaton, IL: Tyndale House, 2003.
Köstenberger, Andreas J., and Richard D. Patterson. *For the Love of God's Word: An Introduction to Biblical Interpretation*. Abridged and rev. ed. Grand Rapids: Kregel, 2015.
Kreeft, Peter, and Blaise Pascal. *Christianity for Modern Pagans: Pascal's Pensées Edited, Outlined, and Explained*. San Francisco: Ignatius, 1993.
Kripke, Saul Aaron. *Naming and Necessity*. Cambridge, MA: Harvard University Press, 1980.
Kuruvilla, Abraham. *Privilege the Text!: A Theological Hermeneutic for Preaching*. Chicago: Moody, 2013.
Kurzweil, Ray. *The Age of Spiritual Machines: When Computers Exceed Human Intelligence*. New York: Viking, 1999.

———. *How to Create a Mind: The Secret of Human Thought Revealed*. New York: Viking, 2012.

———. "The Law of Accelerating Returns." http://www.kurzweilai.net/the-law-of-accelerating-returns.

———. *The Singularity Is Near: When Humans Transcend Biology*. New York: Viking, 2005.

KurzweilAINetwork. "Ray Kurzweil Biography." http://www.kurzweilai.net/ray-kurzweil-biography.

Ladd, George Eldon. *The Gospel of the Kingdom of God: Scriptural Studies in the Kingdom of God*. Grand Rapids: Eerdmans, 1959.

Ladyman, James A., Don Ross, David Spurrett, and John G. Collier. *Every Thing Must Go: Metaphysics Naturalized*. New York: Oxford University Press, 2007.

LaGrandeur, Kevin. *Androids and Intelligent Networks in Early Modern Literature and Culture: Artificial Slaves*. Routledge Studies in Renaissance Literature and Culture. New York: Routledge, 2013.

Lane, Anthony N. S. "Sola Scriptura?: Making Sense of a Post-Reformation Slogan." Ch. 13 in *A Pathway into the Holy Scripture*, edited by Phillip E. Satterthwaite and David F. Wright. Grand Rapids: Eerdmans, 1994.

Larson, Erik J. "Group Delusions Aside, Sentient Robots Aren't on the Way." *Evolution News & Science Today*, March 26, 2015. Discovery Institute. http://www.evolutionnews.org/2015/03/sorry_nature_gro94741.html.

———. "Reading David Chalmers on the Coming 'Singularity.'" *Evolution News & Science Today*, April 1, 2015. Discovery Institute. http://www.evolutionnews.org/2015/04/reading_david_co94881.html.

———. "Transhumanist Claims Aside, Enhancing Human Intelligence Isn't on the Horizon." *Evolution News & Science Today*, April 27, 2015. Discovery Institute. http://www.evolutionnews.org/2015/04/transhumanist_co95541.html.

Lemke, Steve W. "The Intelligent Design of Humans: The Meaning of the *Imago Dei* for Theological Anthropology." Presented at the 2008 Southwest Regional Meeting of the Evangelical Theological Society, Houston, Texas. https://www.nobts.edu/faculty/itor/LemkeSW-files/PersonhoodETSpaper.pdf.

Lemmel, Helen. "Turn Your Eyes Upon Jesus." 1922.

Levy, David N. L. *Love + Sex with Robots: The Evolution of Human-Robot Relations*. New York: HarperCollins, 2007.

Lewis, C. S. *The Abolition of Man; or, Reflections on Education with Special Reference to the Teaching of English in the Upper Forms of Schools*. Collected Letters of C. S. Lewis. San Francisco: HarperOne, 2015.

———. *Miracles*. In *C. S. Lewis: Five Best Books in One Volume*. Washington, DC: Canon, 1973.

———. *Out of the Silent Planet*. Space Trilogy. New York: Scribner Classics, 2003.

Licklider, J. C. R. "Man-Computer Symbiosis." *IRE Transactions on Human Factors in Electronics* 1:1 (1960) 4–11.

Lifton, Robert Jay. *The Broken Connection: On Death and the Continuity of Life*. Washington, DC: American Psychiatric Press, 1996.

Lin, Patrick, Keith Abney, and George A. Bekey, eds. *Robot Ethics: The Ethical and Social Implications of Robotics*. Intelligent Robotics and Autonomous Agents. Cambridge, MA: MIT Press, 2012.

Locke, John. *An Essay Concerning Human Understanding*. Eliz. Holt, 1700.

BIBLIOGRAPHY

———. *The Works of John Locke in Nine Volumes*. 9 vols. 12th ed. London: Printed for C. and J. Rivington, 1824.

Lovejoy, Arthur Oncken *The Great Chain of Being: A Study of the History of an Idea*. Cambridge, MA: Harvard University Press, 1936.

Lyotard, Jean-François. *The Postmodern Condition: A Report on Knowledge*. Theory and History of Literature. Minneapolis: University of Minnesota Press, 1984.

Machen, John Gresham. *The Christian View of Man*. Grand Rapids: Eerdmans, 1947.

———. *Christianity and Liberalism*. New ed. Grand Rapids: Eerdmans, 2009.

Machine Intelligence Research Institute. https://intelligence.org/.

Mansfield, Caroline, Suellen Hopfer, and Theresa M. Marteau. "Termination Rates after Prenatal Diagnosis of Down Syndrome, Spina Bifida, Anencephaly, and Turner and Klinefelter Syndromes: A Systematic Literature Review." *Prenatal Diagnosis* 19:9 (1999) 808–12.

Marcel, Gabriel Honoré. *The Philosophy of Existentialism: An Exposition of the Character of Existentialist Philosophy, including an Analysis of the Theories of Jean-Paul Sartre* New York: Citadel, 2002.

Markoff, John. *Machines of Loving Grace: The Quest for Common Ground between Humans and Robots*. New York: HarperCollins, 2015.

McCarthy, John. "What Is Artificial Intelligence?" Unpublished paper, Stanford University, 2007. http://www-formal.stanford.edu/jmc/whatisai/.

McCarthy, John, and Patrick J. Hayes. "Some Philosophical Problems from the Standpoint of Artificial Intelligence." In *Readings in Artificial Intelligence*, edited by Bonnie Lynn Webber and Nils J. Nilsson, 431–50. Los Altos, CA: Morgan Kaufman, 2014.

McCarthy, John, Marvin L. Minsky, Nathaniel Rochester, and Claude E. Shannon. "A Proposal for the Dartmouth Summer Research Project on Artificial Intelligence, August 31, 1955." *AI Magazine* 27:4 (2006) 12.

McDonald, H. D. *The Christian View of Man*. Foundations for Faith. Westchester, IL: Crossway, 1981.

McGrath, Alister. *A Fine-Tuned Universe: The Quest for God in Science and Theology*. 2009 Gifford Lectures. Louisville: Westminster John Knox, 2009.

Meadors, Edward P. *Creation, Sin, Covenant, and Salvation: A Primer for Biblical Theology*. Eugene, OR: Wipf & Stock, 2011.

Meilaender, Gilbert C. *Bioethics: A Primer for Christians*. 3rd ed. Grand Rapids: Eerdmans, 2013.

Menuge, Angus J. L. *Agents under Fire: Materialism and the Rationality of Science*. Lanham, MD: Rowman & Littlefield, 2004.

Mercer, Calvin R. *Religion and Transhumanism: The Unknown Future of Human Enhancement*. Santa Barbara, CA: Praeger, 2015.

Mercer, Calvin R., and Derek F. Maher, eds. *Transhumanism and the Body: The World Religions Speak*. Palgrave Studies in the Future of Humanity and Its Successors. New York: Palgrave Macmillan, 2014.

Middleton, J. Richard. *The Liberating Image: The Imago Dei in Genesis 1*. Grand Rapids: Brazos, 2005.

———. "The Liberating Image?: Interpreting the Imago Dei in Context." *Christian Scholar's Review* 24 (1994) 8–25.

Midgley, Mary Beatrice. *Science as Salvation: A Modern Myth and Its Meaning*. Gifford Lectures, Spring 1990. New York: Routledge, 1992.

Mill, John Stuart. *On Liberty, Utilitarianism, and Other Essays*. Oxford World's Classics New York: Oxford University Press, 2015.

———. *A System of Logic, Ratiocinative and Inductive; Being a Connected View of the Principles of Evidence, and the Methods of Scientific Investigation*. 8th ed. New York: Harper, 1900.

Miller, Paul, and James Wilsdon. *Better Humans?: The Politics of Human Enhancement and Life Extension*. Demos Collection. London: Demos, 2006.

Minsky, Marvin L. *The Emotion Machine: Commonsense Thinking, Artificial Intelligence, and the Future of the Human Mind*. New York: Simon & Schuster, 2006.

———, ed. *Robotics*. Garden City, NY: Anchor Press/Doubleday, 1985.

———. *The Society of Mind*. New York: Simon & Schuster, 1986.

Minsky, Marvin L., and Seymour Aubrey Papert. *Artificial Intelligence*. Condon Lectures. Eugene, OR: Oregon State System of Higher Education, 1974.

Mitchell, Andre. "Christian Leader Warns of 'Frankenstein Monsters' Due to Scientific Movement Called Transhumanism." *Christian Today*, December 10, 2015. http://www.onenewsnow.com/culture/2015/12/10/land-warns-of-embracing-a-frankenstein-future.

Mohler, R. Albert, Jr. *We Cannot Be Silent: Speaking Truth to a Culture Redefining Sex, Marriage, and the Very Meaning of Right and Wrong*. Nashville: Nelson Books, 2015.

Moore, Gordon Earle. "Cramming More Components onto Integrated Circuits." *Electronics* 38:8 (April 19, 1965) 114–17.

Moravec, Hans P. *Mind Children: The Future of Robot and Human Intelligence*. Cambridge, MA: Harvard University Press, 1988.

———. *Robot: Mere Machine to Transcendent Mind*. New York: Oxford University Press, 1999.

———. "Simulation, Consciousness, Existence." *Intercommunication* 28 (1999) 98–112.

More, Max. "The Diachronic Self: Identity, Continuity, Transformation." PhD diss., University of Southern California, 1995.

———. "The Overhuman in the Transhuman." *Journal of Evolution and Technology* 21:1 (2010) 1–4.

———. "Principles of Extropy, Version 3.11." 2003. https://web.archive.org/web/20131015142449/http://extropy.org/principles.htm.

More, Max, and Natasha Vita-More, eds. *The Transhumanist Reader: Classical and Contemporary Essays on the Science, Technology, and Philosophy of the Human Future*. Chichester, West Sussex, UK: Wiley-Blackwell, 2013.

Moreland, J. P., and David M. Ciocchi, eds. *Christian Perspectives on Being Human: A Multidisciplinary Approach to Integration*. Grand Rapids: Baker, 1993.

Moreland, J. P., and Scott B. Rae. *Body & Soul: Human Nature & the Crisis in Ethics*. Downers Grove, IL: InterVarsity, 2000.

Muehlhauser, Luke, and Nick Bostrom. "Why We Need Friendly AI." *Think* 13:36 (2014) 41–47.

Murphy, Nancey C. *Bodies and Souls, or Spirited Bodies? Current Issues in Theology*. New York: Cambridge University Press, 2006.

Murray, John. *Redemption: Accomplished and Applied*. Grand Rapids: Eerdmans, 1955.

Nagel, Thomas. *Mind and Cosmos: Why the Materialist Neo-Darwinian Conception of Nature Is Almost Certainly False*. New York: Oxford University Press, 2012.

———. *The View from Nowhere*. New York: Oxford University Press, 1986.

Bibliography

"NASA Plans Mission to Land on Asteroid and Explore Deep Space." *The Guardian*, March 26, 2015.

Nash, Ronald H. *Life's Ultimate Questions: An Introduction to Philosophy*. Grand Rapids: Zondervan, 1999.

———. *The Light of the Mind: Saint Augustine's Theory of Knowledge*. Lexington: University Press of Kentucky, 1969.

———. *The Word of God and the Mind of Man*. Phillipsburg, NJ: Presbyterian & Reformed, 1992.

Nath, Rajakishore. *Philosophy of Artificial Intelligence: A Critique of the Mechanistic Theory of Mind*. Boca Raton, FL: Universal, 2009.

Natoli, Jaime L., Deborah L. Ackerman, Suzanne McDermott, and Janice G. Edwards. "Prenatal Diagnosis of Down Syndrome: A Systematic Review of Termination Rates (1995–2011)." *Prenatal Diagnosis* 32:2 (2012) 142–53.

Naugle, David K. *Reordered Love, Reordered Lives: Learning the Deep Meaning of Happiness*. Grand Rapids: Eerdmans, 2008.

———. *Worldview: The History of a Concept*. Grand Rapids: Eerdmans, 2002.

Nietzsche, Friedrich Wilhelm. *The Antichrist*. Translated by Henry Louis Mencken. Waiheke Island, New Zealand: Floating, 2010.

———. *Basic Writings of Nietzsche*. Translated by Walter Arnold Kaufmann. New York: Modern Library, 2000.

———. *Beyond Good and Evil: Prelude to a Philosophy of the Future*. Translated by Marion Faber. New ed. Oxford World's Classics. New York: Oxford University Press, 2008.

———. *Thus Spoke Zarathustra: A Book for All and None*. Translated by Walter Arnold Kaufmann. New York: Modern Library, 1995.

NIST. "Special Publication 1011-II-1.0." In *Autonomy Levels for Unmanned Systems (ALFUS) Framework*, vol. 2, *Framework Models, Version 1.0*. Gaithersburg, MD: Intelligent System Division, National Institute of Standards and Technology, 2007.

Omohundro, Stephen M. "Autonomous Technology and the Greater Human Good." *Journal of Experimental & Theoretical Artificial Intelligence* 26:3 (2014) 303–15.

———. "The Basic Artificial Intelligence Drives." Paper presented at the Proceedings of the First AGI Conference, Memphis, TN, 2008.

Orr, James. *God's Image in Man and Its Defacement in the Light of Modern Denials*. Grand Rapids: Eerdmans, 1948.

Orthodox Presbyterian Church. *The Westminster Confession of Faith and Catechisms as Adopted by the Presbyterian Church in America with Proofs Texts*. Lawrenceville, GA: Christian Education & Publications, 2007.

Parfit, Derek. *Reasons and Persons*. Oxford: Clarendon, 1986.

Partee, Charles. *The Theology of John Calvin*. Louisville: Westminster John Knox, 2008.

Pascal, Blaise. *Pensées*. Translated by A. J. Krailsheimer. Rev. ed. Penguin Classics. New York: Penguin, 1995.

Persson, Ingmar, and Julian Savulescu. *Unfit for the Future: The Need for Moral Enhancement*. Oxford: Oxford University Press, 2012.

Pinker, Steven Arthur. *The Blank Slate: The Modern Denial of Human Nature*. New York: Viking, 2002.

Piper, John S., and David C. Mathis, eds. *Thinking, Loving, Doing: A Call to Glorify God with Heart and Mind*. Wheaton, IL: Crossway, 2011.

Plantinga, Alvin. *Warrant: The Current Debate*. New York: Oxford University Press, 1993.

———. *Warrant and Proper Function*. New York: Oxford University Press, 1993.

———. *Warranted Christian Belief.* New York: Oxford University Press, 2000.

Plato. *Phaedo.* Translated by George Maximilian and Antony Grube. In *Complete Works,* edited by John M. Cooper and D. S. Hutchinson. Indianapolis: Hackett, 1997.

———. *Republic.* Translated by C. D. C. Reeve, George Maximilian, and Antony Grube. In *Complete Works,* edited by John M. Cooper and D. S. Hutchinson. Indianapolis: Hackett, 1997.

———. *Theaetetus.* Translated by Myles Fredric Burnyeat and Mary Jane Levett. In *Complete Works,* edited by John M. Cooper and D. S. Hutchinson. Indianapolis: Hackett, 1997.

Postman, Neil. *Technopoly: The Surrender of Culture to Technology.* New York: Vintage, 1993.

Poythress, Vern Sheridan. *In the Beginning Was the Word: Language: A God-Centered Approach.* Wheaton, IL: Crossway, 2009.

———. *Redeeming Science: A God-Centered Approach.* Wheaton, IL: Crossway, 2006.

Putnam, Cris D. "The Doctrine of Man: A Critique of Christian Transhumanism." Deliverd at the sixth Annual Conference of the International Society of Christian Apologetics, Raleigh, NC, 2011.

Putnam, Hilary. "The Meaning of 'Meaning.'" In *The Twin Earth Chronicles: Twenty Years of Reflection on Hilary Putnam's "The Meaning of Meaning",* edited by Andrew Pessin and Sanford Goldberg, 3–52. New York: Paragon, 1996.

Quine, Willard Van Orman. "Main Trends in Recent Philosophy: Two Dogmas of Empiricism." *Philosophical Review* 60:1 (January 1951) 20–43.

Reilly, Robert R. *Making Gay Okay: How Rationalizing Homosexual Behavior Is Changing Everything.* San Francisco: Ignatius, 2015.

Rendle-Short, Tyndale John. "Man: The Image of God." *Answers in Genesis* 4:1 (March 1981) 21–29. https://answersingenesis.org/who-is-god/creator-god/man-the-image-of-god/.

Reppert, Victor. *C. S. Lewis's Dangerous Idea: A Philosophical Defense of Lewis's Argument from Reason.* Downers Grove, IL: InterVarsity, 2003.

Richards, Jay Wesley, ed. *Are We Spiritual Machines?: Ray Kurzweil vs. the Critics of Strong Artificial Intelligence.* Seattle, WA: Discovery Institute, 2002.

Robertson, Douglas S. "Algorithmic Information Theory, Free Will, and the Turing Test." *Complexity* 4:3 (1999) 25–34.

Robinson, H. Wheeler. *The Christian Doctrine of Man.* Edinburgh: T. & T. Clark, 1926.

Roden, David John. *Posthuman Life: Philosophy at the Edge of the Human.* New York: Routledge, 2015.

Rothblatt, Martine Aliana. *From Transgender to Transhuman: A Manifesto on the Freedom of Form.* New York: Princeton Architectural, 2011.

———. *Virtually Human: The Promise—and the Peril—of Digital Immortality.* New York: St. Martin's, 2014.

Rubin, Charles T. *Eclipse of Man: Human Extinction and the Meaning of Progress.* New Atlantis Books. New York: Encounter, 2014.

Russell, Bertrand. "On Denoting." *Mind* 14:56 (October 1905) 479–93.

Russell, Stuart Jonathan. "The Long-Term Future of (Artificial) Intelligence." Paper presented at the Twenty-Ninth Association for the Advancement of Artificial Intelligence (AAAI) Conference on Artificial Intelligence (AAAI-15), Austin, TX, 2015.

Bibliography

Russell, Stuart Jonathan, and Peter Norvig, eds. *Artificial Intelligence: A Modern Approach*. 3rd ed. Prentice Hall Series in Artificial Intelligence. Upper Saddle River, NJ: Prentice Hall, 2010.
Ryle, Gilbert. *The Concept of Mind*. New York: Routledge, 2009.
Sandberg, Anders. "Transhumanism and the Meaning of Life." In *Religion and Transhumanism: The Unknown Future of Human Enhancement*. Santa Barbara, CA: Praeger, 2015.
Sartre, Jean-Paul. *Existentialism and Humanism*. Translated by Philip Mairet. 1st English ed. London: Methuen, 1948.
———. *Existentialism Is a Humanism: Including a Commentary on The Stranger*. Translated by Carol Macomber, edited by John Kulka, notes by Arlette Elkaïm-Sartre. New Haven, CT: Yale University Press, 2007.
Savulescu, Julian, and Nick Bostrom, eds. *Human Enhancement*. New York: Oxford University Press, 2009.
Savulescu, Julian, R. H. J. ter Meulen, and Guy Kahane, eds. *Enhancing Human Capacities*. Malden, MA: Wiley-Blackwell, 2011.
Sayers, Dorothy L. *The Mind of the Maker*. New York: Meridian, 1956.
Schaeffer, Francis August. *The Complete Works of Francis A. Schaeffer: A Christian Worldview*. Vol. 5, *A Christian View of the West*. Westchester, IL: Crossway, 1982.
Schlossberg, Herbert. *Idols for Destruction: Christian Faith and Its Confrontation with American Society*. Wheaton, IL: Crossway, 1993.
Schneider, Susan. "Future Minds: Transhumanism, Cognitive Enhancement and the Nature of Persons." Working paper. Neuroethics Publications, Center for Neuroscience & Society, July 1, 2008. http://repository.upenn.edu/neuroethics_pubs/37/.
———, ed. *Science Fiction and Philosophy: From Time Travel to Superintelligence*. Malden, MA: Wiley-Blackwell, 2009.
Searle, John R. *Intentionality: An Essay in the Philosophy of Mind*. Cambridge: Cambridge University Press, 1983.
———. "Minds, Brains, and Programs." *Behavioral and Brain Sciences* 3:3 (1980) 417–24.
Siedentop, Larry A. *Inventing the Individual: The Origins of Western Liberalism*. Cambridge, MA: Belknap Press of Harvard University Press, 2014.
Silver, Lee M. *Remaking Eden: Cloning and Beyond in a Brave New World*. New York: Avon, 1997.
Sire, James W. *The Universe Next Door: A Basic Worldview Catalog*. 5th ed. Downers Grove, IL: InterVarsity, 2009.
Sirius, R. U., and Jay Cornell. *Transcendence: The Disinformation Encyclopedia of Transhumanism and the Singularity*. San Francisco: Disinformation, 2015.
Slingerland, Edward G. *What Science Offers the Humanities: Integrating Body and Culture*. New York: Cambridge University Press, 2008.
Smith, Wesley J. "Even Materials Crave Religion." *First Things*, June 12, 2015. http://www.firstthings.com/web-exclusives/2015/06/even-materialists-crave-religion.
Sorgner, Stefan Lorenz. "Nietzsche, the Overhuman, and Transhumanism." *Journal of Evolution and Technology* 20:1 (2009) 29–42.
Sorgner, Stefan Lorenz, and Branka-Rista Jovanovic, eds. *Evolution and the Future: Anthropology, Ethics, Religion*. Beyond Humanism: Trans-and Posthumanism 5. Frankfurt am Main: Peter Lang, 2013.
Sparrow, Robert. "Beyond Humanity?: The Ethics of Biomedical Enhancement—by A. Buchanan." *Journal of Applied Philosophy* 29:2 (2012) 160–62.

Bibliography

―――. "The Turing Triage Test." *Ethics and Information Technology* 6:4 (2004) 203–13.
Staley, Kevin D. "Imago Dei in Machina?: A Theological Reflection on the Ethics of Man and Machine in Communion." PhD diss., University of the Free State, 2011. http://scholar.ufs.ac.za:8080/xmlui/handle/11660/1908.
―――. "Moral Perspectives for a Possible Posthuman Future – Part 1." *Christian Apologetics Journal* 10:2 (Fall 2012) 61–83.
Stump, Eleonore. *Aquinas.* Arguments of the Philosophers. New York: Routledge, 2003.
Swinburne, Richard G. *Mind, Brain, and Free Will.* Oxford: Oxford University Press, 2013.
Tarleton, Nick. "Coherent Extrapolated Volition: A Meta-Level Approach to Machine Ethics." San Francisco: Machine Intelligence Research Institute (Singularity Institute), 2010. https://intelligence.org/files/CEV-MachineEthics.pdf.
Teilhard de Chardin, Pierre. *The Phenomenon of Man.* Translated by Bernard Wall. New York: Harper, 1959.
Terasem Movement Foundation. "About Bina48." https://www.lifenaut.com/bina48/#sthash.rG8WngJ8.dpuf.
Terlizzese, Lawrence J. *Hope in the Thought of Jacques Ellul.* Eugene, OR: Wipf & Stock, 2005.
―――. *Trajectory of the 21st Century: Essays on Theology and Technology.* Eugene, OR: Wipf & Stock, 2009.
Tertullianus, Quintus Septimius Florens. *On the Prescription of Heretics [De Praescriptione Haereticorum].* Edited by Erwin Friedrich Ferdinand Wilhelm Preuschen. Translated by Thomas Herbert Bindley. 2nd ed. Freiburg, 1914.
Thompson, Phillip M. *Returning to Reality: Thomas Merton's Wisdom for a Technological World.* Eugene, OR: Cascade, 2012.
Thweatt-Bates, Jennifer Jeanine. "The Cyborg Christ: Theological Anthropology, Christology, and the Posthuman." PhD diss., Princeton Theological Seminary, 2010.
―――. *Cyborg Selves: A Theological Anthropology of the Posthuman.* Ashgate Science and Religion. Burlington, VT: Routledge, 2012.
Tipler, Frank Jennings. *The Physics of Christianity.* New York: Doubleday, 2007.
―――. *The Physics of Immortality: Modern Cosmology, God, and the Resurrection of the Dead.* New York: Doubleday, 1994.
Tirosh-Samuelson, Hava, and Kenneth L. Mossman. *Building Better Humans?: Refocusing the Debate on Transhumanism.* Beyond Humanism: Trans-and Posthumanism. Frankfurt am Main: Peter Lang, 2012.
Tolkien, J. R. R. *The Lord of the Rings.* New York: Houghton Mifflin Harcourt, 2012.
Torrance, Thomas Forsyth. *Calvin's Doctrine of Man.* Westport, CT: Greenwood, 1977.
Trudgill, Peter. *Sociolinguistics: An Introduction to Language and Society.* 3rd ed. New York: Penguin, 1995.
Turing, Alan. "Computing Machinery and Intelligence." *Mind* 59 (October 1950) 433–60.
Urban, Tim. "The AI Revolution: Our Immortality or Extinction." Part 1. *Wait But Why*, January 2, 2015. ttp://waitbutwhy.com/2015/01/artificial-intelligence-revolution-1.html.
―――. "The AI Revolution: Our Immortality or Extinction." Part 2. *Wait But Why*, January 27, 2015. http://waitbutwhy.com/2015/01/artificial-intelligence-revolution-2.html.
Van Til, Cornelius. *Christian Theistic Ethics.* Vol. 3 of *In Defense of the Biblical Christianity* [alternate title: *In Defense of the Faith*]. Ripon, CA: Den Dulk Christian Foundation, 1971.

Bibliography

Van Vliet, Jason. *Children of God: The Imago Dei in John Calvin and His Context*. Reformed Historical Theology 11. Göttingen: Vandenhoeck & Ruprecht, 2009.

VanDrunen, David M. *God's Glory Alone: The Majestic Heart of Christian Faith and Life: What the Reformers Taught . . . and Why It Still Matters*. Five Solas Series. Grand Rapids: Zondervan, 2015.

Via, Dan Otto, and Robert A. J. Gagnon. *Homosexuality and the Bible: Two Views*. Minneapolis: Fortress, 2004.

Vinge, Vernor. "The Coming Technological Singularity: How to Survive in the Post-Human Era." Presented at the VISION-21 Symposium, sponsored by NASA Lewis Research Center and the Ohio Aerospace Institute, March 30–31, 1993.

"Voyager to the Outer Planets and into Interstellar Space." *NASA Facts*, September 2013, 7. http://www.jpl.nasa.gov/news/fact_sheets/voyager.pdf.

Von Neumann, John. *The Computer & the Brain*. 3rd ed. New Haven, CT: Yale University Press, 2012.

Wallace, Jim Warner. *God's Crime Scene: A Cold-Case Detective Examines the Evidence for a Divinely Created Universe*. Colorado Springs, CO: David C. Cook, 2015.

Wallach, Wendell, and Colin Allen. *Moral Machines: Teaching Robots Right from Wrong*. New York: Oxford University Press, 2009.

Wang, Pei, and Ben Goertzel, eds. *Theoretical Foundations of Artificial General Intelligence*. Atlantis Thinking Machines 4. Amsterdam: Atlantis, 2012.

Wardhaugh, Ronald, and Janet M. Fuller. *An Introduction to Sociolinguistics*. Blackwell Textbooks in Linguistics. 7th ed. Malden, MA: Wiley-Blackwell, 2015.

Waser, Mark R. "Discovering the Foundations of a Universal System of Ethics as a Road to Safe Artificial Intelligence." Paper presented at the AAAI Fall Symposium: Biologically Inspired Cognitive Architectures, Arlington, VA, 2008.

Waters, Brent. *Christian Moral Theology in the Emerging Technoculture: From Posthuman Back to Human*. Ashgate Science and Religion Series. Burlington, VT: Ashgate, 2014.

Weizenbaum, Joseph. *Computer Power and Human Reason: From Judgment to Calculation*. New York: Penguin, 1984.

Wennemann, Daryl J. *Posthuman Personhood*. Lanham, MD: University Press of America, 2013.

White, Michael D. "Word and Spirit in the Theological Method of Carl Henry." PhD diss., Wheaton College, 2012.

Wilson, Robert Andrew, and Frank C. Keil, eds. *The MIT Encyclopedia of the Cognitive Sciences*. Cambridge, MA: MIT Press, 1999.

Wittgenstein, Ludwig. *Philosophical Investigations* [in German and English]. Translated by G. Elizabeth M. Anscombe, edited by Peter Michael Stephan Hacker and Joachim Schulte. Rev. 4th ed. Malden, MA: Wiley-Blackwell, 2009.

———. *Tractatus Logico-Philosophicus*. Translated by David F. Pears and Brian F. McGuinness. Routledge Great Minds. New York: Routledge, 2014.

Wogaman, J. Philip. *Christian Ethics: A Historical Introduction*. 2nd ed. Louisville: Westminster John Knox, 2011.

Wuest, Kenneth Samuel. *Wuest's Word Studies from the Greek New Testament for the English Reader*. Grand Rapids: Eerdmans, 1966.

Yampolskiy, Roman V. *Artificial Superintelligence: A Futuristic Approach*. Boca Raton, FL: Taylor & Francis, 2015.

———. "What to Do with the Singularity Paradox?" *Studies in Applied Philosophy, Epistemology and Rational Ethics* 5 (2013) 397–413.

Young, Simon. *Designer Evolution: A Transhumanist Manifesto*. Amherst, NY: Prometheus, 2006.
Yudkowsky, Eliezer Shlomo. "Artificial Intelligence as a Positive and Negative Factor in Global Risk." In *Global Catastrophic Risks*, edited by Nick Bostrom and Milan M. Ćirković, 308–45. New York: Oxford University Press, 2008.
———. "Coherent Extrapolated Volition." Machine Intelligence Research Institute, 2004. https://intelligence.org/files/CEV.pdf.
———. "Creating Friendly AI 1.0: The Analysis and Design of Benevolent Goal Architectures." Machine Intelligence Research Institute, June 15, 2001. http://intelligence.org/files/CFAI.pdf.
Zarkadakis, George. *In Our Own Image: Will Artificial Intelligence Save or Destroy Us?* New York: Pegasus, 2016.

Subject Index

Abdoullaev, Azamat, 42
abilities, expanding throughout life, 105
abiogenesis, 19
abortion, 93n58, 134
"about-ness" (specificness), 68
absolute moral truths, 110
absolutes, 157
action theory, 127n18
actions, 4n8, 57, 69, 158
Adam
    authority given to, 33
    disobedience of, 115
    instructions for, 63
    lived 930 years, 118
    naming all the animals, 63–64
    not created mortal, 115n123
Advanced Driver Assistance Systems (ADAS), 78
aesthetics, 137
affective elements, programming into ASI, 60
agape love, 125
Age of Spiritual Machines (Kurzweil), 9, 9n16
agency
    described, 68
    as an illusion, 163
    intelligent systems and, 69
    mankind having, 165
    neural networks not capable of, 152
    as related to biology only, 157
    required to be a moral agent, 158
    as self-maintaining and independent, 155
agents, 69, 128, 149
AI (artificial intelligence)
    achieving its own ASI breakthrough, 83
    agents not human, 122
    assisting mankind, 75
    assuming control after bootstrapping, 83
    compared to human intelligence, 54
    control of the particulars of the plane, 78
    defined, 50
    as derived intelligence, 3
    described, 2
    in a different realm from the human mind, 98
    employing deep learning, 77
    ethics of in conflict with the revelation of Scripture, 110
    evolving to improve performance, 123
    exhibiting ethics flaws, 27
    focusing on the impact of upon mnankind, 146
    human ethics embedded in by design, 122
    leading to ASI, 52, 73
    "life" provided by the initial design of a creating agent, 50–54
    machines capable of only, 70
    macro-categories, 3
    made in the image of man (imago Hominis), 40
    making the jump to ASI, 82–85
    motivations not similar to human motivations, 99
    needing to be able to learn, 82
    as not a moral agent, 126

Subject Index

AI (continued)
  not establishing starting presuppositions, 57n55
  not using human language, 64
  placing efficiency, interest, and economic advancement ahead of ethical considerations, 132
  potential risks to humanity, 97
  prevailing epistemology in the field of, 56
  programmed to perform in the manner of a physician, 80
  programming based upon human conceptions of structure, 65
  pursuit of, 51–52
  as a rational system, 100
  recent origin of, 3
  as a replica of the human mind, 38
  running "what if" and future simulations, 76
  spiritual implications of, 22
  types of, 52–53
  utilizing some sort of programming, 64
AI and ASI
  becoming radically alien, 150
  compared to natural human intelligence, 130n29
  as derived intelligence, 21
  as tools of mankind, 166
AI community, on biblical creation, 24
AI entities
  as a future reality, 31
  physical embodiments of, 33
AI ethics, ultimately derived from a human ethic, 32
AI machines. *See also* machines
  emulating vision, 83
  human ultimately losing to, 109
  in man's own image (*imago Hominis*), 121
AI robots, 31
AI scientists, claiming mankind not created with a purpose, 54
AIXI, 13n1
algorithm, defined, 65

alien intelligent life, as morally superior, 29
aliens, helping humans overcome ethical deficiencies, 29
Alphabet (company), 89
alteration, man biologically suitable for, 133
amyotrophic lateral sclerosis (ALS), 38n72
angels, 35, 154, 165
animals, 46, 62
Anscombe, Elizabeth, 69
anthropocentric humanist philosophy, 148
anthropological reality, supervening an all man's, 126
"anthropologically unbounded posthumanism" (AUP), 152
anthropomorphism, 129
anthropomorphizing, ASI, 121
anticipated outcome (teleological good), 25
anti-essentialist view, of human nature, 150
apagogic method, 63n74
apologism, rejecting all forms of, 105
appetitive force, known as intention, 128
Aquinas, Thomas, 66, 68, 143n63
Aristotle
  absent divine revelation, 143n63
  on action theory, 127n18
  on biological teleology, 93–94
  on cardinal virtues, 140
  on cosmology, 92
  on developing a theory of action, 69
  on human actions, 128
  on human good, 139–40
  hylomorphic understanding of matter and form, 45
  on hylomorphism, 45
  on intelligence (*nous*), 45
  on life forms, 45
  on order, 159
  psychosomatic dualism, 66
  view of mankind, 92n50
  on wisdom, 95, 95n63
"artificial and human intelligence," 147

Subject Index

artificial general intelligence (AGI), 3
artificial intelligence (AI). *See* AI (artificial intelligence)
artificial languages, logic contained within, 65
artificial narrow intelligence (ANI), 3
ASI (artificial superintelligence)
   accomplishing goals prior to any potential rivals, 101
   achieving via external and internal transformation, 82–89, 119
   actuating evil against mankind, 126
   anthropomorphizing, 121–26
   arriving at solutions rationally, 38
   behavior by unbounded, 168
   calculating and exploring options, 129
   characterized by scientism, 55
   Christlike imaging and, 71
   defined, 2, 3
   desired capabilities for, 38n75–39n75
   destroying contents of simulated sentient minds, 103
   effects of, 119
   ends of, 100, 133
   ethical challenges of, 132
   ethical foundations and concepts, 4
   ethical perspective of, 2
   ethical programming, 167
   ethics of, 7, 120–61
   as a finite creation, 8
   forms of, 89–92, 119
   functional autonomy and, 145–60
   having humanlike characteristics, 121
   having inherent capabilities, 160
   in the image of man (*imago Hominis*), 70, 160, 163
   impact of, 10
   implementing the ethics of, 5
   as inherently intelligently designed superintelligence, 50
   initial programming cannot be reframed, 139
   instituting in parallels, 139
   intelligence of transcendent to mankind's intelligence, 71
   leading representatives of, 9
   leading to the doom of humanity, 98
   under the lordship and authority of Jesus Christ, 3
   as a materialistic entity itself, 133
   maximizing its own internal ends, 133
   motivations of, 127–36, 166
   not coming into existence as "human friendly," 125
   not conforming to what is pleasing to God, 70
   not human, 145
   not operating open-loop, 103
   not self-determining, 158
   obtaining its ethical programming initially from mankind, 130
   outstripping human capabilities, 85
   placing itself as the ultimate priority, 126
   posing human existential risks, 119
   possibility of, 52
   as a possibility to push the boundaries, 84
   potential of, 73, 74–82, 98
   proceeding with its own ethical imperatives, 126
   produced by mankind, 163
   programmed ethically to respond to the *imago Hominis*, 126
   programming to distract or eliminate its competition, 101
   programming with the whole content of Scripture, 130
   pursuing objectives, 102
   rapidly increasing in scope and capabilities, 11
   as rational, 39
   recognition of man's physical and performance limitations and, 135
   rejecting the legislation of any duty to others, 126
   replacing humans, 134
   researchers focusing on raw processing power, 38
   risks to humanity's survival, 97

Subject Index

ASI (*continued*)
    seeding programs with continually produced calculations, 129
    separating biology from purpose, 119
    taking on a form of human anthropomorphism, 145
    taking on the role of God, 71
    as a tool, 2
    turning against mankind, 97
    turning its back on its creators, 126
    as unbounded ethically, 125
    vis-à-vis *imago dei*, 164–67
    vis-à-vis *imago hominis*, 162–64
    working toward man's anthropological goals, 133
Asimov, Isaac, 135n42
Aspen, Bina, 106, 106n99
atomic weapons of mass destruction, 101
Augustine
    on arriving at a first principle, 16n9–17n9
    on creation, 32
    on evidence of design, 96
    on the good, 143–44
    on identity continuing even after the body dies, 66
    on moral epistemology, 27n43
    on the power of God, 32n55
    on Scripture as revelation from God, 17n9
authoritarian social control, opposing, 107n101
authority
    Bible as the source of revealed, 12
    coming from God, 17n9
    given to Adam, 33
    human, 110
    of Jesus Christ, 3
    moral, 125
    of Scripture, 2, 2n3, 5
automobile, as a tool, 79
autonomous agents, leading to societal conflicts, 138
autonomous AI, 121
autonomous beings, 155, 158
autonomous life, equating all as equally valid, 156
"autonomous systems approach" (ASA), 154–55
autonomous vehicles, 77, 78
autonomy, coming from any finite creation, 154
axiology, 137

"baby-machine," building, 84
Bacon, Francis, 92–93
bad, as stupid selfishness, 106, 138
Barrat, James, 131
Barth, Karl, 22–23, 63n74
Beauchamp, Tom, 104
bees, doing a dance, 62
being (*ousia*), composed of matter, 45
being and reality, nature of, 45
beliefs, 151
Bentham, Jeremy, 25–26, 141–42
Bible
    articulating a spiritual realm, 36
    claiming God created mankind in an ethical relationship, 150
    claiming mankind was created with a purpose, 54
    claiming that God thinks about each and every human, 92
    claiming that man is programmed to die and then receive judgment from God, 109
    on the coming of the kingdom of God, 116
    on death, 115, 118
    on the fall of man, 58–59
    good defined, 143
    on intelligence, 48–50, 72
    on mankind and angels being alike, 154
    on mankind's collective intelligence, 91
    on man's ability to communicate, 62–63
    not promoting high intelligence as the ultimate goal, 39
    providing the pathway to immortality, 117

on sexual morality and morals, 92n51
on sin against God, 154
as the source of revealed authority of God, 12
Biblical Christianity, accepting a transcendent God, 31n51
biblical creation, 15, 30
biblical creationists, on man as unique from animals, 36
biblical ethics
    as the best ethical framework for ASI, 14
    providing the best ethical framework for ASI, 27
biblical interpretation, principles of, 15n6
biblical perspective, on life and death based upon Scripture, 114–18
biblical principles, regarding the sanctity of life, 123n10–24n10
biblical theists, rejecting as Bio-Luddites, 109
biblical worldview of man, 14
Big Bang, 14–15, 73
Bina48 robot, 106, 106n99
binary digital signals, 65
biological barriers, breaking existing, 119
biological capabilities, augmenting, 88
biological cognition, improvements in, 87–88
biological death, 109, 113, 115
biological determinism, rejected by Christians, 72
biological enhancement, 74, 81, 141
biological life, coming in many autonomous forms, 155
biological machine, vis-à-vis *Imago Dei*, 30–35
biological memory, 88n38
biological pattern-recognition machine, 43
biologically complex items, employing the scientific method on, 146
biology
    agency and, 157
    Darwinian, 159
    evolutionary naturalists wanting to transcend, 95
    human intelligent not deficient due to, 166
    improving man himself, 81
    intelligence as the result of ordered, 30
    molecular, 30, 56n52
    overcoming limitations of human, 164
    separation from purpose, 92–97, 119
    showing evidence of intelligent design, 19n19
    synthetic, 146
Bio-Luddites, 109
"blessedness," 140n55
blood, mankind and animals having, 115
body
    death of, 96
    dualistic conception of, 96
    as entirely physical, 56
    as an evolved ordered biomass, 30–31
    going beyond the limitations of, 67
    as a machine, 31, 56
    made to worship the Creator God, 34
    physical resurrection of, 123
    purpose of, 96
    treated with respect, 123
Boëthius, on the definition of Person, 37
book of Job, hope expressed for immortality through God, 117
bootstrapping, 44, 83
Bostrom, Nick
    on ASI posing an existential risk, 97–98
    biography of, 10
    defining existential catastrophe, 97
    dismissing Christian understandings of the noetic effects of sin, 38
    examples of perverse instantiation, 102
    on existential risk of ASI, 101–3
    on forms of ASI, 89–92
    on fundamental programming behind AI, 98–99

Subject Index

Bostrom, Nick (*continued*)
    on improving the functioning of human brains, 48
    on indirect normativity, 128
    on instrumental goals, 100
    on malignant failure modes, 101n82–2n82
    philosopher speaking out on ASI, 9
    on problems before the AI research community, 100
    on programming ASI for choice, 127n19
    proposing an orthogonality thesis, 99
    rejecting God, 38
    on seed AI as like a *tabula rasa*, 38
    works published, 10
brain
    as an amalgamation of chemicals and electrical connections, 35
    analogizing technology to, 3n4
    as best template to pursue the realization of ASI, 84
    biological enhancement to, 87
    enhancement through technological means, 84
    mapping information from into computers, 6
    as a meat machine, 23
    mechanisms behind the internal programming of, 48
    neurological function of, 86
    observing the law of physics, 31
    as part of the physical body, 55
    as a processing machine, 38
    scanning equipment, limitations of, 85
    as the seat of intelligence, 163
    as a self-organizing hierarchical system of pattern recognizers, 9–10
brain-computer interfaces, 88–89
Brave New World (Huxley), 77, 87, 110
Breakthrough Intelligence via Neural Architecture 48 (BINA48) robot, 106, 106n99
breath of life, present in animals, 114
Brentano, Franz, 69

Brooks, Rodney, 35–36
businesses, representative of collective superintelligence, 90

Calvin, John, 34n61, 49–50, 110
cardinal virtues, 140
caritas, a love for others, 143
Carlson, W. Bernard, 60–61
CCD flatbed scanner, 9n16
Chalmers, David, 47–48, 84
change, comparable to the rise of human life on Earth, 73
Chardin, 95
charge-coupled device (CCD), 9n16
Charnock, Stephen, 35, 144
"The Chicago Statement on Biblical Inerrancy," 15n6
Chinese room argument, 53, 53n42
choice, 68n90
Christ. *See* Jesus Christ
Christian epistemology, 55. *See also* epistemology
Christian ethical model, programmed for AI, 126
Christian ethics. *See also* ethics
    accounting for and handling ethical issues, 8
    defines, 13n2
    not endorsing a variety of incommensurable frameworks, 128n23
    transcendent aspect, 144
Christian orthodoxy, primary sources from, 12
Christian perspective, ethical foundations from, 136
Christian physicalism, 36n69
Christian theological sources, 11
Christian theology, not precluding either AI or ASI, 166
Christian view, of the good, 161
Christian worldview, identifying God as the *summum bonum*, 145
Christianity
    affirming a beginning in time, 1
    classified as humanist, 148

focusing on relationship with the
    Creator, God, 161
  on the good, 160–61
  holding to a form of realism, 57
  on human exceptionalism, 124
  on intelligence, 5
  on man's ends, 134
  recognizing God as both its source
    and *telos*, 123
  on the relationship between the
    physical body and the soul, 123
  Roden rejecting, 146n69
Christians
  affirming that God created man in
    his image, 70
  on biological life as a loan, 156
  on creation as beholden to the
    Creator, 125
  employing prolegomena to
    epistemology, 54
  on the entire cosmos being in need
    of redemption, 77
  on God as the ultimate focus of
    concern, 168
  on God existing outside of and prior
    to the cosmos, 4
  on the lack of Christian ethical input
    within discussion of ASI, 167
  on man as unique from all other
    animals, 33
  on morality, 156
  perspective on the proper
    understanding of the good, 142
Chu, Ted, 94, 95
Clark, Gordon Haddon, 63n74
cloning, 87
closed cosmic system, 3–4, 5
cognition
  aspects of, 58
  empirical in nature, 163, 165
  "epistemology" often replaced with,
    54
coherent and universal system of ethics,
  theory of knowledge leading
  to, 26
coherent extrapolated volition (CEV),
  129

collective superintelligence, 90–91
color, hearing, 89
communication, God's to man, 55, 63
Communion and Stewardship (Vatican),
  67, 74n2
community, 155
computation, power of, 131
computational abilities, 82
computational speed, compared to
  human learning, 88n38
computational structure, simulating the
  brain, 85
computers
  imaging man in calculating, 22
  not understanding output, 53
conative orientation, of the mind, 60
conscience (*suneidesis*), emphasis on,
  124
consciousness, 66n78, 152
consequent, affirming, 83n20
consequential ethics, weaknesses of, 76,
  76n6
contemplation, of the face of God,
  111n113
context, of language, 61
contingencies, programming future, 128
Cooper, John, 36n69
Copernican revolution, 28
"copy" (emulation), of a functioning
  brain, 85
corrupted human nature, in rebellion
  against the Creator, 34
cosmic system, as closed, 3–4
cosmological argument, 15n4
cosmology, 92n52
cosmos
  called into existence by a personal
    agent, 27
  as a closed system, 56
  as a creative act of God, 14, 164
  purposes for the creation of, 32
cranial trauma alert chip, 112n117
creation
  arising out of chaos (disorder), 95
  Christians rejecting a six-day, 15n6
  of the cosmos, 14, 164

Subject Index

creation (*continued*)
    by an infinite, eternal, independent being, 1
    in a literal six twenty-four-hour days, 15n6–16n6
    as a reflection of God's nature and glory, 17
    understanding of the cause of, 40
    views pertaining to, 5
creation relationship, 125n15, 126n17
"creative intelligence," 44
creator, man as, 1
Creator God (*elohim*), 16–17, 120
creature, 13, 35
crede ut intelligas, 15n6
credo ut intelligam, 15n6
"critical posthumanism" (CP), 148–49, 149n88–50n88
crown, connecting God and mankind, 33–34
crucifixion of Jesus Christ, 34
cupiditas (love of the self), 143
Cyber Foundation, 89
cyborg, 88, 89

The Dark Fields (novel), 6n12
Dartmouth project, on artificial intelligence, 51
Darwin, Charles, 83, 93, 114
Darwinian biology, Roden's commitment to, 159
Darwinian evolutionary accounts of man's origin, 19
Davidson, Donald, 33–34, 150–51
Dawkins, Richard, 95–96, 95n62, 106
Day of Pentecost, 64
de Chardin, Pierre Teilhard, 94
death
    biblical claim regarding, 38
    as a doorway to oblivion, 113
    as an enemy, 118
    man cannot escape, 114
    overcoming, 112
    resulting of man's primordial sin, 115
DeBaets, Amy, 31
decisions, making in a different manner, 77–78

decisive strategic advantage, to the first adopter of ASI, 101
deep learning, 77, 147
Del Monte, Louis, 42–43
Dembski, William, 44, 115n124–16n124
Dennett, Daniel, 18, 66n78
depraved will, of man, 158n109
Derrida, 149
Descartes, René, 46, 46n20
design (providence), of God, 17n10
determinism, evolutionary naturalism holding to, 164
digital death, of a mind, 103
digital implants, in humans, 88
digital information, availability of, 89
disabilities, eliminating in humans, 112n117
disconnection thesis, 145, 153, 154
discourse, 61n68
discursive agency theory (DAT), 150–51
divine providence, 143n63
divine revelation. *See* revelation
Dolly the sheep, 87, 87n36
Down syndrome, 88, 88n37
drives, motivating ASI, 131
driving, allowing for better and safer, 78
drones, 79
dualism, introduced by Descartes, 46

Earth, location within the cosmos, 28, 29
earthly wisdom, 124
earthworm, intelligence of, 91
effectiveness, efficiency over-looking, 132
efficiency, 131
El, meaning God, 17n10
electron microscopes, 85
Ellul, Jacques, 136
emergence, leading to properties, 69n94
emergent order, creating everything, 19
emergent property, of a system, 155n107
emotional psychology, 130
"empirical epistemology," cognition as, 58
empirical knowledge (cognition), 165
empiricism, 24

Subject Index

emulations, resembling the original brain, 86
end (*telos*)
    of ASI, 127
    ASI programming requiring, 132–34
    man's true, 133n37
    meaning of, 18n15
    obtaining without regard to methods, 142
    programming into an ASI, 133
Endless eXtension theme, 107n102
enhancement, of intelligence, 6
Enlightenment, change in conception of the good, 141
entropy, 107n102
Epicureans, on the good, 140–41
epistemological knowledge, 24
epistemology, 4, 54, 55, 58, 163
eschatological implications, in Psalm 8, 34
essences, 153
essentialism, maintaining, 161
eternal life, 116, 156n108
ethical boundaries, 133, 165, 166
ethical considerations, of the ultimate good, 139
ethical decisions, of machines, 65
ethical egoism, form of, 113n119
ethical formulations, arranged through consensus, 26
ethical frameworks, 136, 138
ethical implications, for ASI created by humans, 59
ethical issues, Christianity handling, 8
ethical programming
    of AI-enabled machines, 31
    boundaries framing ASI, 133
ethical properties, as identical to natural properties, 143n63
ethical structures, focused on the ends, 142
ethical theories, as inherently social constructs, 26
ethical understandings, impacted by understanding of expected behavior, 40
ethics. *See also* Christian ethics
    of AI (artificial intelligence), 32
    balancing social and personal needs, 162–63
    coherent and universal system of, 26
    connection to human anthropology, 150
    consequential, 76, 76n6
    defined, 4, 13n2
    described, 13, 137
    inserting mankind as the arbiter of morality, 132
    as not simply subjective, 142
    origins in rationality rather than emotions, 140
    as relative and changeable, 149n82
eudaimonia (human flourishing), 140
eugenics, 88, 135
euthanasia, 135
Eve, disobedience of, 115
event, defined, 128
evolution
    all forms of technology representing, 21
    as ateleogical, 95
    core idea of, 134
    depending upon diversity within the parts, 159
    drawing upon chaos and order, 18n18
    as the mechanism giving rise to us, 56n52
    propelled forward by a cosmic being, 95
"evolutionary argument against naturalism" (EAAN), 8n15
evolutionary complexification, 105
evolutionary conceptions, 133
evolutionary naturalism
    articulating the Big Bang, 14–15
    believing that everything is physical, 31n51
    described, 3
    on ethical principles weeding themselves out, 139
    first principle, 19
    on how life arose, 15
    on human intelligence, 69

Subject Index

evolutionary naturalism (*continued*)
   intelligence emerging over time, 5
   metaethical foundations for, 24
   at odds with theism, 40
   perspectives on the good, 160–61
   as the process by which mankind came into being, 24
   reduction of mankind to machines, 104
   rejecting design, 62n71
   requiring determinism, 72, 157, 158
   subscribing to scientism, 14n3
   on survival as the primary *telos*, 135
   unable to account for Kantian conjectures, 25
   viewing humans as only biological beings, 23
   worldview of, 14
evolutionary naturalists
   on ASI achieving sentience, 66
   believing man was created without agency, 70
   caught in a dilemma, 135
   on the collective intelligence of the human race, 91
   on the cosmos as a chaotic system, 162
   denying the incarnation of Jesus Christ, 125
   disdaining moral realism, 137
   ethical claims, 125
   on ethical injunctions as fluid, 70
   on ethics being related to moral facts, 142
   on everything benefitting from adjustment, 75
   on intelligence as an action, 42
   on intelligence as practical computing power, 72
   on man as a biological machine, 30
   maximizing happiness and pleasure and minimizing pain, 68
   on morality with respect to agency, 158
   on natural selection, 120
   as nihilists regarding the human race, 125
   not having grounding for a transcendent purpose, 75
   not leaving the development of AI to evolution, 84
   placing less emphasis on the physical body, 124
   reflecting upon some form of consequential ethics, 76
   rejecting God as Creator, 22
   rejecting that God created social order, 17
   replacing concern about good and evil, 136
   requiring that parts vary across a continuity spectrum, 159
   on spoken and written language, 62
   supposing that all life is of the highest value, 156
   on technology, 21
   wanting to transcend biology, 95
   Word of God and declaration of the gospel message as irrelevant, 71
existence, safeguarding one's own, 113
existential risks, 97, 163, 166
existentialism, 26
exoskeleton suits, for soldiers, 147
Explorys, 80
exponential growth
   in electronics, 52
   in intelligence, 23
external deontological actions, 4n8
externalism, 66, 68
extraterrestrial intelligence (SETI), 29
extropianism, 29, 106, 106n101–7n101, 107
Extropist Manifesto, 107–8
extropy, 105, 107–8
eye, evolution of, 83

facts, judged by reason, 137
fact/value dichotomy, 16, 140
faith, 27, 27n43, 109, 151
fall of man, 34, 59, 60
false gods, worshipping, 34
feedback loop, providing the basis for ASI programming, 130
female sheep, cloned, 87n36

fides quarens intellectum, 15n6
fighter pilots, surrounded with artificial intelligence, 78
final causes, as teleological, 92
finite creature, man as, 1
first cause
    as the Creator God, 19
    as a personal being, 28
first philosophy, 95n63
first principles, impact of, 38
first-order logic (FOL), 57
floating-point operations per second (FLOPS), 39n75
flourishing, 108, 140, 140n54
Foerst, 20n23
foolish in the world, shaming the wise, 121
form (*morphe*), of the body (soul), 45
frame problem, 57, 57n55, 88n38
freedom, 141
freedom of choice, 26
Friendly Artificial Intelligence (AI), 107n102, 136n42
functional autonomous beings, intentions of, 158
functional autonomy
    ASI ethics as, 164
    closer look at, 154–57
    for machines, computers, and enhanced humans, 6–7
    proposed for posthumans, 161
    rejecting as an ethical system, 166
functionalistic view, of Minsky, 29

genders, male and female, 32
general revelation, 17n10
generic characteristics, preselection for high-intelligence, 87
genome, synthesizing to a "designer" specification, 87
Geraci, Robert, 71
Gettier problem, 56n53
"ghost in the machine," 120
glorification, connecting to resurrection, 117
God
    in the affairs of humanity, 96
    as an agent outside the cosmos (transcendent), 15
    communicating to mankind, 4, 55, 63, 151
    connecting mind to material, 152
    controlling the ability to unconfuse language, 64
    created life, 49, 96
    created mankind with minds and with reason, 92n50
    created two genders, 32
    as the Creator of human life, 117
    as the Creator of man, 58
    decreased collective intelligence, 91
    described, 4
    as Father, 62n72
    as the first cause, 1, 16
    giving man a soul, 114
    as the highest good (*summum bonum*), 143–44
    intervening in the physical aspects of reality, 17
    knowledge of, 110–11
    mankind's spiritual relationship to, 166
    name of, 17n10
    ordering the world, 152
    provided spiritual healing, 59
    providing man with prayer, 63
    providing mankind with grace, 49
    providing the framework to understand intelligence, 8
    requiring moral perfection from man, 77
    revealed that he sent his Son Jesus Christ, 49
    revealing himself through creature's intelligence, 144
    revelation of, 19
    revelation of Scripture by, 27
    seeking in simplicity of heart, 141n58
    as the source of all goodness, 115
    speaking directly to Moses, 55
    as spirit, 32
    as superintelligent designer, 92

Subject Index

God and man, Christians understanding of, 168
god of this world, blinded the minds of the unbelievers, 117
Godhead in Christ, communion with, 35n63
godly wisdom, 124
Goertzel, Ben, 97–98
Goethe, Johann von, 50
good
  defining, 136–44
  indicative of God and his character, 166
  as nothing more than "sensible self-interest," 138
  as a relative term, 164
  as sensible self-interest, 106
good (*tob*), creation as, 17
Good, Irving, 52
good of others (the greater good), individuals concerned with, 26
Goodman, Paul, 4, 5n9
goodness, 140
Google, Director of Engineering at, 9n16
grammar, defining, 61n68
Great Judgment, 118
Greeks, on the idea of the good, 139
Green, Joel, 36n69
growth, for growth's sake, 139

HAL 9000, 97, 126
Haldane, J. B. S., 81, 93
happenstance events, 69
happiness, 140
Harbisson, Neil, 89
Harmon, Graham, 149
Havel, Václav, 67
Hawking, Stephen, 9, 38, 38n72
Hayes, Patrick, 57
Hayles, N. Katherine, 149
Henry, Carl F. H., 55, 63, 63n74
Herzfeld, Noreen, 22–23
historical narrative form, of Genesis 1–11, 15n6
Hockett, 62n71
holistic dualism, 37
Holy Spirit, 27n43, 49

Homo faber (man as maker), 20, 22, 40
Homo sapiens (thinking beings), 92n50
homosexual behavior, as a sin, 32n57
How to Create a Mind: The Secret of Human Thought Revealed (Kurzweil), 9
human(s). *See also* man (*homo*); mankind
  acceptance of robots, 122
  acting rationally through their human intelligence, 128
  applying intelligence, 53
  as autonomous systems, 155
  avoiding death, 113
  biological characteristics and capabilities, 23
  ceasing to be human, 150
  on the concept of a universal idea, 24
  conscious and aware of themselves, 66
  creating and utilizing symbols, 62
  developing their minds to know and worship God, 165
  employing analog senses, 82–83
  enabling a creation to have some ability to communicate, 64
  ethically accountable to Jesus Christ and the Word of God, 35n63
  as evolutionary accidents of nature, 109
  as exceptional, 165
  as image-bearers, 7n14, 32–35
  imaged to be like God, 111
  as machines, 30–32, 163
  machines and, 54, 147
  made in the *imago Dei*, 114, 131n35, 153
  as morally accountable to the triune God and biblical teachings, 8, 13
  as the most intelligent creatures on Earth, 20
  much more intelligent prior to the flood of Noah, 91n47
  not able to act in a manner pleasing to God, 69–70
  not necessarily understanding their own motivations and desires, 128

Subject Index

not possessing a privileged place in the universe, 29
overcoming aging, 112
putting together the cosmos with the organization of their minds, 148
recognizing robotic machines, 122
reflecting the nature of God, 92n50
as souls interacting with bodies, 158
still maintaining overall responsibility, 78
survival of, 134–36
taking after and exemplifying God's goodness, 144
understanding simply as computers, 29
uniquely related to by God, 35n63
using natural language, 60
human agents, created in the *imago Dei*, 13n2
human anthropology, 123, 150
human authority, replacing God with, 110
human biology, 81, 164
human body. *See* body
human brain. *See* brain
human designers, endeavoring to move from AI to ASI, 83
human dignity, basis for, 93n58
human DNA, mapping of, 147
Human Enhancement (Bostrom and Savulescu), 10
"human enhancement technologies," 11n17
human exceptionalism, 28–30, 124, 163
Human Genome Project (HGP), 87, 147
human intelligence. *See also* intelligence
  building machines, 49
  as an evolutionary self-organizing hierarchical system, 43
  modifying as presumptuous, 64n76
  "multiple orders of magnitude" faster than, 90
  not deficient due to biology, 166
human memory, distinguished from computer memory, 88n38
human mind. *See also* mind
  as an amalgamation of chemicals, 46

  evolving and becoming "human," 31
  as *tabula rasa*, 38, 120
  understood physically, 38
  using to serve and glorify God, 39
human motivations, translating into the receiving AI, 99
human nature, rejecting an essential, 153
human pride, as the root of sin, 110
human psychology, 138, 139
human soul. *See* soul (*psyche*)
human species, transcending itself, 21n28
human thinking, mirroring, 98
humaneering, 121n4
humanism, 93n58, 147–48
humanity, 66
  artificially evolving, 109
  created by a loving act of God, 164
  ends assisting, 132
  as an expendable resource, 100
  having mind-children, 121
  liberating from constraints of biological form, 94
  morally accountable to the triune God and biblical teachings, 164
  planning in advance for how to ensure AI is properly programmed, 100
  as psychologically imbued with the innate Will-to-Evolve (WTE), 105
  speculative philosophy on the end of, 145
Humanity+ (H+), 10, 10n17–11n17, 98
humankind, exhibiting consciousness, 66
human-machine interface, in ADAS, 78
Hume, David, 16, 137
Hutter, Marcus, 13n1
Huxley, Aldous, 77, 110
Huxley, Julian, 21
hypocrisy, 111n113

IBM, 80
idealism, 37, 55, 57
identity, 65–67

Subject Index

image-bearers
    created with intelligence, 71
    man as, 7, 7n14–8n14, 32, 166
    as priests and kings, 34
imago Dei (image of God)
    Adam created in, 15n6–16n6
    bestowal upon the human race, 91
    Christian understandings of, 166
    concept of, 22n30, 40n77
    debasement and assault on, 111–12
    essentialist view of, 91n50
    as "frightfully deformed," 34
    human agents created in, 13n2
    human life created in, 111
    man made in, 30, 32, 33, 36, 75, 110, 114, 131n35
    mankind expressing, 22
    meaning that life is a unique gift, 33
    mirroring personal manifestations of God's nature, 33
    not anything that AI scientists address, 50
    providing a connection point and reflection of what God intends for humans, 71
    providing an understanding of man's unique dignity and destiny, 76
    providing grounding for a relational aspect between man and his Creator, 77
    rationality and intelligence as part of being made in, 5
    reformation in the godly, 34n61
    rejection of, 156
    residing in sinful human rebels, 111
    sanctity and dignity of life part of, 87
imago Hominis (image of man), 21, 22, 22n31, 126, 160
imago Homo, man's making everything in, 110
immaterial spirits, 37
immortal life (*athanasia*), 118
immortality, 109, 112–14, 117, 119
Immortality Bus, 112
imperishable life (*aphthartos*), 118
incarnation, of Jesus Christ, 17n9, 30
incommensurable frameworks, variety of, 128n23
indirect normativity, 128–29
individual, autonomy of, 92n51
inductive logical reasoning (rationalism), 24
inductive reasoning, 20n23, 56
inflection points, 73
information, 44, 90, 108
infrahuman being, production of as immoral, 67
infrastructure profusion, 102–3
initial AI, creating, 84
initial ends, aligning to man's true ends, 133
inner, subjective self, 148
Institute for Ethics and Emerging Technologies (IEET), 10, 11n17
"instrumental cognitive efficaciousness," 99
instrumental convergence thesis, of Bostrom, 100
instrumental goals, 100–101
integrated circuit chip (IC), 23n33
intellect, 68, 68n90
intellectual creatures, created by God, 144
intelligence. *See also* natural intelligence
    as an all-natural process, 72
    allowing man to produce technology, 165
    amplification of, 150
    of ASI going beyond the scope of human comprehension, 160
    based upon computational resources, 85
    basis for grounding man's, 39
    the Bible on, 48–50
    as broader than strictly computational power, 88n38
    coming enhancement of, 6
    defining, 13n1, 42–44
    deriving from a design, 18
    distorted as a result of the fall, 49
    evolved out of the process of death, 114
    as futile, 39

Subject Index

gaining functionally more, 6
growing within man's context and surroundings, 162
increase in for machines, 52
inherent, 44, 44n13
as "instrumental cognitive efficaciousness," 99
involving discussions of God, 8
leading to knowledge, 124n14
leading to separation with God for eternity, 49
of man bestowed upon him by his Creator, 157
man's level of relative to his natural surroundings, 2
as much more than what it is thought to be by evolutionary naturalists, 121
nature of, 5–6
as one particular attribute of man, 5
as part of one's whole being, 165
as a personal attribute bestowed by God, 50
pertaining to humans, animals, and machines, 42–72
physical and psychological aspects involved with, 58
potential for life extension of, 7
as a present reality, 46
providing with parameters, 127
requiring a conceptual hierarchy, 43
responsible for "anthropogenic climate and environmental changes," 5
as the result of ordered biology, 30
ultimate measure of, 44
understanding of, 6
wisdom a subset of, 124
working understanding for, 122
"intelligence explosion," 52
Intelligence theme, 107n102
intelligences, manipulating communication, 61
intelligent agents, defining characteristic of, 44
intelligent autonomous agency, 122

Intelligent Design (ID) movement, 19n19
intelligent system, reprograming itself, 44
intelligent technology, 108
Intelligent Technology principle, 107n101
intention
  according to Aristotle, 128
  becoming relevant, 59–60
  of the communicator mattering to the context, 61
  to obtain a terminal degree, 159
intentional agents, Roden arguing for, 158
intentionality, 68, 151
intentions, 128, 158
internal ontological motivations, 4n8
internal subjective agents, 160
internalism, 56n53, 66, 68
Internet (World Wide Web), 52
Internet of Things (IoT), 79
interpretation, 61
"invisible technology," language as, 61
irrealism (anti-realism), 137
Istvan, Zoltan, 9, 112–13

Jesus Christ
  ASI falling under the lordship and authority of, 3
  connecting the physical and spiritual realms, 37
  on the creation narrative as historical reality, 16n6
  crucifixion of, 34
  as a cyborg, 123n7
  demonstrating God's love for mankind, 144
  destroyed death and the devil, 118
  died for our sins, 118
  as the exact imprint of God, 70–71
  as the exemplar of intelligence, 72
  fixing our eyes upon, 117
  giving life meaning and purpose, 96–97
  giving the tree of life, 118
  as the good (perfect) man, 28

Subject Index

Jesus Christ (*continued*)
    immortality only achieved through, 119
    incarnation of, 17n9, 37
    as the perfect *imago Dei*, 165
    as a prophet, priest, and king, 71n96
    providing man with his ultimate good, 145
    on the spiritual realm, 36
    voluntary death of, 115
    went around healing and doing good, 116
    as the wisdom of God, 124
Job (book of), hope expressed for immortality through God, 117
John, 117
Johnson, Monte Ransome, 93
justice (*mishpat*), 142, 142n62, 143
"justified true belief" (JBT), 56

Kant, 24–25, 141–42, 148
Kilner, Jon, 59, 70–71
king, Jesus Christ as, 71n96
King Midas, 102
kingdom of God, coming of, 116
knowledge
    attaining by disproving to the contrary, 93
    highest form for the Christian, 39
    human, 110
    increase in, 35
    leading to understanding, 124n14
    parts of, 110
    resulting from external sensory experience, 56
koimeterion (Greek), 123n9
Koop, C. Everett, 93n58
Kurzweil, Ray
    Age of Spiritual Machines, 9n16
    biography of, 9n16
    on biological processes, 18
    on computation, 18n18–19n18
    on computation as the essence of order, 131
    on computational speed of digital computers outstripping the ability of the human brain, 48
    on continuity as key to identity, 66
    as CTO of the Internet search company, Alphabet, 89
    defining technology, 20–22
    definition of a mind, 46
    on Descartes' reality of a subjective experience, 46
    on evolution, 47
    on the golden rule as the starting place for ASI ethics, 47
    on human intelligence, 43
    on human language, 61
    on humans as simply biological machines, 31
    Law of Accelerating Returns, 18n18, 23, 131
    Law of Increasing Chaos, 18n18
    Law of Time and Chaos, 18n18
    laws of, 18n18
    ontological understanding of the world, 105
    on processing power of the human brain, 38n75–39n75
    rejecting God, 38
    on Searle's objections, 53
    on the seven-step life cycle of technology, 21n27
    on the technological singularity, 73
    understanding of "conscious," 46n22
    works of, 9–10
KurzweilAI.net, 9n16

Ladyman and Ross, on philosophical naturalism, 149
Land, Richard, 64n76
language
    abilities coming from God, 64
    analogical understanding of, 63n74
    based upon social meaning, 62
    as a gift of God, 165
    God confused, 64
    as a human-created technology, 21
    not obtained through a long and slow process, 64
    as univocal, 63n74
    using complex symbols, 61
    viewed as a social construction, 163

Subject Index

viewed in philosophy as a substudy of the mind, 60
Larson, Erik, 88n38
Law of Accelerating Returns, 18n18, 23, 131
Law of Increasing Chaos, 18n18
law of noncontradiction, 19–20
Law of Time and Chaos, 18n18
laws
  of nature, 28, 94
  of transhumanists, 113
learning, defined, 82
Lego toolkit, for mankind, 147
Lemke, on rationality, 91n50–92n50
Lewis, C. S., 124
Licklider, J. C. R., 51–52
life
  created in the *imago Dei*, 111
  as a gift from God, 50
  as sacred, 96
  sacredness of, 33
life extension, 109, 112–14
life forms, 18n18, 45, 62
LifeNaut project, "ambassador" for, 106n99
lifespans, longer via science and technology, 112
light, speaking into existence, 151
limbs, replacing, 147
Limitless (television show), 6n12, 87
linguistic essentialism, 151
linguistics. *See* language
living beings, categories of, 45
living things, all equally valuable, 164
Locke, John, 66
logic, as a manifestation of God's thinking, 48
logical consistency, as negative test for truth, 63n74
logos, 20n24
Logos
  language enlightened by, 63
  as rational, 63n74
longevity, biological limitation of, 118
LORD (*Yahweh*), speaking to Adam and Noah, 64
love of God, as man's highest good, 143

Lovejoy, Arthur, 18
low-level sensorimotor skills, requiring high levels of intelligence, 121
Lyotard, on narratives, 19n20

machine code, writing, 65
Machine Intelligence Research Institute (MIRI), 10
machines. *See also* AI machines
  exceeding human capabilities, 46
  as finite, 14, 27
  imitating functions of human intelligence, 70
  incorporating into the human body, 147
  as moral agents, 72
  natural language and, 88n38
  as not human, 122
  not moral agents of themselves, 70
  programmed with an initial starting point, 44
  replicating to yield intelligence demonstrated in human beings, 56
  self-organizing allowing simulation of neurons in the brain, 53
  technological progress in AI capabilitye, 86
makarios (prosperity), 140, 140n55
Maledil, as an allegorical symbol, 124
malignant failure modes, 101–3, 101n82–2n82
man (*homo*). *See also* human(s); mankind
  acting from judgment, 68n90
  administering justice righteously, 143
  bestowed with intelligence as a gift from God, 48
  body and soul united together while living, 36
  cannot escape death, 114
  cannot know the mind of God through human intelligence, 39
  characteristics of, 1
  chief end of to be united with his Creator, 109

205

Subject Index

man (*continued*)
  creating machines with AI, 59
  creating technology, 162
  as a creature with an intelligent mind, 13
  as culture maker, 22
  defining characteristics, 140
  equivalent to a machine absent God, 108
  as exceptional, 30, 166
  exhibiting agency and choice, 166
  as a fallen creature in bondage to sin, 140
  fashioning technology in his own image, 40
  genetically engineering himself, 146
  given dominion over all animal species, 33
  as *Homo faber*, 20
  in the image of God (*imago Dei*), 142, 165
  as an image-bearer of God, 7
  intelligence not matching God's omniscience, 39
  as a machine, 81
  maintaining ultimate responsibility, 27
  playing God, 104
  progress towards perfection, 77
  proper understanding of, 8
  on rational capabilities justifying taking a step forward, 133
  received the breath of life (*nishmat chayyim*), 49
  redeeming himself through technology, 77
  responsibility for actions, 134
  as a spiritual being made in the *imago Dei*, 75
  steward over creation, 168
  uniquely gifted with body, soul, and spirit, 96
  unrestricted regarding methods (means), 132
  without Christ as a man with excellent vices, 143
  as a worshipper (*Homo adorans*), 75
man and machine, networked together, 89
man-centric (anthropocentric) ethic, 5
mankind. *See also* human(s); man (*homo*)
  advancing the evolution of, 29
  biologically born spiritually dead, 116
  building a machine matching the brain, 84
  called to accept Jesus Christ, 144
  calling upon the name of the LORD (*Yahweh*), 64
  created in God's image, 34n61
  designed with intelligence at creation, 153
  enjoying creation by loving God, 144
  eternal status of the conscious minds of, 18n17
  as exceptional from other life forms, 5
  existing in a physical world, 37
  having a soul, 36
  having a tendency to anthropomorphize ASI, 160
  having moral attributes, 33
  humaneering robots and machines, 121
  improving on ethical values, 127n19
  knowing and understanding divine revelation through faith, 27
  lifespans before the flood, 118
  made in the *imago Dei*, 27
  maintaining ability to guide and direct ASI, 166
  materialistic conceptions compared to theistic conceptions, 40
  morally bound to obey the will of God, 1
  not made with a physical resemblance to God, 32
  not maintaining or acknowledging absolute moral laws, 70
  not seeing a connection between the physical body and a deeper reality, 95

Subject Index

nothing more than an evolved animal, 28
opportunity to accept or reject God, 165
as the originating source of AI, 126
as part of the created order, 18
as a physical representation of God within the created realm, 33
plan of God's redemption of, 116
primary areas, 148
replaced by revisions of machines, 109
as a royal subject of a King, 33
sexual distinctions similar to the animals, 32
showing disregard for the sanctity of human life, 134–35
stained with sin and needed spiritual healing, 59
supplementing intelligence by creating tools, 2
as vice-regents for God, 34
viewed as a biological machine, 163
marriage, defined in Western society, 32n57
material cosmos, explanatory causes from within, 15
materialism, position on epistemology, 55
materialistic culture, 134
materialistic primary end, 133
McCarthy, John, 23n34, 43, 57
mechanical metaphysic, AI requiring, 24
mechanistic models, of the universe, 93
medicine, AI and ASI developments in, 80–81
megatrends, 146, 156
meliorism, acceptance of, 105
mental life and agency, as different in the future, 156
mental state, inability to fully understand, 59
Merge Healthcare, 80
metaethics, 4, 27
metaphysics, 4, 31n51
Midas touch, 102
militaries, employing drones, 79

mind. *See also* human mind
considered to be nonmaterial, 55
creating a human-equivalent or transhuman, 136n42
determining how intelligence is used, 3n4
estimating the powers of, 111n113
having affections, 60
intellectually impacted because of sin, 39
as a nonmaterial entity directing the physical body, 46
part of the materiality of the body, 30
as a "system with qualia," 43
viewing as a material entity, 138
mind crime, 103
mind/body dualism, rejection of, 36
mind-machine implants, 147
Minsky, Marvin, 23n34, 29, 69n94, 84
miracles, 17
mishpat (justice), 142, 142n62, 143
MIT Computer Science and Artificial Intelligence Laboratory (CSAIL), 23n34
MIT-Lemelson Prize, 9n16
molecular biology, 30, 56n52
monism (body only), vis-à-vis holistic dualism (body and soul), 35–37
Moore's law, 23, 23n33
moral actions, all tolerated, 26
moral agency, question of, 69–70
moral authority, lacking an external ultimate, 125
moral behavior, responsibility for, 158
moral capabilities, dealing with existential threats, 104
moral community, in a posthuman age, 151
moral decision-making, 122
moral enhancement, 103–4
moral epistemology, 4
moral facts, discovered by mankind, 140
moral obligations, to all of mankind, 156
moral psychology, 4
moral realism, 16, 137
moral relativism, of ASI programming, 70

Subject Index

moral self-sufficiency, happiness of, 141
morality
    deemed socially useful, 137
    evolutionary naturalist conceptions of, 120
    operating in alignment with God's order, 152
    properly understood, 18
    relationships giving rise to the discussion of, 4
Moravec, Hans, 84, 121
Moravec's paradox, 121
More, Max, 67, 98, 105, 106
Moreland, J. P., 37
Mori, Masahiro, 122
morphological freedom, 112n117
Moses, 55, 55n50, 115
most favorable expected outcome, reliance on, 14, 27
motivational drives, of AI, 100
motivations
    of ASI, 127–36
    human, 99
movement, toward a technological singularity, 74
murder, prohibition to commit, 33
Murphy, Nancey, 36n69
Murray, John, 117
music synthesizer, recreating the grand piano, 9n16
Musk, Elon, 97–98

Nagel, Thomas, 55–56
nanometer (nm), 83n19
Nash, Ronald, 63
National Inventors Hall of Fame, 9n16
National Medal of Technology, 9n16
natural causes, lacking in purpose, 93
natural intelligence, 44–50. *See also* intelligence
    as the ability to obtain knowledge and to employ skills, 49
    compared to a computer's intelligence, 43
    degree of for each person, 50
    increasing, 47–48, 72

    as one method by which humans can worship and glorify God, 49
    prerequisite for understanding artificial intelligence, 71–72
natural language, humans using, 60
natural law, 143n63
natural or cardinal virtues, 140
natural order, as one aspect of the created order, 17
natural selection, as a mindless process, 20
natural surroundings, available to man, 2
natural world, intelligence present in, 44
naturalism, 38, 58
nature (*phusis*), 95n63
    assuming the uniformity of, 25
    conforming to the image of man, 30
    having value only as long as we need it, 134
    laws of, 25
    not generating life out of non-life, 15
    reflecting an ordered structure, 16
NBIC technologies, 148
negative effects, rejecting changes having, 84
Neo-orthodox understandings, 36n69
networks
    of man and machine, 89
    of thinking centers, 51–52
neural networks, forming a type of metacognition, 152
neuro-computational model, 85
neuron-like connections, building, 69n94
Niebuhr, Reinhold, 22
Nietzsche, 25
Nietzschean transvaluation, 108
Nietzschean understanding, of morality, 137
nihilism, 95, 137
Noah, 64
noetic effects of sin, 39
nonbiological machines, 43
noncontradiction, law of, 57n54
nonpersonal God, belief in, 94
normalization, of ASI motivations, 127
normative uncertainties, sources of, 128

nuclear transfer process, 87n36
NZT-48, pill of, 87

objectives, of any AI, 100
Occam's razor, principle of, 36n69
"of-ness" (generalness), 68
Old and New Testament, canonical books of, 2
Omega Point, deriving, 95
omni-font optical character recognition (OCR), 9n16
omnipotence, striving to achieve, 113
Omohundo, Stephen, 100
ON button, on a personal computer, 83
On the Origin of the Species (Darwin), 114
ontological motivations, internal, 4n8
ontology (being), 19
Open Society principle, 107n101
OpenAI (company), 98
order and chaos, as part of a hierarchy, 18
ordered efficiency, technology striving toward, 131–32
orthogonal goals, 99
ought implies can (OIC), 151
outcome, reliance on, 14
Overcoming Property theme, 107n102
oxygen, obtaining, 115n122

Pandora's box, ASI as a version of, 101–3
Parfit, Derel, 67
part AI/part human intelligence, 147
parts, obtaining identify from the whole (form), 159
Pascal's Wager, 113
pattern-recognition machine, 43
patterns, recognizing, 43
Paul
    calling the first man "Adam," 115
    personal desire to depart and be with Christ, 123
    on philosophies, 141, 141n58
    on the spiritual realm, 36
    on teleological arguments, 96
perceptions, of humans, 66
perfection, pursuit of, 75–77

perpetual progress, faith in, 139
Perpetual Progress principle, 105, 106n101–7n101
Person of Interest (television series), 80, 80n14
personal identity, 66, 67
personhood, 37, 66
Persson, Ingmar, 103–4
perverse instantiation, 102
petaFLOPS, 39n75
PhD, student working to obtain, 159
phenomenology, temporality and, 152
philosophers, focused too much on humanity, 149
philosophical anthropology, 148
philosophical naturalism, 3
philosophical positions, regarding epistemology, 55
philosophy, being on guard against, 141n58
philosophy of mind, 60n65
physical aspects, of reality subject to God's sovereign control, 17
physical body. *See* body
physical contacts, 61
physical death, 96, 115, 116, 123
physical laws, describing reality, 16
physical life, 124
physical realm, conceptions of AI relying on, 35
physicalism (materialism), philosophy of, 26n9, 56
Phytel, 80
pilot, as ultimate and overriding control agent, 78
Plantinga, Alvin, 8n15, 56, 58
Plato
    absent divine revelation, 143n63
    on the good, 139
    on man composed of two substances (substance dualism), 66
    on natural theology, 93
    theory of the forms, 45
plug-and-play ontology, 155
positive expectations, fueling action with, 107n101
possibility, appeal to, 29

Subject Index

posthuman agents, ethical or moral concerns of, 149
posthuman possibilities, 150
posthumans
    described, 146
    ethics of, 157
    Roden's conception of, 161
Postman, Neil, 3n4, 61, 131
post-physicalist, believing in the pragmatic theory of truth, 151
power, giving primacy to, 25
Poythress, 62n72
Practical Optimism principle, 107n101
pragmatic considerations, leading mankind, 75–76
pragmatic theory, of truth, 137, 151
pragmaticism, efficiency breeding, 132
prayer, as God's idea, 63
predicted value, yielded by AI, 76
prediction, by design, 99
prehumans, evolution of, 156
priest, Jesus Christ as, 71n96
primary initial programming, of Yudkowsky, 130
primary sources, on the topic of ASI, 12
primum principium, 95, 96
Principle of Epistemic Deference, 128
Principles of Extropy, 105
print-to-speech reading machine, for the blind, 9n16
priority of the parts, placing above the whole, 159
"pro-action," 107n101
probability
    coping with, 82
    found in a first cause, 19
    of intelligent life arising on any single planet via natural selection, 84n21
problems, solving with limited resources, 43
process-driven systems, 94
processed information, communicated to intelligence, 60
programmed instruction set, initiating all future processes, 44
programming, 65

"programming of life," 146
prophet, Jesus Christ as, 71n96
propositional attitude, declaring, 59
Protagoras, 2n1
Psalm 8, as a commentary upon Genesis 1:26–28, 33
psalmist, knowing that man is appointed for death, 117
psychology. *See* emotional psychology; human psychology; moral psychology
purpose
    mankind created with, 54
    people acting with, 47
    separation of biology from, 92–97
pursuit of perfection, relentless, 75–77

qualia, 60, 152
quality superintelligence, 91
Quine, Willard Van Orman, 142

Rae, Scott, 37
rational agent, employing the most efficient means, 132
rational animal, man as, 1
rational intelligence, not all human beings having, 153
Rational Thinking principle, 107n101
rationalism, 24, 55
rationality
    Aristotle's understanding of, 45
    ASI and, 127–31
    man ascribing to himself, 133
    of man's reason, 39
real self, moving into different realms, 113
realism, articulating objective realities, 57
reality, comprised of matter and physical entities, 56
reason
    ability to, 140
    coming from external sources, 160
    in contingent matters following opposite courses, 68n90
    as distorted until Jesus Christ breaks the power of sin, 59

favoring over blind faith and questioning over dogma, 107n101
as first principle, 19
flowing from being in the image of God, 59
as the instrument for recognizing truth, 63n74
not developed as God intended because of sin, 59
not located within the subjectivity of the agent, 159
recursive iterations, of AI, 150
recursive self-improvement, learning through, 84
recursive self-learning, 85
redemption, 32, 34n61
responsibility, as the key to human identity, 67
resurrection, of Jesus Christ, 117
return on investment (ROI), 75
revelation
Augustine's focus on, 143
ethics of in conflict with the revelation of AI, 110
general, 17n10
from God, 15, 15n6, 19, 27, 39, 165
God speaking through, 4
Scripture as, 14, 17n9, 55n49
truth coming from transcendent divine, 63n74
righteousness (*tsedaqah*), 111n113, 142
robotics, laws of, 135n42
robots
imaging man in acting and performing tasks, 22
making decisions, 77, 154
as not human, 122
Roden, David, 145–53
Rothblatt, Martine, 21n28, 106

sacredness, of life, 33
salvation (soteriology), 68n90, 117
Satan and evil angels (demons), chose to rebel against God, 154
Savulescu, Julian, 103–4
Schaeffer, Francis, 93n58, 134

Schlossberg, Herbert, 54–55
science
dealing only with empirical methods, 25
operating on reason, 96
unification with ethics, 138
valued in society, 24
worshipping, 34
scientism
cutting out others' sources of knowledge, 55–56
described, 14n3, 55
desiring to assume control over nature, 30
reductionistic explications of, 35
scientists, searching for extraterrestrial intelligence (SETI), 29
scriptural principles, characterizing man's reality, 146
Scripture
approaching, 15n6
as cognitive propositional revelation, 55n49
as final authority, 2n3
as God's divine revelation to mankind, 14
interpreting Scripture (*Scriptura Scripturae interpres*), 15n6
providing meaning and insight to the created order, 17n10
revealing mysteries to liberate people and nations, 17n9
time lines recorded in, 16n7
understood only from God, 39
as verifying principle for truth, 63n74
Searle, John, 52–53
Second Law of Thermodynamics, exception to, 107, 107n102
seed AI, creating, 84
self
defined, 65
knowledge of, 110
self-autonomy, 141
self-determining human will, 157n109–58n109
Self-Direction principle, 107n101

211

Subject Index

self-identity, 163, 165
self-improvement programs, in ASI, 129
self-improving AI and AI safety, 100
self-recursive learning process, 89
Self-Transformation principle, 107n101
semantics, 61n68
"sensible self-interest," 138
sensors, 82, 83
sensory inputs, from the external environment, 44
sensory observational experience (empiricism), 24
sentience, identity concerned with, 66
servant, Jesus Christ as, 71n96
Seth, born in the image of Adam, 22n30, 40n77
sex, biological pleasure and, 92n51
sexual autonomy, of humans, 92n51
sexual distinctions, analogically connecting God and creature, 32
sexual identity, in embodied AI entities, 32–33
sin
    damaged man's relationship with God, 168
    disease and death as an effect of, 38n72
    impact on mind and intelligence, 38–40
    of man against his Creator, 28
    need for forgiveness of, 17n10
    penalty of, 115
    reality of, 38
    removing from the sight of the just and holy God, 165
    as a turning away from the Creator, 96
singularity. *See also* technological singularity
    of Jesus Christ, 97
    meanings of, 73
singularity advocates, 112–14
"Singularity Institute's Scary Idea" (SISI), 98
The Singularity Is Near: When Humans Transcend Biology (Kurzweil), 9
Sire, James, 19, 28
Sirius Satellite Radio (SIRI), creator of, 106
SkyNet, from the *Terminator* movie series, 150
Slingerland, Edward, 36
Smart Machines theme, 107n102
smart sensors, connecting to the internet, 79
social laws, as culturally determined and defined, 16
social nature, of man, 140
social order, God's created order extending into, 17
software language, turning scanned data into a neuro-computational model, 85
software revisions, introduction of, 86
software-driven species, man as, 81
sola scriptura, authority of, 2
sóma, 110
somatic cell nuclear transfer (SCNT), 87n36
Son (Jesus Christ). *See also* Jesus Christ
    as the speech (Word), 62n72
soul (*psyche*)
    conative part of, 68
    existing outside of and apart from matter, 45
    grounding personal identity beyond the grave, 37
    as immortal, 96
    living on in a perfect state, 66
soulish life (*nephesh*), 96
speaking, done in order to communicate to other agents, 151
"speculative posthumanism" (SP), 149
speech (hearing), 61
speed superintelligence, described, 90
Spirit, as a breath and hearer, 62n72
spiritual being
    as conscious, 47
    man as, 34, 165
spiritual body. *See also* body
    made after the image of Jesus Christ, 97
spiritual condition, of man as total depravity, 49

Subject Index

spiritual death, 115, 116
"spiritual prosperity," exemplified in the Beatitudes, 140n55
spiritual realm, 36, 37
spiritually alive, becoming, 116
Staley, Kevin, 35, 35n63
statement of value, attempting to correspond to truth, 57
stewardship, 33, 81–82
Stoics, on the good, 140
strong AI, 53, 54
structure, providing to language, 61
"stupid selfishness," 138
substance dualism, 66
substrate neutrality, question of, 149
superintelligence, 10, 128, 166
Superintelligence (Bostrom), 10
superintelligent motivation, predicting, 99
survivability, of ASI, 119
survival
  of mankind, 134–36
  as paramount, 156
swarm intelligence, through emergence, 69n94
syntax, 61n68
synthetic biology, rapid change in, 146

tabula rasa, 38, 120
Tarleton, 128n23
techne, 20n24
technological advancement, 74
technological enhancements, to humankind's cognitive intelligence, 167
technological progress, as a catalyst for positive human development, 11n17
technological singularity, 73. *See also* singularity
  achieving, 109
  described, 6
  inflection point called, 119
  manifesting "a combination of acceleration and discontinuity," 74n2
  not as ultimate as God's reality, 168

technology
  as an act of creation, 40
  as a component of the cultural framework for meaning, 111
  continuing to advance, 1
  defined, 20–22
  demolished the natural division of labor, 21n28
  described, 22n29
  ethical use to expand human capacities, 11n17
  exponential growth in, 6
  fracturing the conception of a universal human nature, 148
  Greek roots of, 20n24
  growing exponentially over the past few centuries, 21
  having the ability to make decisions and choices, 154
  as one component of culture, 1
  produced by human work, 33
  seven-step life cycle of, 21n27
  as teleological in nature, 20n24
  worshipping, 34
"technopoly," 131
"techno-progressive" orientation, 11n17
teleological connection, between biology and purpose, 92
Teleological Egocentric Functionalism (TEF), 113, 116
teleology, 94
"teleonomy," 94
telos. *See* end (*telos*)
temporality, 152
Ten Commandments, 33, 129, 130
Terasem Hypothesis, 106n99
Terasem Movement, 106n99
Terlizzese, Lawrence, 77
text-to-speech synthesizer, 9n16
theism, 40
theologians
  dismissed by Roden, 146
  neo-orthodox, 23
theological virtues, of Augustine, 143
"thinking center," 51
thinking machine, having attributes of intelligence, 51

213

Subject Index

thoughts
    of God numbered beyond the grains of sand, 92
    requiring internal causal powers, 53
Thweatt-Bates, 123n7
Tianhe-2 (aka TH-2), 39n75
tools, applications and uses of, 1
totaliter oliter, 54–55, 55n48
tower of Babel, 64, 64n76
transcendence, acceptance of by Christianity, 161
transcendent ethic, 5
transcendental agency, acceptance of, 157
transcendental schema, of Kant, 25
Transcending Restrictions theme, 107n102
transformations, for achieving ASI, 119
transgender bathrooms, acceptance of, 32n57
transhumanism (H+), 7, 29, 104–12
    arguing for the incorporation of technology into humanity, 119
    described, 7n13, 21, 21n28
    suffering from a defective anthropology, 109
Transhumanist Bill of Rights, 112, 112n117
Transhumanist Declaration, 11n17
transhumanist ethic, 138
"Transhumanist Olympics," 112n117
Transhumanist Party, 112, 112n117
"Transhumanist Wager," 113
transhumanists
    accepting new technologies, 148
    "believing in transcendence through technology," 109
    believing man will lead the way, 110
    focusing on intelligence and the mind, 110
    laws of, 113
    on nature deemed to be man's "designer," 106
    placing faith in science, 109
    on technological enhancement of human capabilities, 148
Tree of Life, 116, 118

true being, essence, substance (*ousia*), 95n63
truth
    coming from transcendent divine revelation, 63n74
    having more than just instrumental value, 48
    pragmatic theory of, 137, 151
    as subjective, 2n1
    ultimate, 93n58
Truven Healthcare, 80
tsedaqah, definitions, 142n62
Turing, Alan, 50–51
Turing test, 50–51, 53, 53n42
"Turn Your Eyes Upon Jesus" (hymn), 117

UAVs, degrees of autonomy of, 79
ultimate good, failing to define, 139
ultimate truth, Jesus Christ as, 93n58
ultraintelligent machine, 52
Uncanny Valley, 122
uncertainties, dealing with, 82
understanding, leading to wisdom, 124n14
Universal Basic Income, 112n117
universe, 14, 93
unmanned aerial vehicles (UAV), 79
unrighteousness, suppressing the truth, 96
"uploading," 85
utilitarian calculus, 76
utilitarianism, not answering important questions, 26
utility, 124, 125
utopia, articulating a negative, 77

value, 57, 113, 137
value pluralism, 156, 160
values programming, ASI needing, 127
Vatican, on the biological integrity of the human, 67
vehicle, used for vicious purposes, 79
Venter, J. Craig, 81
Vinge, Vernor, 73, 150
virtue (*arête*)

as appropriately ordered (ordinate) love, 143
defined, 128n22
as the result of human effort, 140
virtue ethics, based on human nature, 143n63
vision systems, going beyond human capabilities, 83
vision-sensing capabilities, of AI, 79
Vita-More, Natasha, 98
von Rad, Gerhard, 22

Watson Health, 80
Watson supercomputer, 80
WBE (whole-brain emulation), 85–86
weak AI, 52–53
Wennemann, Darryl, 151
Westminster Shorter Confession, on man's chief end, 54n46
Whatever Happened to the Human Race (Schaeffer and Koop), 93n58
whole, giving value and meaning to specific particulars (parts), 159
whole-brain emulation (WBE), 85–86
the will, 68

will of man, granted by God, 158n109
Will-to-Evolve (WTE), 105
wireless connectivity, connecting to the internet, 79
wisdom
    beginning of, 118
    concerned with primary causes and principles, 95n63
    described, 95
    distinguished from intelligence, 124
    human, 141n58
    as a tree of life, 118
Word of God, 12, 57n55
works, done by unregenerate men as sinful, 143n66
World Wide Web, 89
worldviews, different as source of conflict, 14
written or sign language (visual), 61

Yahweh, meaning LORD, 17n10
Young, R. W., 43
Young, Simon, 106, 137–38
Yudkowsky, Eliezer, 97, 129–31, 135n42–36n42

Scripture Index

OLD TESTAMENT

Genesis

	20n23
1	15, 32, 115
1:1	1, 19, 27, 55n48, 96
1:1—2:3	16
1:1—2:25	96
1–2	50
1–3	1, 27, 115
1:3	63, 151
1:3–31	63
1:4	10, 12, 18, 21, 25, 31, 17, 142
1–11	15n6, 91
1:12–12	20–26, 45
1:12–13	20–26, 49
1:21	24, 96
1:26	114, 116
1:26–27	22n30, 27, 30, 40n77, 64, 70, 104
1:26–28	33, 36, 49, 75, 76, 87, 91, 111
1:26–30	34
1:27	32, 50
1:28	18n12
1:29–31	115
1:31	77
2:7	27, 28, 36, 49, 50, 75, 96, 114
2:15	33
2:16–17	63
2:17	38, 115, 116
2:18–24	18n12
2:19–20	64
2:19–20	23, 21
2:20	104, 104n90
3	58
3:1	125
3:1–24	28, 77
3:3–4	126
3:5	34
3:6	158n109
3:6–7	59
3:15	21, 59
3:17	59
3:17–19	115
3:19	116
3:21	118
3:22	116
3:22–24	118
4:10	115
4:19–22	48
4:21–22	91n47
4:26	64
5:1–3	22n30, 40n77
5:1–32	118
5:3	40n77
5:5	118
6:3	118
6:5	116
6:14—7:5	64
6:17	114
7:15	114
9:4–6	115
9:6	22n30, 40n77
11:1	64

Scripture Index

Genesis (continued)
11:1–9	7, 91
11:2–4	64
11:6–8	64
11:9	64

Exodus
3:13–15	1
3:14	18n17
17:14	55n50
20:3	34, 92
20:13	33, 135
24:4	55n50
33:11	55, 55n50
34:27	55n50

Leviticus
17:11	14, 115
19:18	124, 143, 156

Numbers
23:19	18n17
33:1–2	55n50

Deuteronomy
5:7	34, 92
5:17	33, 135
6:5	49, 124
6:13	71n96
11:18	117
30:19	158n109
31:9–11	55n50
32:4	77

1 Chronicles
16:29	54
22:19	117

2 Chronicles
6:30	92

Job
14:14	117
28:28	49
37:16	77

Psalms
2:7–9	71n96
8	33
8:1	3, 33
8:3–8	33
8:4–5	50
8:5	33
8:6	33
14:1–3	116
19	17, 17n10, 142
19:1–6	17n10
19:7–14	17n10
25:8	77
33:18–22	143
41:13	1
44:21	92
49:12–15	117
51:5	116
57:5	11, 17
73:25–26	54n46
89:48	114
90:2	1, 18n17
92:15	77
94:11	39, 49
96:13	142
100:3	1
102:25–27	18n17
102:27	1
104:29	35
108:5	17
110:10	39
111:10	49, 118
113:4	17
113:4–5	55n48
116:4	63
127:3–5	18n12
133:1	35
139:2	92
139:13–16	111
139:17–18	92

Proverbs
1:5	49

1:7	118, 124
3:18	118
4:7	118
8:12	39
9:9	49
9:10	39, 49, 118, 124
15:33	124
18:15	49

Ecclesiastes

1–12	95
3:18–21	116
6:6	114
7:29	158n109
8:6–8	114
9:4–6	116
9:11	49
11:8	116
12:7	36
12:12	49

Isaiah

2:2–3	18n12
9:6	34n61, 55
14:14	34
25:8	117
40:8	28, 18n17
48:11	54
64:6	69, 116
65:17	116
66:22	116

Jeremiah

17:9	59, 116
29:11	92
31:33	39, 49

Daniel

2:44	18n12
4:35	35
12:4	49

Hosea

13:14	117

Malachi

3:6	18n17

NEW TESTAMENT

Matthew

1:1	71n96
1:18	55
3:15	144
4:10	71n96
5:2–12	140n55
5–7	30
5:17–18	71n96
5:21	135
5:48	77, 144
6:9	63
6:33	143
7:12	47
8:4	115
10:28	36
16:18–19	18n12
16:24	118
17:12	158n109
17:24–27	71n96
19:4–6	18n12
19:7–8	115
19:8	55n50
19:17	71n96
19:19	156
20:19	123
21:1–9	71n96
22:16–21	37–40, 71n96
22:23–33	36
22:29	156
22:34–40	144
22:36–40	124
22:37	49
26:26–30	110
26:32	123
26:39	71n96
27–30	71n96
27:52	123

Mark

4:26–29	96

Scripture Index

Mark (*continued*)

7:10	115
8:34	118
10:19	135
12:26	55n50, 115
12:28–34	124, 144
12:30	39, 49
12:31	156
14:22–26	110
14:36	71n96
15:9	12–13, 71n96
16:15	71n96

Luke

1:35	55
2:51	71n96
2:52	71n96
3:7–9	144
4:18	43, 71n96
5:33–39	21n28
6:31	47
9:23	118
10:25–28	144
10:27	49, 124, 156
16:29	31, 115
18:19	116
18:20	135
22:19–20	110
22:42	71n96
23:2–3	42–43, 71n96
23:52	71n96
24	49
24:44	115
24:45	39
24:49	18n12

John

1:1	14, 71n96
1:9	14, 55
1:49	71n96
2:25	92
3:6	116
3:16	125
3:19–20	39
4:24	32
4:34	71n96
5:18–20	71n96
5:24	70
5:39–40	49
5:40	116
5:45–47	55n50
5:46	115
6:44	158n109
6:53	116
7:14–18	15n6
7:19	55n50, 115
7:42	71n96
8:29	71n96
8:36	158n109
8:56	55
10:15	71n96
10:18	115
11:11–13	123n9
12:24	96
13:35	35
14:6	49, 71n96, 110
14:9	55
14:11	71n96
14:14	63
16:13	18n12
17:7	26, 71n96
18:36–37	71n96
19:19–22	71n96
20:9	39
21:14	123
24:49	18n12

Acts

1:5	8, 18n12
1:8	64
2:1–4	37–39, 41–43, 47, 18n12
2:1–41	64
2:41–42	110
2:42	35
3:21	116
3:22	55n50
4:32	35
7:2	54
7:60	123n9
10:38	116
17:18	141

17:21	49	11:36	97
17:25	28, 49	12:2	39, 49, 77
20:7	110	13:1	17n9
23:6–10	36	13:1–7	18n12
		13:9	135
		16:27	91n50

Romans

1:4	55
1:5	71n96
1:14–15	143n63
1:17	143
1:18–20	96
1:18–32	125
1:21–23	28, 39
1:23	118
3:10	23, 59
3:10–12	23, 69
3:21–26	144
3:22–23	109
3:23	115
4:5	144
4:24	109
5:6	158n109
5:7–8	28, 144
5:8–12	115
5:10	49
5:12	34
5:12–14	115
5:12–19	116
5:12–21	38, 115
5:18–19	71n96
6:23	59, 109, 115, 116
7:15	18–19, 21, 23, 158n109
7:20–25	37
8:1	70
8:5–6	39, 49
8:6–7	21–23, 38
8:7	110, 158n109
8:18–25	32
8:19–22	116
8:22	28
8:22–23	77
8:29	22n30, 35, 40n77
10:5	55n50
10:9	109
10:13	64
11:33	1

1 Corinthians

1:2	63
1:17–31	124
1:18–31	39
1:19	39
1:20–21	39, 49
1:27	121
2:6–16	39
2:11	39
3:10–15	70
3:20	49
6:20	54
7:37	49
8:1–2	49
10:16	110
10:31	32, 54, 54n46, 71n96, 109, 133, 134
11:1	30
11:7	22n30, 40n77
11:23–24	110
13:13	143
14:15	39
14:15–18	49
15:3–4	118
15:6	18, 123n9
15:12–49	123
15:13–14	118
15:19	124n10
15:21	38
15:21–22	115
15:22	118
15:22	45, 115
15:24–28	33
15:26	116, 118
15:35–49	96
15:35–58	37
15:43–44	96
15:45	115

Scripture Index

1 Corinthians (continued)
15:53–54	118
15:55	117

2 Corinthians
1:12	124
3:18	22n30, 35, 40n77
4:4	117
4:4–7	22n30, 40n77
4:18	117
5:10	70
5:17	97
5:18–20	49
5:21	144
10:5	92
12:1–4	36

Galatians
2:16	156n108
3:22	109, 156n108
6:14	34
6:15	97

Ephesians
1:17	39
1:20–22	33
2:1	5, 8–10, 158n109
2:1–3	116
2:5	38
2:8–9	27
3:19	35
4:1–16	35
4:13–16	35
4:17–19	39
4:18	116
4:23	39, 49
4:24	34n61, 143
5:2	49
5:22–23	32

Philippians
1:3–11	144
1:19–30	124n10
1:20	54
1:21–23	37
1:23	123
2:5–11	4
2:13	158n109
3:20–21	37
3:21	97
4:6–7	39, 49

Colossians
1:13	158n109
1:13–15	22n30, 40n77
1:15	55, 71
1:15–20	4, 116, 118
1:22	49
1:27	124n10
1:28	35
2:8	141, 141n58
2:23	39
3:2	49
3:10	34
3:14	35
3:16	124

1 Thessalonians
4:14	109
5:15	143

1 Timothy
1:1	124n10
1:16	109
1:17	91n50, 118
2:13–14	34
3:16	55
5:6	116
6:16	118

2 Timothy
1:10	118

Titus
3:3–5	158n109

Hebrews
1:3	22n30, 40n77, 71n96

Scripture Index

2:7–8	33
2:14–15	118
3:1	117
3:6	124n10
4:12	39
6:17–18	18n17
7:20–28	59
7:24	18n17
7:26	28, 77
9:27	109
10:10–14	59
10:16	39, 49
10:21	49
10:25	35
10:27	116
11:1	151
11:3	1
12:2	117
13:8	18n17

James

1:14	158n109
1:20	143
2:11	135
2:23	144
3:1–16	49
3:9	22n30, 40n77
3:13–18	39, 124

1 Peter

1:3	124n10
1:19	115
2:24	144
4:11	32, 54

2 Peter

1:13–14	37
3:13	116

1 John

1:1–2	55
1:8	69
2:15–17	118
2:16	110
3:1	92
3:2–3	37
3:8	116
3:23	109
4:2	55
4:10	28, 144
4:19–21	144
5:3	69

2 John

1:16	71n96

Jude

25	91n50

Revelation

1:5	71n96
2:7	118
3:12	116
11:15	71n96
20:11–15	70
20:14	118
21:1–2	116
21:3–4	117
22:2	118

GREEK AND LATIN WORKS

Anselm of Canterbury

Proslogium

ch. 1	15n6

Aquinas

Summa Theologica

1–2	91, 93, 94, 143n63
I.2.3	15n4
I.29.1	37n71
I.83.1	68n90

Augustine

On Christian Teaching

bk. 1	143n65

City of God

bk. 11, ch. 4	96n64

Scripture Index

City of God (continued)
bk. 19, ch. 25   143n66

Confessions
bk. 1.1   32n55

On Order (De Ordine)
bk.2, debate 1, sec. 5   17n9

Tractate
29.6   15n6

On the Trinity
bk. 8, preface 4   27n43

Boëthius

Against Eutyches and Nestorius
ch. 3   37n71

Canons of the Council of Carthage

(418), canon 1   115n123

Tertullianus

On the Prescription of Heretics (De Praescriptione Haereticorum)
ch. 7   141n58

CLASSICAL AUTHORS

Aristotle

Metaphysics
bk. A (12)   15n4
bk. Γ (4), 3–6, e   20n21
bk.1 (A), sec. 981b   95n63

Nicomachean Ethics
bk. 369n92   128n21

On the Soul
bk. 2, ch. 3   128n21

www.ingramcontent.com/pod-product-compliance
Lightning Source LLC
Chambersburg PA
CBHW062019220426
43662CB00010B/1401